WEB APPLICATIONS
WITH ASP.NET CORE BLAZOR

WEB APPLICATIONS
WITH ASP.NET CORE BLAZOR

*Create Powerful, Responsive, and
Engaging Web Applications*

Brian Ding

MERCURY LEARNING AND INFORMATION
Boston, Massachusetts

Publisher: David Pallai
MERCURY LEARNING AND INFORMATION
121 High Street, 3rd Floor
Boston, MA 02110
info@merclearning.com
www.merclearning.com
800-232-0223

B. Ding. *Web Applications with ASP.NET Core Blazor: Create Powerful, Responsive, and Engaging Web Applications.*
ISBN: 978-1-50152-267-3

Library of Congress Control Number: 2024939129

242526321   This book is printed on acid-free paper in the United States of America.

TO

My beloved parents:
Zhong Ding,
Yi Hu,
&

My wife, Haoran Diao

Contents

PREFACE

This book covers many different aspects of developing Blazor applications, a modern way to build rich UI web applications. The book introduces how to leverage .NET and its eco-systems to build a modern enterprise application. It introduces WebAssembly and how it enables web applications to be written in any programming language. It also compares different Blazor hosting models and the strategy to select a model that suits its business requirements. The book is designed for web developers, software engineers, and tech enthusiasts looking to build robust, interactive web applications using ASP.NET Core Blazor.

Using a demonstrative approach for Blazor learners, every chapter includes numerous code examples and a Blazor source code analysis. It covers basic Blazor directives and components and how these concepts can be combined together to build a more complex customized component. This book also explains some advanced techniques to control component rendering and improve performance.

The book is divided into 13 chapters. It begins with the introduction of WebAssembly and covers the basic concepts in Blazor Framework. It includes some advanced techniques you may find handy when developing production-ready applications, as well as explaining source code structures and designing patterns and styles. So, readers can learn the basics of how a Blazor application is running. The chapter details are listed below.

Chapter 1: WebAssembly Introduction

Discover the power of WebAssembly and why it was introduced despite the capabilities of JavaScript. This chapter includes a hands-on demonstration of compiling C/C++ source code into WebAssembly and calling WebAssembly functions from JavaScript. It also explores the WASM binary format, various sections of the binary code, and popular languages that produce WebAssembly modules, including ASP.NET Core Blazor.

Chapter 2: Choosing Your Hosting Model

Learn about WebSocket and compare it to HTTP. Explore SignalR, a .NET library that implements WebSocket with a fallback to long polling for compatibility. Understand the basic structure of a Blazor application and compare three Blazor hosting models: Blazor Server, Blazor WebAssembly, and Blazor Hybrid.

Chapter 3: Implementing Razor and Other Components

Explore the basic components of Blazor applications, including directives, binding, cascading, and event handling. This chapter explains the lifecycle of a typical component and introduces layouts, a special component type useful for building applications with multiple functional spaces. Discover popular third-party libraries for building enterprise applications.

Chapter 4: Advanced Techniques for Blazor Component Enhancement

This chapter discusses advanced component features and source code. Learn how to reference, preserve, and template components, and how to define a CSS style specific to a component using CSS isolation.

Chapter 5: File Uploading in Blazor

Understand common file transfer protocols and their differences. Learn about the component used to upload files in the Blazor framework, complete with source code explanations and detailed usage examples.

Chapter 6: Serving and Securing Files in Blazor

Gain insights into one of the most important mechanisms in ASP.NET Core: middlewares. Learn how middlewares handle client requests, serve static and dynamic files in Blazor, and apply basic security rules to protect servers from attacks.

Chapter 7: Collecting User Input with Forms

Master web forms, which are essential for data input from application users. This chapter covers default data validation, customizing validation rules and error prompts, and key events and concepts in Blazor forms, including submission, context, and state.

Chapter 8: Navigating Over Applications

Explore page navigation in a Blazor application. Understand the key routing components in the Blazor framework, different types of routing with parameters, navigation events, and asynchronous navigation for enterprise-level applications.

Chapter 9: .NET and JavaScript Interop

Learn about serialization and deserialization with JSON for communication between web services, and its application in .NET and JavaScript interop. This chapter covers loading customized JavaScript code, calling JavaScript from .NET and vice versa, and advanced interop topics such as cache, element reference, and type safety.

Chapter 10: Connecting to the World with HTTP

Discover the HTTP protocol, its role in front-end and back-end separation, and the challenges of CORS. This chapter explains the built-in types HttpClient and HttpClientFactory for external communication and covers RPC and gRPC with practical examples.

Chapter 11: Data Persistence with EF Core

Explore data persistence using EntityFramework Core, comparing stateless and stateful concepts. Understand the design ideas behind EF Core and analyze its source code to learn patterns supporting various databases. Key concepts such as entity, context, query, and migration are explained with detailed examples.

Chapter 12: Protecting Your Application with Identity

Learn about authentication and authorization in Blazor applications. This chapter covers the authentication mechanism, the AuthenticationStateProvider source code for customized authentication, and different authorization approaches, including role-based and policy-based authorizations, with code examples.

Chapter 13: Deploying with Docker and Kubernetes

Master modern deployment techniques using Docker and Kubernetes. Learn how to containerize Blazor applications and deploy them using Azure Kubernetes Services and Azure Container Registry.

Companion files with code samples and color figures from the book are available for downloading by writing to info@merclearning.com.

Transform your web development skills with ASP.NET Core Blazor. Successful coding!

ACKNOWLEDGMENTS

This book would not exist without the help of many people, mostly including the continuous support from my parents and my wife's encouragement for writing the book. They've taken most of the housework so that I can focus on writing it — I could have never completed this book without their support. My gratitude also goes to the team at my publisher for being supportive enough to provide me with quite a long time to finish the book. This is my first book ever, and I would like to thank them for their professionalism, guidance, and patience along the way.

ABOUT THE AUTHOR

Brian Ding has over 8 years of experience in TypeScript and .NET development, specializing in areas such as WinForm, WPF, ASP.NET, and ASP.NET Core. Currently employed at BMW Archermind Information Technology Co. Ltd., he holds the position of tech leader, where he focuses on creating engaging digital driving experiences for BMW customers. Throughout his career, Brian has worked in diverse domains including software development, DevOps, automation tools, and cloud technologies. His passion lies in coding and developing scalable solutions that are adaptable and easy to maintain.

ABOUT THE REVIEWER

Trilok Sharma is a seasoned technical architect with 14 years of expertise in designing, developing, and implementing enterprise-level solutions on the Microsoft technology stack. Throughout his career, Trilok Sharma has demonstrated mastery in Microsoft technologies, including Blazor Server, Blazor Web Assembly (WASM), .Net 7.0, Net Core, C#, Angular, React, SQL Server, Azure, and AWS. He has a strong command over object-oriented programming principles and has leveraged their knowledge to architect scalable and efficient applications. Trilok holds a bachelor's degree in computer science and MBA in Project +IT Management. With his strong technical understanding, attention to detail, and commitment to quality, Trilok Sharma continues to make valuable contributions as a technical reviewer in the Microsoft technology space.

1

WebAssembly
Introduction

INTRODUCTION

This chapter introduces the concept and roadmap of WebAssembly and how it enables Web applications to be written in any programming language. It also discusses a few popular WebAssembly languages and illustrates the benefits of building a Web application with ASP.NET Core Blazor.

STRUCTURE

This chapter discusses the following topics:

- What is WebAssembly?
- How is a WebAssembly module compiled?
- What does a WebAssembly module look like?
- What is .NET Core with WebAssembly?

OBJECTIVES

This chapter is intended to guide readers briefly through the world of WebAssembly, get familiar with WebAssembly modules, and explain how .NET Core is involved with WebAssembly. Readers will learn how to install Emscripten SDK and will also get familiar with emcc command. The chapter will explore the world of WebAssembly binary format and help readers understand how a module was constructed. Finally, the chapter will introduce the new generation of .NET—.NET Core with the WebAssembly framework, ASP. NET Core Blazor.

WHAT IS WEBASSEMBLY

WebAssembly (abbreviated as Wasm) is a target for modern languages for compilation of more than one language, designed to be highly efficient while maintaining a safe sandbox environment. The definition seems to be too official. When broken down into two words *Web* and *Assembly*, one might get a better understanding of WebAssembly. *Web* is a familiar word to most in this era of prevalent Internet use. For example, people can buy goods from *Amazon.com*, watch videos on *Youtube.com*, and check out how friends' lives are on *Facebook.com*.

Assembly, however, might not be that obvious to those who do not work with computer science. In recent years, most developers write programs with advanced programming languages like *Golang, C#,* or *Java*. Prior to using advanced languages, programmers used to write code with Assembly, which is more specific to the hardware platform. For example, writing Assembly code for x86 CPU and ARM CPU will have different key words and syntax. As a language that is closer to the hardware level, Assembly language usually has higher runtime efficiency than advanced languages.

HISTORY OF WEBASSEMBLY

The first Web was created in the early 1990s. At that time, the Web was mainly used by scientists to share information. The Web was designed to be the media of static content. HTML defines the content. URL locates the resources on the World Wide Web. The client (browser) would then send a HTTP request to the server through a URL and then render the HTML content returned by the server. In this process, all the information transported was static, and that means there was no way that a user could interact with the Web.

In 1995, Branden Eich designed a new language called `JavaScript` in only ten days. It looks like Java, but is easier to use than Java, and even nonprofessional Web site workers can understand it. Eich seemed to dislike JavaScript. He was of the belief that everything that is excellent is not original, and everything original is not excellent. With *Chrome* getting more popular, JavaScript soon appeared everywhere on the Web. Currently, Engine V8 from Google is enabling JavaScript to be used in large and complex projects.

HELLO WORLD! WITH WEBASSEMBLY

JavaScript has been efficient, then why create another "Assembly Language" for the Web? JavaScript is a dynamic language, which means the type of variable could be changed in runtime, unlike C# or Java. For programmers or developers, it is very convenient to write code, but it becomes cumbersome when it comes to the interpreter. The interpreter must judge which type of variable is being used while running code. Even armed with JIT compiler, compiling JavaScript into machine code sometimes requires it to be rolled back to the original code under some circumstances. For this reason, many companies that build browsers are looking for a more performance-enhanced solution.

In April 2015, the WebAssembly Community Group was founded. Two years later, WebAssembly became one of the W3C standards. In 2019, WebAssembly became one of the standard Web languages, along with HTML, CSS, and JavaScript. Through the years, most of the popular Web browsers have supported WebAssembly.

Many languages, for example, C/C++, C#, and Go can now be compiled to WebAssembly.

Using C/C++ as an example, write a simple C++ program that says `Hello World`. Save it as `hello.cpp` under `my-hello-world-demo`:

```
#include <stdio.h>


int main() {

    printf("Hello World!\n");

}
```

Emscripten SDK is an open-source SDK that compiles C/C++ to WebAssembly, and auto-generates JavaScript code that can run the `.wasm` file. Install the SDK following the instructions here *https://emscripten.org/docs/ getting_started/downloads.html* and compile the code with the following command:

```
emcc hello.cpp -o hello.html
```

There will be three output files, `hello.html`, `hello.js` and `hello.wasm`, shown as follows:

```
my-hello-world-demo
├──hello.cpp
└──hello.html
└──hello.js
└──hello.wasm
```

`hello.html` is the default Web page, and `hello.js` is the code logic running on it, designed by the Emscripten SDK.

Next, install Python from *https://www.python.org*. Open the command line or terminal and move to `my-hello-world-demo` and enter `python -m http.server`, Python will start a server listening on port `8000`. Open the browser and navigate to *http://localhost:8000*, it will show the files under `my-hello-world-demo`, then click `hello.html`, a default front-end page provided by `emscripten` will show. Refer to Figure 1.1.

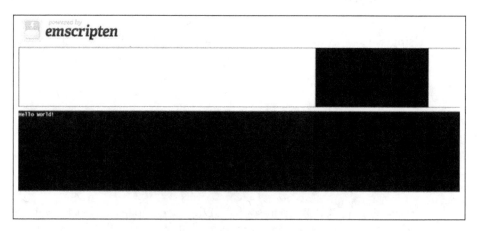

FIGURE 1.1 Default front-end Web page.

In the black box area, it shows `Hello World!` that we printed. A program that is running the C++ code. If we open the DevTools and switch to Console Tab, `Hello World!` is also printed there.

CALL WEBASSEMBLY FROM JAVASCRIPT

Write a simple C++ function that can be called by the page using JavaScript. Create another file called `function.cpp` and write the following code:

```
#include <emscripten.h>


extern "C"

{

    EMSCRIPTEN_KEEPALIVE

    int myAddFunc(int a, int b)

    {

        int c = a + b;
        return c;

    }


    EMSCRIPTEN_KEEPALIVE

    int myMinusFunc(int a, int b)

    {

        int c = a - b;
        return c;

    }

}
```

There are two functions here, `myAddFunc` will get the sum of two integers and `myMinusFunc` will get the subtraction. Similarly, compile with the command:

```
emcc function.cpp -o function.html
```

The folder would look like:

```
my-hello-world-demo

├───function.cpp

└───function.html
```

```
└──function.js
└──function.wasm
└──hello.cpp
└──hello.html
└──hello.js
└──hello.wasm
```

Use Python to start a server again and go to *http://localhost:8000/function. html*. Nothing is printed in the black box area this time, and that's because nothing was printed in the function. Call the two math functions provided by WebAssembly this time. Open the DevTools, switch to the `Console` tab and write `_myAddFunc(1,2)` and 3 will be the result. In fact, when `_myAddFunc` the IntelliSense will tell rhw user that the function does exist in the context of page function.html. Try `_myMinusFunc` and it will also work. How exactly did the Web page load the two math functions? Take a look at the generate `function.html` and `function.js`:

```
<script type='text/javascript'>

    var statusElement = document.getElementById('status');
    var progressElement = document.getElementById('progress');
    var spinnerElement = document.getElementById('spinner');

    var Module = {

        preRun: [],

        postRun: [],

        print: (function() {

            var element = document.getElementById('output');

            if (element) element.value = ''; // clear browser cache

            return function(text) {

                if (arguments.length > 1) text = Array.prototype.
slice. call(arguments).join(' ');

                console.log(text);
```

```
          if (element) {

               element.value += text + "\n";

               element.scrollTop = element.scrollHeight; //
focus on bottom

          }

     };

  })(),

  canvas: (function() {

     // draw canvas

  })(),

  setStatus: function(text) {

     // set status

  },

  totalDependencies: 0,

  // some code here

  };

  Module.setStatus('Downloading...');

  // some code here

</script>

<script async type="text/javascript" src="function.js"></script>
```

In the HTML body, it defines the front-end layout and page logic. We will focus on the script section. It first initiated a module object, which has a few properties, for example, print, canvas, `setStatus`. Print shows `Hello World!` in the previous code example on the Web page by changing the value of the element with ID "output" and printing it to the console as well with `console.log(text)`; `setStatus` is actually called when the page is first loaded, and if the page is refreshed a few times quickly, a caption that says `Downloading` will appear. It is downloading the WebAssembly file `function.wasm`. The following explains how the `function.wasm` was loaded and how the function was called:

```
var asm = createWasm();

function createWasm() {

    function receiveInstance(instance, module) {
        var exports = instance.exports;

        Module['asm'] = exports;
    }

    function receiveInstantiationResult(result) {
        receiveInstance(result['instance']);
    }


    function instantiateArrayBuffer(receiver) {

        return getBinaryPromise().then(function (binary) {

            return WebAssembly.instantiate(binary, info);

        }).then(function (instance) {
            return instance;
        });

    }


    function instantiateAsync() {

        if (!wasmBinary && typeof WebAssembly.instantiateStreaming
== 'function' &&

            !isDataURI(wasmBinaryFile) && !isFileURI(wasmBinaryFile)
&& !ENVIRONMENT_IS_NODE &&

            typeof fetch == 'function') {

            return fetch(wasmBinaryFile, { credentials: 'same-
origin'}).then(function (response) {

                var result = WebAssembly.instantiateStreaming
(response,info);

                return result.then(
                    receiveInstantiationResult,
                    function (reason) {
                        return
```

```
instantiateArrayBuffer(receiveInstantiationResult);

                });

            });

        } else {

            return instantiateArrayBuffer(receiveInstantiation
            Result);

        }

    }


    if (Module['instantiateWasm']) {

        var exports = Module['instantiateWasm'](info,
        receiveInstance); return exports;

    }


    instantiateAsync();
    return {};
}


function createExportWrapper(name, fixedasm) {

    return function () {

        var displayName = name;

        var asm = fixedasm;
        if (!fixedasm) {
            asm = Module['asm'];

        }

        if (!asm[name]) {

            assert(asm[name], 'exported native function `' +
displayName + '` not found');

}

  return asm[name].apply(null, arguments);

    };

}
```

```
var _myAddFunc = Module["_myAddFunc"] =
createExportWrapper("myAddFunc");

var _myMinusFunc = Module["_myMinusFunc"] = createExportWrapper
("myMinusFunc");
```

Here is the key code of `function.js`, and it is fairly self-explanatory. A call to `createWasm()` starting the process. Inside this function, it goes to `instantiateAsync()` and onw can guess from the function name that it will initiate the WebAssembly. It does provide two ways to instantiate. If possible, it will fetch the wasm file through `http` protocol, in this case, `function.wasm`.

In this way, the wasm was loaded as a network stream, so `WebAssembly.instantiateStreaming` was used to process the http response. If the user opens DevTools, switches to the `Network` tab, and refreshes the page again, they will notice a request to *http://localhost:8000/function.wasm and it returns 200.* Refer to Figure 1.2.

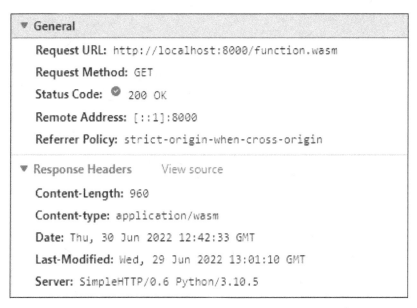

▼ **General**

   Request URL: http://localhost:8000/function.wasm

   Request Method: GET

   Status Code: ⊘ 200 OK

   Remote Address: [::1]:8000

   Referrer Policy: strict-origin-when-cross-origin

▼ **Response Headers**   View source

   Content-Length: 960

   Content-type: application/wasm

   Date: Thu, 30 Jun 2022 12:42:33 GMT

   Last-Modified: Wed, 29 Jun 2022 13:01:10 GMT

   Server: SimpleHTTP/0.6 Python/3.10.5

FIGURE 1.2 Fetch function.wasm.

`WebAssembly.instantiateStreaming()` will be responsible for compiling and initiating the WebAssembly module, and it will be more efficient than loading the wasm code directly by `WebAssembly.instantiate()`. In practice, most of the WebAssembly frameworks will choose `WebAssembly.instantiateStreaming()` to load the WebAssembly, and this explains why some Web sites built by WebAssembly will be take longer to load for the first time than a Web site built with only JavaScript, since they will download the `.wasm` file through the network.

Otherwise, it will fall back to `WebAssembly.instantiate()` inside `instantiateArrayBuffer()`, and the name of the function indicates that it is load the binary format of `.wasm` directly.

Once the WebAssembly module was loaded, the `receiveInstantiation-Result()` will be the callback to handle the instance of WebAssembly, and `instance.exports` will be assigned to `Module['asm']` to save the exports from the WebAssembly. Finally, two lines of code generated by the Emscripten SDK call `createExportWrapper()`, and it will find the exported functions by name in `Module['asm']`. Function apply will be used to run the desired function with arguments.

It can be proved by opening DevTools, switching to Console tab and type: `_myAddFunc(2,3)` and press enter. As expected, the result is 5. Alternatively, one could use `Module['asm']` directly: `Module['asm']['myAddFunc'] (4,5)` and it shows 9 correctly. This is how the WebAssembly runs on the Web, but what exactly is in the `function.wasm`? Can it be manually loaded?

Introducing .WASM binary format

Here is another example:

```
#include <emscripten.h>


extern "C"

{

    MSCRIPTEN_KEEPALIVE

    int myMultiplyFunc(int a, int b)
```

```
    {

        int c = a * b;
        return c;

    }

}
```

This time, compile it to `.wasm` only, without generating `html` and `js` file.

In the terminal, type:

```
emcc manual.cpp -O3 -no-entry -o manual.wasm
```

Notice that `-no-entry` is required since there is no `main()` function and users will build in STANDALONE_WASM mode. The folder will look as follows:

```
my-hello-world-demo
 ├────function.cpp
 └────function.html
 └────function.js
 └────function.wasm
 └────hello.cpp
 └────hello.html
 └────hello.js
 └────hello.wasm
 └────manual.cpp
 └────manual.wasm
```

Open `manual.wasm` with a binary viewer or VS Code with appropriate extensions.

```
00000000  00 61 73 6d 01 00 00 00 01 17 05 60 00 01 7f 60    .asm… …`..▨`
00000010  00 00 60 02 7f 7f 01 7f 60 01 7f 00 60 01 7f 01    ..`.▨▨.▨`.▨.`.▨.
00000020  7f 03 07 06 01 02 00 03 04 00 04 05 01 70 01 02    ▨. ...........p..
00000030  02 05 06 01 01 80 02 80 02 06 09 01 7f 01 41 90    ............▨.A.
```

```
00000040 88 c0 02  0b 07 80  01 08 06 6d 65 6d 6f 72 79 02    .........memory.
00000050 00 0e 6d  79 4d 75  6c 74 69 70 6c 79 46 75 6e 63    ..myMultiplyFunc
00000060 00 01 19  5f 5f 69  6e 64 69 72 65 63 74 5f 66 75    .._indirect_fu
00000070 6e 63 74  69 6f 6e  5f 74 61 62 6c 65 01 00 0b 5f    nction_table..._
00000080 69 6e 69  74 69 61  6c 69 7a 65 00 00 10 5f 5f 65    initialize...__e
00000090 72 72 6e  6f 5f 6c  6f 63 61 74 69 6f 6e 00 05 09    rrno_location...
000000a0 73 74 61  63 6b 53  61 76 65 00 02 0c 73 74 61 63    stackSave...stac
000000b0 6b 52 65  73 74 6f  72 65 00 03 0a 73 74 61 63 6b    kRestore...stack
000000c0 41 6c 6c  6f 63 00  04 09 07 01 00 41 01 0b 01 00    Alloc......A....
000000d0 0a 30 06  03 00 01  0b 07 00 20 00 20 01 6c 0b 04    .0........ . .l..
000000e0 00 23 00  0b 06 00  20 00 24 00 0b 10 00 23 00 20    .#..... .$....#.
000000f0 00 6b 41  70 71 22  00 24 00 20 00 0b 05 00 41 80    .kApq".$. ....A.
00000100 08 0b                                                 ..2
```

Refer to the following code consisting of the magic number:

```
00000000 00 61 73 6d 01 00 00 00 01 17 05 60 00 01 7f 60
         ^^ ^^ ^^ ^^
```

The first four bytes are called the magic numbers, 0x00 0x61 0x73 0x6d representing \0asm if converted by ASCII code. It means that this is a .wasm file.

```
00000000 00 61 73 6d 01 00 00 00 01 17 05 60 00 01 7f 60
                     ^^ ^^ ^^ ^^
```

The next four bytes are the version number: 0x01 0x00 0x00 0x00 (little endian), version 1 here:

```
00000000 00 61 73 6d 01 00 00 00 01 17 05 60 00 01 7f 60
                                 ^^ ^^ ^^ ^^ ^^ ^^ ^^ ^^
00000010 00 00 60 02 7f 7f 01 7f 60 01 7f 00 60 01 7f 01
         ^^ ^^ ^^ ^^ ^^ ^^ ^^ ^^ ^^ ^^ ^^ ^^ ^^ ^^ ^^ ^^
00000020 7f 03 07 06 01 02 00 03 04 00 04 05 01 70 01 02
         ^^
```

The ninth byte is the start of a section, which composes the binary format of WebAssembly. The starting byte of a section represents the section type, and the next byte would be the length of the section. Refer to Table 1.1 for more possible values.

TABLE 1.1 WebAssembly module sections.

Id	Section
0x00	custom section
0x01	type section
0x02	import section
0x03	function section
0x04	table section
0x05	memory section
0x06	global section
0x07	export section
0x08	start section
0x09	element section
0x0a	code section
0x0b	data section
0x0c	data count section

Sections usually start with 01 – type section. In this section, `.wasm` defines signatures of functions or type information. In the first line of the first code discussed in this chapter, 0x01 flags the start of the type section, and the following byte 0x17 indicates that this section has length 23 (excluding type byte and length byte) till byte 0x20. The next byte 0x05 indicates there are five functions, so users could find 5 0x60 following:

```
00000010: 00 01 7F 60 00 00 60 02 7F 7F 01 7F 60 01 7F 00

              ^^ ^^ ^^ ^^ ^^ ^^
```

Bytes 0x16 to 0x1b define a function (0x60) with 2 (0x20) i32 (0x7F) parameters, and 1 (0x01) i32 (0x7F) output, and this would be the function that calculates multiplication, and the function signature is exactly two integers (int a, int b) and an integer result (int c).

There is nothing imported here, so there is no import section. Jump to function section (0x03):

```
00000020 7f 03 07 06 01 02 00 03 04 00 04 05 01 70 01 02
            ^^ ^^ ^^ ^^ ^^ ^^ ^^ ^^ ^^
```

This section would be of length 7 (0x07). The next byte indicates there are six (0x06) function indices, and the array of indices is 1 (0x01), 2 (0x02), 0 (0x00), 3 (0x03), 4 (0x04), 0 (0x00):

```
00000020 7f 03 07 06 01 02 00 03 04 00 04 05 01 70 01 02
                        ^^ ^^ ^^ ^^ ^^ ^^

00000030 02 05 06 01 01 80 02 80 02 06 09 01 7f 01 41 90
            ^^

00000030 02 05 06 01 01 80 02 80 02 06 09 01 7f 01 41 90
               ^^ ^^ ^^ ^^ ^^ ^^ ^^ ^^

00000030 02 05 06 01 01 80 02 80 02 06 09 01 7f 01 41 90
                                 ^^ ^^ ^^ ^^ ^^ ^^ ^^

00000040 88 c0 02 0b 07 80 01 08 06 6d 65 6d 6f 72 79 02
            ^^ ^^ ^^ ^^
```

The next is a table section with id 4 (0x04) and length 5 (0x05), and it defines the JavaScript objects mapping, for they could not be accessed by WebAssembly directly and this helps to ensure that WebAssembly runs in a safe sandbox environment. Followed by section with id 5, (0x05) represents memory information, which defines the minimum and maximum memory usage. After that would be the global section (0x06) of length 9 (0x09), which defines 1 (0x01) global i32 (0x7f) variable and the variable is mutable (0x01). Readers should be familiar with the global variables concept in many other advanced languages. This variable is initialized with the following instructions (0x41 0x90 0x88 0xc0 0x02 0x0b):

```
00000040 88 c0 02 0b 07 80 01 08 06 6d 65 6d 6f 72 79 02
            ^^ ^^ ^^ ^^ ^^ ^^ ^^ ^^ ^^ ^^ ^^ ^^

00000050 00 0e 6d 79 4d 75 6c 74 69 70 6c 79 46 75 6e 63
            ^^ ^^ ^^ ^^ ^^ ^^ ^^ ^^ ^^ ^^ ^^ ^^ ^^ ^^ ^^
```

```
00000060 00 01 19 5f 5f 69 6e 64 69 72 65 63 74 5f 66 75
         ^^ ^^ ^^ ^^ ^^ ^^ ^^ ^^ ^^ ^^ ^^ ^^ ^^ ^^ ^^ ^^

00000070 6e 63 74 69 6f 6e 5f 74 61 62 6c 65 01 00 0b 5f
         ^^ ^^ ^^ ^^ ^^ ^^ ^^ ^^ ^^ ^^ ^^ ^^ ^^ ^^ ^^ ^^

00000080 69 6e 69 74 69 61 6c 69 7a 65 00 00 10 5f 5f 65
         ^^ ^^ ^^ ^^ ^^ ^^ ^^ ^^ ^^ ^^ ^^ ^^ ^^ ^^ ^^ ^^

00000090 72 72 6e 6f 5f 6c 6f 63 61 74 69 6f 6e 00 05 09
         ^^ ^^ ^^ ^^ ^^ ^^ ^^ ^^ ^^ ^^ ^^ ^^ ^^ ^^ ^^ ^^

000000a0 73 74 61 63 6b 53 61 76 65 00 02 0c 73 74 61 63
         ^^ ^^ ^^ ^^ ^^ ^^ ^^ ^^ ^^ ^^ ^^ ^^ ^^ ^^ ^^ ^^

000000b0 6b 52 65 73 74 6f 72 65 00 03 0a 73 74 61 63 6b
         ^^ ^^ ^^ ^^ ^^ ^^ ^^ ^^ ^^ ^^ ^^ ^^ ^^ ^^ ^^ ^^

000000c0 41 6c 6c 6f 63 00 04 09 07 01 00 41 01 0b 01 00
         ^^ ^^ ^^ ^^ ^^ ^^ ^^
```

Now comes the export section (0x07) with length 129 (0x80 + 0x01). Contrary to the import section, it defines the functions, tables, memory, or global variables that will be exported to the world of JavaScript. In manual.wasm, we have 8 (0x08) exported objects. A closer look may help one notice that bytes from 0x51 to 0x61 define the multiplication function. The following code can help find the function:

```
00000050 00 0e 6d 79 4d 75 6c 74 69 70 6c 79 46 75 6e 63
            ^^ ^^ ^^ ^^ ^^ ^^ ^^ ^^ ^^ ^^ ^^ ^^ ^^ ^^ ^^

00000060 00 01 19 5f 5f 69 6e 64 69 72 65 63 74 5f 66 75
            ^^ ^^
```

The 5th (0x05) exported function is named 0x6d 0x79 0x4d 0x75 0x6c 0x74 0x69 0x70 0x6c 0x79 0x46 0x75 0x6e 0x63. If the user looks them up in the ASCII table, they will find out that the function name is myMultiplyFunc. The last two bytes claims that the exported object type is function (0x00) and the index of the function is 1 (0x01):

```
000000c0 41 6c 6c 6f 63 00 04 09 07 01 00 41 01 0b 01 00
            ^^ ^^ ^^ ^^ ^^ ^^ ^^ ^^ ^^ ^^
```

Since the `manual.cpp` is compiled with the command –no-entry, skip the start section (0x08) and jump directly to the element section (0x09):

```
000000d0  0a 30 06 03 00 01 0b 07 00 20 00 20 01 6c 0b 04
          ^^ ^^ ^^ ^^ ^^ ^^ ^^ ^^ ^^ ^^ ^^ ^^ ^^ ^^ ^^ ^^

000000e0  00 23 00 0b 06 00 20 00 24 00 0b 10 00 23 00 20
          ^^ ^^ ^^ ^^ ^^ ^^ ^^ ^^ ^^ ^^ ^^ ^^ ^^ ^^ ^^ ^^

000000f0  00 6b 41 70 71 22 00 24 00 20 00 0b 05 00 41 80
          ^^ ^^ ^^ ^^ ^^ ^^ ^^ ^^ ^^ ^^ ^^ ^^ ^^ ^^ ^^ ^^

00000100  08 0b
          ^^ ^^
```

The code section (0x0a) defines 6 (0x06) functions. The first one takes 3 (0x03) bytes (0x03), has no (0x00) parameters and the next two bytes would be the instructions code. The next function takes 7 (0x07) bytes and no parameters as well.

Readers should now have a basic understanding of the WebAssembly binary format and should try to run `manual.wasm` manually in the browser.

Case 1: In a browser, open DevTools and switch to the Console tab. Enter the following code all in once, and it will print out a log that says "3 * 4 = 12"

```
var array1 = [0,97,115,109,1,0,0,0,1,23,5,96,0,1,127,96,0,0,96,2,127,127
,1,127,96,1,127,0,96,1,127,1,127,3,7,6,1,2,0,3,4,0,4,5,1,112,1,2,2,5,6,1
,1,128,2,128,2,6,9,1,127,1,65,144,136,192,2,11,7,128,1,8,6,109,101,109,1
11,114,121,2,0,14,109,121,77,117,108,116,105,112,108,121,70,117,110,99,0
,1,25,95,95,105,110,100,105,114,101,99,116,95,102,117,110,99,116,105,111
,110,95,116,97,98,108,101,1,0,11,95,105,110,105,116,105,97,108,105,122,1
01,0,0,16,95,95,101,114,114,110,111,95,108,111,99,97,116,105,111,110,0,5
,9,115,116,97,99,107,83,97,118,101,0,2,12,115,116,97,99,107,82,101,115,1
16,111,114,101,0,3,10,115,116,97,99,107,65,108,108,111,99,0,4,9,7,1,0,65
,1,11,1,0,10,48,6,3,0,1,11,7,0,32,0,32,1,108,11,4,0,35,0,11,6,0,32,0,36,
0,11,16,0,35,0,32,0,107,65,112,113,34,0,36,0,32,0,11,5,0,65,128,8,11];
```

```
var array2 = Uint8Array.from(array1);

WebAssembly.instantiate(array2).then(({instance}) => {
  console.log(`3 * 4 = ${ instance.exports.myMultiplyFunc(3, 4)}`);
});
```

```
> var array1 =
  [0,97,115,109,1,0,0,0,1,23,5,96,0,1,127,96,0,0,96,2,127,127,1,127,96,1,127,0,96,1,127,1
  ,127,3,7,6,1,2,0,3,4,0,4,5,1,112,1,2,2,5,6,1,1,128,2,128,2,6,9,1,127,1,65,144,136,192,2
  ,11,7,128,1,8,6,109,101,109,111,114,121,2,0,14,109,121,77,117,108,116,105,112,108,121,7
  0,117,110,99,0,1,25,95,95,105,110,100,105,114,101,99,116,95,102,117,110,99,116,105,111,
  110,95,116,97,98,108,101,1,0,11,95,105,110,105,116,105,97,108,105,122,101,0,0,16,95,95,
  101,114,114,114,110,111,95,108,111,99,97,116,105,111,110,0,5,9,115,116,97,99,107,83,97,118,
  101,0,2,12,115,116,97,99,107,82,101,115,116,111,114,101,0,3,10,115,116,97,99,107,65,108
  ,108,111,99,0,4,9,7,1,0,65,1,11,1,0,10,48,6,3,0,1,11,7,0,32,0,32,1,108,11,4,0,35,0,11,6
  ,0,32,0,36,0,11,16,0,35,0,32,0,107,65,112,113,34,0,36,0,32,0,11,5,0,65,128,8,11];

  var array2 = Uint8Array.from(array1);

  WebAssembly.instantiate(array2).then(({instance}) => {
    console.log(`3 * 4 = ${ instance.exports.myMultiplyFunc(3, 4)}`);
  });
< ▶ Promise {<pending>}
  3 * 4 = 12                                                          VM484:6
>
```

FIGURE 1.3 Manually run WebAssembly.

Case 2: Manipulate the `manual.wasm` a little, changing the function name from `myMultiplyFunc` to `yourManilupate`. The new bytes would be:

```
00  61  73  6d  01  00  00  00      01  17  05  60  00  01  7f  60
00  00  60  02  7f  7f  01  7f      60  01  7f  00  60  01  7f  01
7f  03  07  06  01  02  00  03      04  00  04  05  01  70  01  02
02  05  06  01  01  80  02  80      02  06  09  01  7f  01  41  90
88  c0  02  0b  07  80  01  08      06  6d  65  6d  6f  72  79  02
00  0e  79  6f  75  72  4d  61      6e  69  70  75  6c  61  74  65
00  01  19  5f  5f  69  6e  64      69  72  65  63  74  5f  66  75
6e  63  74  69  6f  6e  5f  74      61  62  6c  65  01  00  0b  5f
69  6e  69  74  69  61  6c  69      7a  65  00  00  10  5f  5f  65
72  72  6e  6f  5f  6c  6f  63      61  74  69  6f  6e  00  05  09
73  74  61  63  6b  53  61  76      65  00  02  0c  73  74  61  63
6b  52  65  73  74  6f  72  65      00  03  0a  73  74  61  63  6b
41  6c  6c  6f  63  00  04  09      07  01  00  41  01  0b  01  00
```

```
0a  30  06  03  00  01  0b  07      00  20  00  20  01  6c  0b  04

00  23  00  0b  06  00  20  00      24  00  0b  10  00  23  00  20

00  6b  41  70  71  22  00  24      00  20  00  0b  05  00  41  80

08  0b
```

```
> var array1 =
  [0,97,115,109,1,0,0,0,1,23,5,96,0,1,127,96,0,0,96,2,127,127,1,127,96,1,127,0,96,1,127,1
  ,127,3,7,6,1,2,0,3,4,0,4,5,1,112,1,2,2,5,6,1,1,128,2,128,2,6,9,1,127,1,65,144,136,192,2
  ,11,7,128,1,8,6,109,101,109,111,114,121,2,0,14,121,111,117,114,77,97,110,105,112,117,10
  8,97,116,101,0,1,25,95,95,105,110,100,105,114,101,99,116,95,102,117,110,99,116,105,111,
  110,95,116,97,98,108,101,1,0,11,95,105,110,105,116,105,97,108,105,122,101,0,0,16,95,95,
  101,114,114,110,111,95,108,111,99,97,116,105,111,110,0,5,9,115,116,97,99,107,83,97,118,
  101,0,2,12,115,116,97,99,107,82,101,115,116,111,114,101,0,3,10,115,116,97,99,107,65,108
  ,108,111,99,0,4,9,7,1,0,65,1,11,1,0,10,48,6,3,0,1,11,7,0,32,0,32,1,108,11,4,0,35,0,11,6
  ,0,32,0,36,0,11,16,0,35,0,32,0,107,65,112,113,34,0,36,0,32,0,11,5,0,65,128,8,11];

  var array2 = Uint8Array.from(array1);

  WebAssembly.instantiate(array2).then((({instance}) => {
    const { myMultiplyFunc } = instance.exports
    console.log(`3 * 4 = ${ myMultiplyFunc(3, 4)}`)
  });
< ▶ Promise {<pending>}
⊗ ▶Uncaught (in promise) TypeError: myMultiplyFunc is not a function        VM494:7 🔍
    at <anonymous>:7:27
  >
```

FIGURE 1.4 Run-manipulated WebAssembly.

It will state that `myMultiplyFunc` is not a function, because it has been changed. WebAssembly is like any other language, and emscripten is just one of the tools that could convert existing code to WebAssembly. Compiled and instantiated by `WebAssembly.instantiate` or `WebAssembly.instantiateStreaming` as a preferred way, WebAssembly runs in a safe sandbox in a more efficient and faster way.

WEBASSEMBLY IN THE FUTURE

In the future, it is likely that anything that can possibly be compiled targeting WebAssembly, eventually, will be compiled to WebAssembly. WebAssembly was designed for the Web initially, but it is not limited to the Web; it could be running on the server as well. There is a possibility that one day in the future, all computing units will be running WebAssembly, regardless of the selected language, both for the client side and the server side.

POPULAR WEBASSEMBLY LANGUAGES

Many popular languages have been supported; for example, C/C++, Rust, C#, Golang, and many more. Some of these supports are still experimental. Alternatively, some have been used in a production environment for a long time. This book uses C#, and experienced users will find building a WebAssembly application with C# will be a very smooth process. For inexperienced C# users the book will cover all the knowledge and concepts needed.

.NET CORE

In the 2000s, .NET Framework was born. It is a reaction from Microsoft to the world of Java. The initial name was *Next Generation Windows Services (NGWS)*. It was designed to be a new platform that could run not only one selected language, but also run in a secure and extensible way, and adapt to the Web, which was born one or two decades earlier. With the framework of ASP. NET, programmers can develop Web sites by easily dragging and dropping Web controls, and that greatly lowers the efforts required to build an enterprise-level Web site. Since then, C# and .NET Framework has been evolving. In Build 2015, Microsoft has pronounced a new .NET platform called .NET Core, which is available to run on every platform including *Windows, Linux*, and *MacOS*, and the new world of C# begins. C# is not closely coupled with the Windows Server anymore. It could be run in a docker container, more cloud native, and obviously, more adapted to the new world of the Web, again.

ASP.NET CORE

ASP.NET Core was born with the new .NET Core platform, which aims to upgrade from the old ASP.NET. By providing a default and replaceable dependency injection container, as well as a newly designed middleware mechanism, it has quickly become a popular framework for the microservice architecture. Basically, it is another normal .NET Core console application, except that when it starts, it will run a few configurations and listens for http requests.

WHEN TO CHOOSE ASP.NET CORE BLAZOR

ASP.NET Core Blazor was the framework aiming to build a client Web application running both on WebAssembly, Server, and even native apps, while enjoying the benefits of an existing C# ecosystem. For example, entity objects could be shared between a client app and backend services running on Linux servers, enjoying also the secure and efficiency brought from WebAssembly, and enjoying the interactions with your application build upon C# instead of JavaScript, and enjoying the Web standards that allow your application to be run on any modern browsers, even on a mobile device.

Blazor has been one of the top WebAssembly enthusiasts. There are many active open sources projects that are contributing to the communities, providing many UI components and libraries available to users. This book will cover every corner you need to build your production-ready Blazor application.

CONCLUSION

WebAssembly is crafted to be a target for programming languages compiler to be target with. It is now one of the W3C standards with *HTML, CSS,* and *JavaScript*, making it available to run on the most modern Web browsers like *Chrome, Edge, Safari,* and *Firefox*, not only on PC, but on mobile devices as well.

WebAssembly is safe to be executed in a sandbox environment, while maintaining efficiency and speed. It could be executed at a near native speed. It is open and debuggable with help from its textual format. Remember, despite having started with "Web," WebAssembly is not limited to building Web applications, it is possible to run WebAssembly with backend services as well.

The next chapter introduces WebSocket, another communication protocol between clients and servers other than http; and SignalR, a .NET Core library that helps users build a WebSocket server. Three major Blazor hosting models will be discussed. Blazor Server executes in the server based on the SignalR WebSocket connection, while Blazor WebAssembly, as its name suggests, leverages WebAssembly to run in the client environment. Also discussed is Blazor Hybrid, a new model that combines Blazor with native application development so that users can share their code between Blazor Server or Blazor WebAssembly as well as applications run in desktops or mobile devices.

2

Choose Your Hosting Model

INTRODUCTION

Chapter 1 briefly introduced ASP.NET Core Blazor and explained that Blazor is becoming one of the most popular frameworks for front-end developing. This chapter will continue exploring and comparing three different Blazor hosting models. One model, Blazor WebAssembly is a framework dedicated to WebAssembly. The following sections explore the different Blazor hosting models.

STRUCTURE

This chapter discusses the following topics:

- WebSocket and HTTP
- using SignalR to create a WebSocket server
- Blazor Server
- Blazor WebAssembly
- Blazor Hybrid

OBJECTIVES

This chapter aims to introduce one of the most important protocols that will be used in Blazor, WebSocket and the three common hosting models provided by Blazor.

Before going into the world of hosting models, a few useful concepts are introduced.

WEBSOCKET

When opening a Web page, for example, *https://www.google.com*, the browser sends a GET HTTP request to one of Google's servers, and the server responds with HTML, CSS, or JavaScript that are required to render the page. Before the existence of WebSocket, all the requests were imitated by the client, or Web browser. The server is not able to send a message to the client initially. How could a Web application, for example, a web chatting room allow users to chat with their friends remotely, get the notification that the friend sent them a message? Figure 2.1 depicts the protocol between clients and servers in the most natural way.

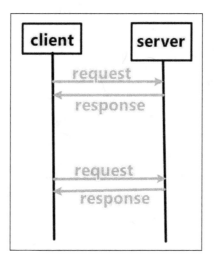

FIGURE 2.1 HTTP model.

An easy way to implement this is to loop sending check requests to the server with Ajax. The shorter the loop, the more "instantly" the user receives their friends' messages. Imagine an app with hundreds of thousands of users, each having hundreds of friends; millions of check requests will be sent to the app servers, and those are only the requests to check if there are new message yet. No reasonable servers could handle such a large quantity of requests.

A request sent from the user's browser to the server goes through the Internet by the HTTP protocol based on a TCP connection. After the server responds to the request, it may or may not close the TCP connection. If it decides to close the connection, the next time the client sends the request, a new TCP connection must be built again. It is called a *Request/Response model.*

WebSocket is not entirely independent of the HTTP protocol. The client first sends a handshake request to the server based on the HTTP protocol, with predefined standard headers, including WebSocket Key which is used to identify the client and the server, version, and subprotocol that is aligned between the client and the server so that they will both communicate based on the aligned subprotocol. If the server is compatible with WebSocket, it will respond to the client with predefined headers as well. The client will not communicate with the server again until it validates the response from the server, and a WebSocket connection is built. With this WebSocket connection, the client and the server can talk in a bidirectional way. They both can actively send messages to on another as shown in Figure 2.2.

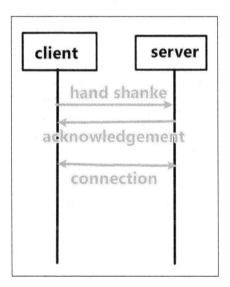

FIGURE 2.2 WebSocket model.

Both HTTP and WebSocket protocols are based on TCP, so in general, it would be easy for the server to support WebSocket, and the default ports are 80 and 443 for the WebSocket. WebSocket soon became popular in online games, chat rooms, and many other applications which are dependent on real-time or live interactions between users and the platforms.

In general, almost all the real-time services are exchanging information on the WebSocket connection, while the stateless HTTP protocol is more popular with RESTful API services. An HTTP connection can be set up directly, while the WebSocket must have a handshake request first before establishing the connection. HTTP protocol contains more overheads in each transport than WebSocket. In addition, WebSocket supports sending binary messages.

SIGNALR

WebSocket is apparently more popular in real-time applications. Even so, implementing a WebSocket from scratch might be both complex and time-consuming. In addition, some old version browsers might not have WebSocket supported. You can't force customers to upgrade, therefore it would be more complicated if a server tries to switch between long-polling and WebSocket for different clients. It would be optimal if there was a library that could both help users build a real-time server based on WebSocket while also being compatible with older browsers where long polling is the only solution to be real timing.

An open-source library, *ASP.NET Core SignalR*, emerges. SignalR library is an enabler that an application could leverage to send messages in both directions, from the client to the server, invoking code on the client side through *remote procedure calls (RPC)*, or vice versa, and most importantly, if the application is facing customers with older browsers, SignalR automatically falls back to long-polling if conditions were not met, and of course, users could customize the fallback priorities. While sending messages simultaneously to all the clients, users could also send a message to a specific client. Sounds familiar? Nowadays, a typical instant chatting app would require those capabilities to create chat rooms and private chats. SignalR is not only saving time on the building of a WebSocket server like many popular WebSocket libraries for .NET or other languages, but it also provides an automatic fallback mechanism that saves the user and user applications from worrying about compatibilities.

Following is a demo that displays easy set-up:

notification receiving boards with SignalR.

cd *to a fold of your desire for this demo:*

```
dotnet new webapi -o NotificationApp
code .\NotificationApp\
```

The previous command creates a new ASP.NET Core Web API project and opens the project by VS Code. Add the SignalR capabilities to it.

```
cd .\NotificationApp\
```

Or open the terminal window and it will be automatically located in the project directory.

```
var builder = WebApplication.CreateBuilder(args);
var app = builder.Build();

app.MapGet("/", () => "Hello World!");

app.Run();
```

This is generated from the ASP.NET Core Web template and it doesn't display much other than "Hello World!." To provide a Web page UI interface to users, create a folder called wwwroot, and add a file index.html:

```
<!DOCTYPE html>

<html lang="en">

<head>

    <meta charset="utf-8" /

    <title>SignalR</title>

</head>

<body>

    <h1>Notification App</h1>

    <p>This is an application to send/receive centralized
notifications.</p>

</body>

</html>
```

To serve this html page, ASP.NET Core provides two methods: `UseDefaultFiles()` and `UseStaticFiles()`. The first method enables the default file path mapping, and that is where to put the `index.html`. The second method enables the server to host the static files, and index.html is one of them.

Now, the `Program.cs` looks like the following, and the user should comment out the `MapGet`, otherwise it will show `"Hello World!"` by default.

```
var builder = WebApplication.CreateBuilder(args);


var app = builder.Build();
app.UseDefaultFiles();
app.UseStaticFiles();


// app.MapGet("/", () => "Hello World!");

app.Run();
```

Type `dotnet run` in the command line and it will say that the server is listening on a certain port. Navigate to that URL in the Web browser, in this case it is *http:// localhost:5044*, which will render the HTML page.

Next, use SignalR to implement a WebSocket server that could push notifications to clients.

First, register SignalR into the container. A container in ASP.NET Core is a box, or a provider that one could register multiple interfaces, classes, or instances, and retrieve back later. It is an implementation of the design pattern, inverse of control. The idea behind is that the user is not depending on a concrete implement layer anymore. Instead, the user relies on a contract or an interface that promises to fulfil their requirements. Basically, there are two ways, inject and retrieve, to interact with the container, or ASP.NET Core calls it ServiceProvider.

```
    /// <summary>
    /// Adds SignalR services to the specified
<see cref="IServiceCollection" />.
```

```
/// </summary>

/// <param name="services">The <see cref="
IServiceCollection" /> to add services to.</param>

/// <returns>An <see cref="ISignalRServerBuilder"/> that
can be used to further configure the SignalR services.</returns>

public static ISignalRServerBuilder AddSignalR(this
IServiceCollection services)

{

    if (services == null)

    {

        throw new ArgumentNullException(nameof(services));

    }


    services.AddConnections();
    // Disable the WebSocket keep alive since SignalR has
      it's own

    services.Configure<WebSocketOptions>(o =>
o.KeepAliveInterval =TimeSpan.Zero);

    services.TryAddSingleton<SignalRMarkerService>();

            services.TryAddEnumerable
(ServiceDescriptor.Singleton<IConfigureOptions<HubOptions>,
HubOptionsSetup>());

    return services.AddSignalRCore();
}
```

The static method `AddSignalR`, like many other dependency injection extension methods, put the required dependencies into the container, for example, `SignalRMarkerService`. Generally, these registrations are structured under the namespace `Microsoft.Extensions.DependencyInjection`, even when users are creating their own libraries, for example, `NLog` takes this pattern to register itself as well.

Now, we add SignalR to our notification application by simply calling `AddSignalR()`.

```
var builder = WebApplication.CreateBuilder(args);


// Add SignalR
builder.Services.AddSignalR();


var app = builder.Build();
```

`IServiceProvider` plays an important role in dependency injection in ASP.NET Core. As the name of this interface suggests, it is a provider for all kinds of services that are registered into the container:

```
namespace System
{
    //
    // Summary:
    //     Defines a mechanism for retrieving a service object;
that is, an object that
    //     provides custom support to other objects.
    public interface IServiceProvider
    {
        //
        // Summary:
        //     Gets the service object of the specified type.
        //
        // Parameters:
        //     serviceType:
        //     An object that specifies the type of service
        object to get.
        //
        // Returns:
        //     A service object of type serviceType. -or- null
```

```
if there is no service object
        //      of type serviceType.
        object? GetService(Type serviceType);
    }
}
```

To take the dependencies out of the box, .NET defines a method `GetService` in the interface `IServiceProvider`. It takes the `Type` required as a parameter and will return the instance of that `Type` if possible.

Second, create a folder called `Hubs` under root path and add a new file called `NotificationHub.cs`:

```
using System.Collections.Concurrent;
using Microsoft.AspNetCore.Http.Features;
using Microsoft.AspNetCore.SignalR;


public class NotificationHub : Hub
{
    private static ConcurrentDictionary<string, string>
Connections = new ConcurrentDictionary<string, string>();

    public async Task Notify(string notification)
    {
        var caller = Clients.Caller;

        await Clients.All.SendAsync("onReceived", $"{DateTime.
Now. ToShortTimeString()}: {Connections[Context.ConnectionId]}
notifies:{notification}");
    }

    public override async Task OnConnectedAsync()
    {
        var feature = Context.Features.Get<IHttpConnectionFeature>();
        Connections[Context.ConnectionId] = $"{feature.
```

```
RemoteIpAddress}: {feature.RemotePort}";


        await base.OnConnectedAsync();

        await Clients.All.SendAsync("onReceived", $"{DateTime.Now.
ToShortTimeString()}: {Connections[Context.ConnectionId]} joins.");

    }

}
```

A hub in SignalR works as a communication manager. It defines the methods that will be called by the clients, and calls the methods defined by the clients. All the dirty work beyond that is handled by the SignalR library as we introduced before. In this `NotificationHub` defines a method `Notify` with a string parameter, and the client will invoke this method to send a notification to the centralized notification manager. Meanwhile, the hub will invoke the function `onReceived` on the client side with one parameter as well. Notice the override `OnConnectionedAsync` from the base `Hub` class to log the connected clients, so that the user knows where the notification is coming from.

The final step on the server side is mapping the hub to the asp.net core middleware pipelines by calling `MapHub` in `Program.cs`.

```
app.UseStaticFiles();



app.MapHub<NotificationHub>("/Notification");
```

the set-up on the server side is completed. Now it is time to turn to the client side.

```
microsoft-signalr - Libraries - cdnjs - The #1 free and
open source CDN built to make life easier for developers
```

First, update the index.html to import the SignalR JavaScript client code and the customized `index.js`. `signalr.min.js` makes it possible to build a connection with the SignalR server and send messages back and forth. To allow users to notify all the clients, users add a text input element with id `txt` and a button input with id `btn`. Finally, a bullet element is added to show all the notifications received.

```html
<!DOCTYPE html>
<html lang="en">

<head>
    <meta charset="utf-8" />
    <title>SignalR</title>
    <script src="https://cdnjs.cloudflare.com/ajax/libs/
microsoft- signalr/6.0.8/signalr.min.js" integrity="sha512-
nERale4S3QuybfgFv0L+n k/8D55/5rNuDTewZkDsbVtFd0e5++
Q7V9sQEG2yAfRfTQB0gyDGSC70lKV68PAgVg==" crossorigin="anonymous"
referrerpolicy="no-referrer"></script>
    <script src="index.js"></script>
</head>


<body>
    <h1>Notification App</h1>
    <p>This is an application to send/receive centralized
notifications.</p>

    <div>
        <input type="text" id="txt" />
        <input type="button" id="btn" value="Notify" />
    </div>

    <br />

    <div>
        <ul id="notifications"></ul>
    </div>
</body>


</html>
```

In `index.js`, build a connection with URL defined in ASP.NET Core pipeline. In case the connection is break out, restart the connection again in the `onclose` handler. When a user clicks the Notify button, it will invoke the method `Notify` defined in the `NotificationHub`, which will in turn invoke the `onReceived` handler and append a new item in the bullet list.

```
const connection = new signalR.HubConnectionBuilder()
    .withUrl('/Notification')
    .configureLogging(signalR.LogLevel.Information)
    .build();


async function start() { try {
        await connection.start();
        console.log('SignalR Connected.');
    } catch (err) { console.log(err);
        setTimeout(start, 5000);
    }
};


// Listen for `DOMContentLoaded` event
document.addEventListener('DOMContentLoaded', (e) => {
    document.getElementById('btn').addEventListener('click', send);
});


async function send(e) {
    const message = document.getElementById('txt').value;
    console.log(message);

    try {
        await connection.invoke('Notify', message);
    } catch (err) {
        console.error(err);
    }
}
```

```
connection.on('onReceived', (message) => {
    const li = document.createElement('li');
    li.textContent = message;
    document.getElementById('notifications').appendChild(li);
});


connection.onclose(async() =>
    { await start();
});


// Start the connection.
start();
```

Type `dotnet run` in the terminal to run the app. This time, bring up two browser clients and navigate to *http://localhost:5044*. In the first browser window, users will see two clients joining messages. Try sending notifications in these two browsers and both clients get notified. Refer to Figure 2.3.

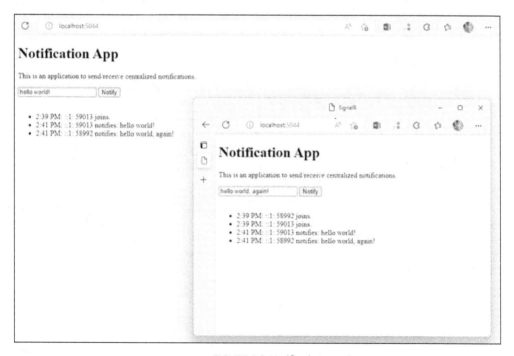

FIGURE 2.3 Notification app.

This example is shown using Microsoft Edge Version 104.0.1293.46 on Windows 11 and it supports WebSocket, so SignalR will utilize WebSocket and RPC to implement these notifications. If users are using an older browser that does not support WebSocket, they will notice that they are able to get notifications as well since SignalR can fallback communication strategies automatically.

BLAZOR SERVER

All different Blazor hosting models leveraged Razor components. (This will be explained more in Chapter 3, Implementing Razor and Other Components.). Where the components were hosted determines the hosting model. If the components run on the server side, it is called Blazor Server. Saying components run on the server side means that the app is executed in the ASP.NET Core application, and Blazor Server heavily depends on SignalR to update UI, handle events, and execute JavaScript.

Create a Blazor Server app and see how SignalR helps here. Type the commands in the terminal to generate a new Blazor Server app in the folder `BlazorServerDemo`.

```
dotnet new blazorserver -o BlazorServerDemo
cd ./BlazorServerDemo
```

In `Program.cs` there is that one line code that looks familiar, which was introduced in the SignalR section.

```
using Microsoft.AspNetCore.Components; using
Microsoft.AspNetCore.Components.Web; using
BlazorServerDemo.Data;


var builder = WebApplication.CreateBuilder(args);


// Add services to the container.
Builder.Services.AddRazorPages();
builder.Services.AddServerSideBlazor();
builder.Services.AddSingleton<WeatherForecastService>();


var app = builder.Build();
```

```
// Configure the HTTP request pipeline.
If (!app.Environment.IsDevelopment())
{
    app.UseExceptionHandler("/Error");

    // The default HSTS value is thiry days. Users may want to
change this for production scenarios (see https://aka.ms/
aspnetcore-hsts).
    App.UseHsts();

}


app.UseHttpsRedirection();

app.UseStaticFiles();

app.UseRouting();

app.MapBlazorHub();
app.MapFallbackToPage("/_Host");


app.Run();
```

It is reasonable to guess that `MapBlazorHub` will map an endpoint for the `BlazorHub` class, just like what we did in our previous SignalR notification application.

`aspnetcore/ComponentEndpointRouteBuilderExtensions.cs` at `main dotnet/aspnetcore (github.com)`

Check the open-source code on GitHub, and the assumption is verified. `MapBlazorHub` has a few overloads that will finally map the class `ComponentHub` to the default URL `_blazor`. It can be easily proved if users start the `BlazorServerDemo` application, browse to the home page and switch to the Console tab in the developer tools. The console log states `Information: Normalizing '_blazor' to 'https:// local-host:7267/_blazor'`. Further evidence is that when users register Blazor in the container, the open-source code shows that it is calling the method `AddSignalR` under the hood to register SignalR as well.

It is worth pointing out that while the application is running on the server, a circuit that represented the connection between a client and the server persisted until disconnection. Each connection established with the server will open a new circuit, and that includes opening a new browser on the same page. The circuit will be closed when the user closes a page or navigates to the external URL. Even better, one can inherit the `CircuitHandler` to customize the lifecycle handlers for the circuits. By taking notes of each connected client (as shown in the SignalR example), users can show how many clients are reading their blogs or watching their videos.

Users usually choose Blazor Server if they want to take advantage of the .NET ecosystem, for example, .NET API, libraries, or tool chains. In addition, with Blazor Server, users release the clients from downloading heavily as compared to Blazor WebAssembly. On the other side, since the application is running on the server, all the client interactions will be handled by the user's server as well, and that would definitely hurt their server's performance, and they can't even leverage CDN to boost static resource loading.

BLAZOR WEBASSEMBLY

Blazor WebAssembly is running in the Web browser on the client side. It is based on a .NET WebAssembly runtime, and it will be downloaded by the browser for the very first visit. Unlike Blazor Server, all the events, or UI interactions are running on the client threads.

For example, look at the default Blazor WebAssembly app. Create a demo app with the following commands:

```
dotnet new blazorwasm -o BlazorWebAssemblyDemo
```

Then in the folder `BlazorWebAssemblyDemo`, files similar to Figure 2.4 will be generated:

```
> ls
App.razor  BlazorWebAssemblyDemo.csproj  Pages  Program.cs  Properties  Shared  _Imports.razor  wwwroot
```

FIGURE 2.4 Code generated by dotnet new.

Then run another command in BlazorWebAssemblyDemo to run the Balzor WebAssembly application:

```
dotnet run
```

Browse to the URL displayed in the terminal, open the network tab in DevTools, and one should see many `dotnet` libraries are being sent to the client as shown in Figure 2.5.

FIGURE 2.5 dotnet libraries sent to clients.

Some of these are exactly the same libraries that are normally required when users run a local dotnet console application, such as System.IO.dll, while others are dedicated for a Blazor application, such as Microsoft.AspNetCore. Components.WebAssembly.dll. When users run a local console application, those `dll` libraries are consumed by a .NET runtime. Similarly, Blazor WebAssembly provides such a runtime, `dotnet.wasm`, sent to the client as well in Figure 2.3, and this runtime makes it possible to consume unchanged dotnet libraries just as in a console application.

As was introduced in the last chapter, the `wasm` code is initiated by `blazor. webassembly.js`. In this JavaScript file, it wraps a method to call the recommended `WebAssembly.instantiateStreaming` and falls back to array instantiation.

Here, is where the core code is picked up to help users understand the process which will enable them to build a better connection with the WebAssembly introduced in Chapter 1:

```
await async function (e, t) {
    if ("function" == typeof WebAssembly.instantiateStreaming)
        try {
```

```
        return (await WebAssembly.instantiateStreaming
(e.response,t)).instance

      } catch (e) {

        console.info("Streaming compilation failed.
Falling back to ArrayBuffer instantiation. ", e)

      }

    const n = await e.response.then((e => e.arrayBuffer()));

    return (await WebAssembly.instantiate(n, t)).instance

}(t, e)
```

Other than the WebAssembly loading, take a closer look at the starting point of a Blazor WebAssembly application, `Program.cs`:

```
var builder = WebAssemblyHostBuilder.CreateDefault(args);

builder.RootComponents.Add<App>("#app");
```

First, it creates a `WebAssemblyHostBuilder`, and it is responsible for configuring and creating a `WebAssmeblyHost`. The next line of code configures the `RootComponent` for the application, which is an `app` component, followed by a parameter of CSS selector. It will select a HTML element with id app as in `index.html` under the `wwwroot` folder:

```
<!DOCTYPE html>

<html lang="en">


<head>

    <meta charset="utf-8" />

    <meta name="viewport" content="width=device-width, initial-
scale=1.0, maximum-scale=1.0, user-scalable=no" />

    <title>EShop</title>

    <base href="/" />

    <!-- <link href="css/bootstrap/bootstrap.min.css"
    rel="stylesheet"
/> -->
```

```
    <link href="https://cdn.jsdelivr.net/npm/bootstrap@5.2.1/
dist/css/bootstrap.min.css" rel="stylesheet" integrity=
"sha384- iYQeCzEYFbKjA/T2uDLTpkwGzCiq6soy8tYaI1GyVh/UjpbCx/
TYkiZhlZB6+fzT" crossorigin="anonymous">

    <link rel="stylesheet" href="https://cdn.jsdelivr.net/npm/
bootstrap-icons@1.9.1/font/bootstrap-icons.css">

    <link href="css/app.css" rel="stylesheet" />

    <link href="EShop.styles.css" rel="stylesheet" />
</head>


<body>
    <div id="app">Loading...</div>


    <div id="blazor-error-ui">
        An unhandled error has occurred.
        <a href="" class="reload">Reload</a>
        <a class="dismiss">✖</a>
    </div>

    <script src="_framework/blazor.webassembly.js"></script>

    <script src="https://cdn.jsdelivr.net/npm/bootstrap@5.2.1/
dist/js/ bootstrap.bundle.min.js" integrity="sha384-u1OknCvx-
WvY5kfmNBILK2hRnQC3Pr 17a+RTT6rIHI7NnikvbZlHgTPOOmMi466C8"
crossorigin="anonymous"></script>
</body>


</html>
```

This index.html works as a blueprint for the Blazor WebAssembly application. It works the same way as any other Web application. In the body section, we defined a div element with id app. The component added to the RootComponents in builder will be inserted here.

App.razor defines two sections for found route and not found route, and intuitively, they are for a defined route in the application and what a 404 response should look like. More about the `Router` component will be discussed in a later chapter. In the project root folder, there is another file, `_Imports.razor`. It defines global `@using` directive. Any directive added to this file applies to all the components in the project folder.

Users usually choose Blazor WebAssembly when they desire to have an application that can work offline when there are no network connections. Users can also benefit from CDN distributing static resources, or even as a whole, serving their applications. Blazor WebAssembly also helps to reduce the server performance pressure since all the event handling, UI interactions, and heavy calculations are now the responsibility of the clients. In addition, the applications could be installed as a progressive Web app on the clients' machines, and users can leverage all the capabilities of PWA, for example, notification.

BLAZOR HYBRID

Blazor Hybrid has recently joined the Blazor family. It is a hybrid way to build native applications with HTML and CSS technologies. Users can unlock all the capabilities that are not available on the Web-alone platform, combined with .NET MAUI, WPF, and Windows Forms. Blazor Hybrid will not be covered in the following chapters; however, readers are encouraged to experiment with it in their own way, especially when they have a production-ready Web application that is built with Blazor. It will greatly reduce workload when developing a corresponding native app.

CONCLUSION

This chapter began with a protocol WebSocket. It is proposed to help build a full duplex communication channel between the client and server. It is very popular in real-time Web applications, for example, instant messaging and gaming. Then the chapter introduced a .NET library, SignalR. It is aimed to help users build real-time applications with high performance. This chapter continued by providing information for developing a demo on how clients can send notifications to each other online.

Blazor Server is heavily dependent on SignalR to build connections with clients, and all the handlers are running on the server side, while Blazor WebAssembly offloads this work to the browsers. The key benefits of these two models were described. Blazor Hybrid is another hybrid way to develop native applications based on Web technologies, and it will overall increase productivity if users already have a Web based on Blazor, or if they want to develop an app targeting multiple platforms, including Web, desktop, and mobile at the same time.

In the next chapter, the core building block in the world of Blazor, Razor Component, is introduced. The text will dive deep into how components are implemented and how they can be combined to render UI, partial pages, and layouts.

CHAPTER 3

IMPLEMENTING RAZOR AND OTHER COMPONENTS

INTRODUCTION

This chapter introduces Razor components and discusses one of the special components, layout, which shares many common properties with other components as well. The text jumps into details of how components are implemented and how to use them on a page. In addition, the community has been providing plenty of open-source libraries, which will be looked at.

STRUCTURE

In this chapter, the following topics are discusssed:

- directives
- one-way binding
- two-way binding
- cascading
- event handling
- lifecycle
- layout
- libraries

OBJECTIVES

In this chapter, readers will understand the process of creating a customized component and understand the binding between components and models to create an interactive application.

Next, readers will be taught event handling for components and know the lifecycle of components to customize components' behavior. Readers will also learn how to reuse components by layouts.

Starting from this chapter, readers will build an e-shop Web application step by step, with the topics that have been discussed in each chapter, and eventually they will deploy it on the cloud.

Regardless of which Blazor model users choose, Razor components will be the common building blocks used to build an application from the ground up.

RAZOR COMPONENTS

Components are usually developed by the file with the extension `.razor`. It will be the bricks when building the application house. Razor syntax is based on both HTML and C#, while HTML defines how to render the components, and alternatively, C# defines the logic of the components. The following is one of the simplest razor components to be used as an example.

Before creating the first components, a Blazor project is created by typing `dotnet new blazorwasm` a preferred terminal. The example here uses Microsoft terminal. Run the default application with dotnet run and browse to the Web page with port; here it is *https://localhost:7045* which will show a Web page like the one in Figure 3.1.

FIGURE 3.1 Blazor WebAssembly home page.

Create a simple head component to replace `Hello, world!` with `This is my new head!` First, go to the `shared` folder under the root and create a new file called `MyHeader.razor`:

```
<h1>@head</h1>
@code {

    private string head = "This is my new head!";

}
```

Update the `Index.razor` under the `Pages` folder to use the newly created component:

```
@page "/"


<PageTitle>Index</PageTitle>

@* <h1>Hello, world!</h1> *@

<MyHead />
```

Welcome to your new app.

```
<SurveyPrompt Title="How is Blazor working for you?" />
```

We commented on the old h1 label and replaced with newly created components. Now run the app again with `dotnet run` and refresh the browser. Notice that on the home page there is a header that says, `This is my new head!`:

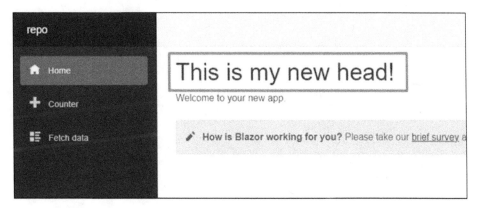

FIGURE 3.2 Home page with the new header.

In the Razor component, users should extensively use @ sign prefixed to a keyword representing a directive or a directive attribute.

DIRECTIVE

A directive changes how a component is parsed. Take the simple head component `MyHead` as an example. Inside the `h1` label, there is an @ sign followed by the variable head. If @ sign is removed, users will see "head" on the home page.

In this section build an order model where users can update the number of items in the cart.

First, create a shop item model and an order model, which contains key information, for example, which items your customers are buying and the quantity of those items:

```
namespace EShop.Models
{
    public class ShopItem
    {
        public string Name { get; set; }
        public string Description { get; set; }
        public double Price { get; set; }
        public ShopItem(string name, string description, double price)
        {
            Name = name;
            Description = description;
            Price = price;
        }
    }
}
```

The next model is `CartItem`. It represents an item in the customers' shopping cart, including how many of that specific item:

```
namespace EShop.Models
{
    public class CartItem
    {
        public ShopItem Item { get; set; }
        public int Count { get; set; }
        public CartItem(ShopItem item, int count)
        {
            Item = item;
            Count = count;
        }
    }
}
```

A final model is the `Cart`. A customer can add numerous `CartItem` in the Cart:

```
namespace EShop.Models
{
    public class Cart
    {
        public List<CartItem> Items { get; set; } = new
List<CartItem>();

        public void Add(CartItem item)
        {
            Items.Add(item);
        }
```

```
public void Remove(CartItem item)
{
    Items.Remove(item);
}

public void Clear()
{
    Items.Clear();
}
}
}
```

Next, create a Cart.razor page in the Pages folder to show the CartItems that the customer added to the Cart.

```
@page "/cart"

<PageTitle>Cart</PageTitle>

<h1>Cart</h1>

<button class="btn btn-danger" @onclick="Buy">Buy</button>

<div class="list-group">
@foreach (var item in _cart.Items)
{
  <div class="list-group-item">
    <div class="d-flex w-100 justify-content-between">
      <h5 class="mb-1">@item.Item.Name</h5>
      <small>3 days ago</small>
    </div>
    <p class="mb-1">@item.Item.Description</p>
```

```
        <small>

            <div class="d-flex flex-row mb-3">

                <i class="p-2 bi bi-dash-square" @
onclick="()=>Remove(item)"></i>

                <p class="p-2">@item.Count</p>

                <i class="p-2 bi bi-plus-square" @onclick="()=>
                Add(item)"></i>

            </div>

        </small>

    </div>

}

</div>


@code {

    private Models.Cart _cart = new Models.Cart();
    private void Buy()

    {

        _cart.Add(new Models.CartItem(new Models.ShopItem
("T-shirt","One of the tops", 5), 1));

    }


    private void Add(Models.CartItem item)

    {

        item.Count++;

    }


    private void Remove(Models.CartItem item)

    {

        item.Count--;

    }

}
```

DIRECTIVE ATTRIBUTE

A directive attribute is mostly applied to a Razor component and will affect parsing or the functionalities. It is more like a booster to the Razor components.

One of the directive attributes that one might find extremely useful is `@bind`. It builds a data binding between the view and the model behind the scenes. When the application updates the model data, the front-end will render to reflect the change. This is suggestive of MVVM.

ONE-WAY BINDING

Blazor provides a data binding feature, and users can bind the user input to their model.

For example, if a customer would like to change their item count in the shopping cart from 1 to 100, with the former implementation, they might have to click on the add button 99 times, which is definitely not a user-friendly experience. Users can use binding with an input element so that this customer can enter any value they like.

Replace the `<p>` label with a `<input>` html element and bind it to `item.Count`. To verify that the model value is updated correctly, write a `Print` method to log the count of the updated item:

```
@page "/cart"

@* some code *@

        <div class="d-flex flex-row mb-3">
            <i class="p-2 bi bi-dash-square" @
onclick="()=>Remove(item)"></i>
            <input class="p-2" type="text" @bind="item.Count" />
            <i class="p-2 bi bi-plus-square" @onclick="()=>
Add(item)"></i>
            <p class="p-2">@item.Count</p>
        </div>


@* some code *@
```

Buy a T-shirt, change the count to 100, and users should be able to see the label next to the plus button is 100 now as well.

BINDING EVENT

In the previous example, after changing the value of the item count, only when users click somewhere else will the next label be updated to the new value. This may confuse customers because if they don't click anywhere, the value will not be updated, and they will pay for an order with an undesired amount of items. It can be easily fixed with the directive `@bind:event`.

This directive defines under which event trigger the binding will update value. By default, `@bind:event` is implicitly set to the `onchange` event. Defined in the HTML standards, `onchange` will be triggered when two conditions are met. The first is that content is changed, and the second one is when the element loses focus. In this case, when a customer clicks `onelement` and the item count input box loses focus and the `onchange` event is triggered, this leads to the model value updated behind the scenes.

To improve user experience, one could set this bind directive on the input element to be `oninput` event: `<input class="p-2" type="text" @bind="item.Count" @ bind:event="oninput" />`, which is similar to the `onchange` event, and it will be fired immediately when the value changes, meaning every time a customer presses any key, it will be triggered, and the binding model will be updated more frequently. It is a balance between the `onchange` or `oninput` event. If frequent updates fired by the `oninput` event will be a performance bottleneck for the application, one might consider using the default `onchange` event.

BINDING FORMAT

Another useful binding directive might be `@bind:format`. It defines the format to display the binding model. For example, the product owner decides to display an update time for each item in the cart with customized format, showing either when the item was put in the cart or when the item count was updated.

To show the time, add a `DateTime` property `UpdateTime` to the `CartItem` model and update it when the `Count` changes:

```
namespace EShop.Models
{
    public class CartItem
    {
        // some code

        private int _count;
        public int Count
        {
            get => _count;
            set
            {
                _count = value; UpdateTime = DateTime.Now;
            }
        }

  public DateTime UpdateTime { get; set; } = DateTime.Now;

        // some code
    }
}
```

Bind the `UpdateTime` to a `readonly` `<input>` element on the `Cart` Razor page:

```
@* some code *@

    <div class="d-flex w-100 justify-content-between">
      <h5 class="mb-1">@item.Item.Name</h5>
      <small><input readonly @bind="item.UpdateTime"></input>
      </small>
</div>

@* some code *@
```

When the format directive is not set, the application Web page will display the default `DatetTime` string:

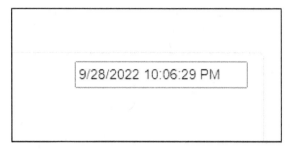

FIGURE 3.3 Default DateTime format.

To match product owner's requirements, we could add a format directive to the element, `<small><input readonly @bind="item.UpdateTime"` `@ bind:format="HH:mm:ss"></input></small>` and it will only display time but no date anymore:

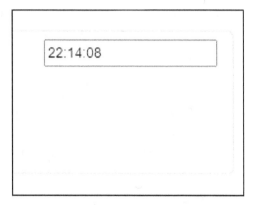

FIGURE 3.4 Customized DateTime format.

As of the time of writing, format directive only supports `DateTime` expressions. To display more value formatting, developers have to add a customized string property for binding purposes.

UNPARSED VALUE

If customers enter a string instead of a number for the item count, binding directives will revert the value back to the last one automatically. In the example, users bind the value to the Count property of type int, and if they enter 10 first, and keep typing "H" on the keyboard, it will stay with 10 and has no effect.

Another customized way to handle unparsed value is to bind with a string value, and then code the get and set methods to convert the binding string to the model data in a unique way or format, as bind directive will call the get and set methods upon the binding event as specified.

TWO-WAY BINDING

The small label section is used for each item Count, and now it might be a good chance to refactor the Cart page and create a CartItemCount Razor component dedicated to the item count.

Create a new folder called Components and a customized component CartItemCountComponent.razor under it:

```
<small>
    <div class="d-flex flex-row mb-3">
        <i class="p-2 bi bi-dash-square" @onclick="Remove"></i>
        <input class="p-2" type="text"
@bind="Count" @ bind:event="oninput" />
        <i class="p-2 bi bi-plus-square" @onclick="Add"></i>
        <p class="p-2">@Count</p>
    </div>
</small>


@code{
    [Parameter]
    public int Count { get; set; }
```

```
    public void Add()
    {
        Count++;
    }


    public void Remove()
    {
        Count--;
    }
}
```

Add a `Count` property and a `Parameter` attribute with it. This `Parameter` attribute tells Blazor that `Count` will be exported as a parameter that can be bound to just like any other HTML attribute.

The cart page will also be updated accordingly to use the newly created component:

```
@page "/cart"
@using EShop.Components;

<PageTitle>Cart</PageTitle>

<h1>Cart</h1>

<button class="btn btn-danger" @onclick="Buy">Buy</button>

<div class="list-group">
@foreach (var item in _cart.Items)
{
```

```
<div class="list-group-item">

  <div class="d-flex w-100 justify-content-between">

    <h5 class="mb-1">@item.Item.Name</h5>

    <small><input readonly @bind="item.UpdateTime" @
bind:format="HH:mm:ss"></input></small>

  </div>

  <p class="mb-1">@item.Item.Description</p>

  <CartItemCount Count="@item.Count" />

</div>

}

</div>


@code {

    private Models.Cart _cart = new Models.Cart();


    private void Buy()

    {

        _cart.Add(new Models.CartItem(new Models.ShopItem
("T-shirt","One of the tops", 5), 1));

    }

}
```

Run the EShop application, buy a T-Shirt, and try to update the item count. The label next to the input element is updated as well, however, there is a bug when observed closely, and the updated time element does not sync with the typing. It never updates!

If the user moves the code from the page to a Razor component that is used by this page, and the count label shows the correct number, the count does update. Take one step back and check the code to see where to update the Updated Time. Assign a new value to the UpdateTime property when the Count of CartItem is updated, and that gives the user two potential reasons why the time is not displaying correctly in the browser. The first one is that the user did not actually set the Count property, and the other one is that the user updated the time but failed to render it. The first one can be easily proved. In the set method, add one line of code to print a log in the console,

Console.WriteLine("sssssssssssssssssssssssssssssssssssssss ssssset");, and set a debug breaking point on the set method. Now we run the application and enter some value in the input element. Neither the breaking point is hit nor the console prints ssssssssssssssssssssssssssssss ssssssssssssset.

That is the essential difference between one-way and two-way binding directives. In one-way binding, users pass the data into the Razor components as a parameter. No matter how the components update the parameter, the world outside of the components will not be notified, and that explains why the time is never updated further.

To fix this, one must officially introduce the two-way binding. Modify the CartItemCount Razor component first.

```
<small>
    <div class="d-flex flex-row mb-3">
        <i class="p-2 bi bi-dash-square" @onclick=
        "RemoveAsync"></i>
        <input class="p-2" type="text" value="@Count"
        @oninput="OnInput" />
        <i class="p-2 bi bi-plus-square" @onclick="AddAsync"></i>
        <p class="p-2">@Count</p>
    </div>
</small>


@code{
    [Parameter]
    public int Count { get; set; }


    [Parameter]
    public EventCallback<int> CountChanged { get; set; }
    public async Task AddAsync()
    {
        Count++;
        await CountChanged.InvokeAsync(Count);
```

```
    }


    public async Task RemoveAsync()

    {

        Count--;

        await CountChanged.InvokeAsync(Count);

    }


    public async Task OnInput(ChangeEventArgs args)

    {

        if (args.Value is null || string.IsNullOrWhiteSpace(args.
Value.ToString()))

        {

            Count = 1;

        }

        else

        {

            Count = int.Parse(args.Value.ToString());

        }

        await CountChanged.InvokeAsync(Count);

    }

}
```

There are a few highlights in this version of `CartItemCount` component. The first is that users provide an `EventCallBack` event. With the `Parameter` attribute, this is the event that users expose to the parent component. The parent component will handle the notification event with the generic payload to implement further logic.

In the example, expose a `CountChanged` event, and invoke this event everywhere the Count value gets changed. From the page side, upgrade the one-way binding to two-way binding, with the following code, `<CartItemCount @bind-Count="item.Count" @bind-Count:event="CountChanged" />`. Unlike assigning `item.Count` to the `Count` property directly, we use the bind directive to bind the `Count` property with `item.Count` in two directions. If the value from the `item.Count` changed, the child item's property will be updated as usual. This time, if the child component's `Count` property is changed, since the user invoked the notification event every time, the parent page will also be notified, and the set method of the `CartItem` model will be invoked as well, so that time displayed on the top right corner will reflect the latest changes.

Pay attention to the syntax here. Component parameters bind in a parent component using `@bind-{PROPERTY}`, and `{PROPERTY}` represents the property to bind. In this case, the property is `Count`, with the `Parameter` attribute. You also must implement an `EventCallback`, named by `{PROPERTY}Changed` with the `Parameter` attribute as well. These two "Parameters," together with the `@bind` syntax achieve the two-way binding between components.

CASCADING

Passing parameters to low-level components has been proved to be a powerful tool to build up a system with different levels. It helps to maintain clean code and clear business logic. Passing them just one level down is simply not enough. Sometimes, users need to refer to the context from more than one level up, as the application evolves, and as more features or requirements emerge. If users find themselves in a situation with complex business rules, they will usually choose to refactor code to be more object-orientated with more than one-level hierarchy.

Based on this reason, the developing team decided to refactor the Cart page once again. This time, they will build a dedicated Cart Razor component, which will use a few `CartItem` components to represent the items customers selected for their cart.

A new challenge is to take the data context from `_dart` object to the components deep down, with Parameter attributes; users are only allowed to pass the parameter one level down. To go further than that, they will introduce another attribute, `CascadingParameter`. With `CascadingParameter` and `CascadingValue`, users can identify a uniformed data context throughout the components tree. A typical example would be to define a general CSS style for all the components in the hierarchy tree.

The UI designed has defined a uniform `fontsize` for the EShop Cart page, and this `fontsize` standard will be passed to all the components referenced:

```
@using Models


<h3>@Cart.User</h3>


<div class="list-group">
  @foreach (var item in Cart.Items)
  {
    <div class="list-group-item">
      <div class="d-flex w-100 justify-content-between">
        <p class="mb-1" style="@FontSize">@item.Item.Name</p>
        <small><input readonly @bind="item.UpdateTime" @
bind:format="HH:mm:ss"></input></small>
      </div>
      <p class="mb-1">@item.Item.Description</p>
      <CartItemCount @bind-Count="item.Count" @bind-
Count:event="CountChanged" />
</div>


  }
</div>


@code {
  [Parameter]
  public Cart Cart { get; set; }


  [CascadingParameter(Name = "FontSize")]
  public string FontSize { get; set; }


  [CascadingParameter(Name = "FontStyle")]
  public string FontStyle { get; set; }
}
```

Add the cascading properties to the `CartItemCountComponent` Razor component:

```
<small>
    <div class="d-flex flex-row mb-3">
        <i class="p-2 bi bi-dash-square" style="@FontSize" @
onclick="RemoveAsync"></i>
        <input class="p-2" style="@FontSize font-style: italic;"
type="text" value="@Count" @oninput="OnInput" />
        <i class="p-2 bi bi-plus-square" style="@FontSize" @
onclick="AddAsync"></i>
        <p class="p-2" style="@FontSize">@Count</p>
    </div>
</small>


@code{
    [Parameter]
    public int Count { get; set; }


    [Parameter]
    public EventCallback<int> CountChanged { get; set; }


    [CascadingParameter(Name = "FontSize")]
    public string FontSize { get; set;}


    [CascadingParameter(Name = "FontStyle")]
    public string FontStyle { get; set;}


    @* some code *@
}
```

Define the `CascadingValue` in the most parent Razor pages.

```
@page "/cart"

@using EShop.Components;
```

```
<PageTitle>Cart</PageTitle>

<h1>Cart</h1>

<button class="btn btn-danger" @onclick="Buy">Buy</button>
<CascadingValue Value="@_fontSize" Name = "FontSize">
  <CascadingValue Value="@_fontStyle" Name = "FontStyle">
    <CartComponent Cart="@_cart" />
  </CascadingValue>
</CascadingValue>

@code {
    private Models.Cart _cart = new Models.Cart("Brian");

    private string _fontSize = "font-size: 30px;";

    private string _fontStyle = "font-style: italic;";

    private void Buy()
    {
        _cart.Add(new Models.CartItem(new Models.ShopItem
("T-shirt", "One of the tops", 5), 2));

        _cart.Add(new Models.CartItem(new Models.ShopItem
("Jacket", "The most popular", 17), 1));
    }
}
```

The key idea is to wrap components in a `CascadingValue` label. In this label, users will define a data context that will be passed downward throughout the entire components tree. Each child component, which is intended to take the data context, can define a property with a `CascadingParameter` attribute. If users have more than one `CascadingValue`, they will give the `Name` attribute a value, and wrap the `CascadingValue` one inside another, and the child components will be placed innermost. Components' `CascadingParameter` will also catch the data by assigning a `Name` field.

In this example, users defined a universal `fontsize` and a universal `font-style` in the page level and passed these standard styles into the tree. The children are now also rendered with the new style. In general, `CascadingValue` will be the best option to set up a global theme or style, as the theme or style built in this way can take effect easily for the entire application.

EVENT HANDLING

Another popular feature in components is event handling. In the world of Blazor components, users can define an event using `EventCallback` seen in the two-way binding section, where users notify the parent component that data has been updated. Unlike the event keyword in normal .NET world, in components, users define an event with the help of the struct `EventCallback`. `EventCallback` can only be subscribed by one method, and this will be the only one method that will be invoked, when users emit an event. While in normal .NET, an event can be subscribed to by multiple methods, and these methods will be invoked together while emitting the event.

A new user story comes from the product owner. EShop will allow customers to remove items from the card and record the log when an item is removed, so that the business operation can analyze the data and improve customers' experience.

Add an `EventCallback` `OnCartItemRemoved` to the `CartComponent` razor component:

```
@using Models

<h3>@Cart.User</h3>

<div class="list-group">
  @foreach (var item in Cart.Items)
  {
    <div class="list-group-item">
      <div class="d-flex w-100 justify-content-between">
        <p class="mb-1" style="@FontSize">@item.Item.Name</p>
        <small>
```

```
        <div>
            <input readonly @bind="item.UpdateTime" @
bind:format="HH:mm:ss"></input>
            <i class="p-2 bi bi-x-octagon-fill" @
onclick="()=>Remove(item)"></i>
        </div>
      </small>
    </div>
    <p class="mb-1">@item.Item.Description</p>
    <CartItemCountComponent @bind-Count="item.
Count" @bind- Count:event="CountChanged" />
  </div>
  }
</div>


@code {
  [Parameter]
  public Cart Cart { get; set; }

  [CascadingParameter(Name = "FontSize")]
  public string FontSize { get; set; }

  [CascadingParameter(Name = "FontStyle")]
  public string FontStyle { get; set; }

  [Parameter]
  public EventCallback<CartItem> OnCartItemRemoved { get; set; }

  private void Remove(CartItem item)
  {
    OnCartItemRemoved.InvokeAsync(item);
  }
}
```

Pass a method as a delegate to the `OnCartIteAlibaba` and back:

```razor
@page "/cart"
@using EShop.Components;


<PageTitle>Cart</PageTitle>


<h1>Cart</h1>


<button class="btn btn-danger" @onclick="Buy">Buy</button>
<CascadingValue Value="@_fontSize" Name = "FontSize">
  <CascadingValue Value="@_fontStyle" Name = "FontStyle">
    <CartComponent Cart="@_cart" OnCartItemRemoved=
"OnCartItemRemoved"/>
  </CascadingValue>
</CascadingValue>


@code {
    private Models.Cart _cart = new Models.Cart("Brian");
    private string _fontSize = "font-size: 30px;";
    private string _fontStyle = "font-style: italic;";
    private void Buy()
    {
        _cart.Add(new Models.CartItem(new Models.ShopItem
("T-shirt","One of the tops", 5), 2));
        _cart.Add(new Models.CartItem(new Models.ShopItem
("Jacket", "The most popular", 17), 1));
    }


    private void OnCartItemRemoved(Models.CartItem item)
    {
      _cart.Remove(item);
    }
}
```

In the `CartComponent`, users expose an `EventCallback` if `CartItem` was a parameter, so the page could call the component and assign a method to this callback just like any other parameters defined before. Later on, users can invoke this callback in the child component at any time, given a `CartItem` instance as the callback argument. In the method that subscribes, it will be executed while users invoke the callback. In this way, users implemented the removing of `CartItem` in the page, when they click on the remove button in the child component.

LIFECYCLE

In a Razor component, there are multiple virtual methods that users can choose to override to alter the rendering behavior for this component. These virtual methods are, in the lifecycle order, `SetParametersAsync`, `OnInitializedAsync`, `OnParametersSetAsync`, `ShouldRender`, `BuildRenderTree`, `OnAfterRenderAsync` `SetParametersAsync` will wrap all the parameters set to this component in the `ParameterView` object, and users can get the parameter by its name. This is a good chance now to retrieve data from the backend API with parameter values. Next, call the base `SetParametersAsync`, in the base method implementations, it invokes `OnInitializedasync` if this is the first time creating this component instance, and then immediately invokes `OnParametersSetAsync`. Untill now, users can get the component's state and parameters set.

When users want to explicitly rerender a component, they can call `StateHasChanged` to trigger the rendering. Blazor will then check with `ShouldRender`. This method returns a Boolean value to inform Blazor whether a rendering will take place or not. If users return `false` in this method, they will prevent Blazor from rerendering this component, to improve users' experience and build up a high-performance application. `BuildRenderTree` is another virtual method one can override if no markup code has been written yet for this component. In this method, users may define how to render the component specifically by coding. Once Blazor completes the rendering, `OnAfterRenderAsync` will be invoked, and it will now be safe to call the ref component here. The last method in component lifecycle is `Dispose` if the component implements `IDisposable` interface. When the component is removed from the rendering tree, Blazor will invoke this method, and it will be good chance for the user to dispose all of the resources.

LAYOUT

With three default pages and the Cart page, there are a total of four pages currently in the EShop application, and they all share the same top head and side navigation bar. This is implemented by a layout in Blazor. If one is building a complex Web application, it tends to have more than one page, and it is important to keep a consistent head or navigation menu throughout the application. Layout can be displayed on every page, and it saves the user from duplicated code, and makes it easy to maintain the shared consistency.

A layout is in fact a special component in Blazor. All the layouts will inherit from the `BlazorLayoutComponent`, which inherits `ComponentBase`, the same base class that a normal component will inherit. It provides a special Parameter of type `RenderFragment`, Body. In the implemented layout, one can render the @body anywhere. Therefore, it is likely that users will add top head and side navigation menus in the layout, just like the default Blazor example and render the body in an article element:

```
@inherits LayoutComponentBase
<div class="page">
    <div class="sidebar">
        <NavMenu />
    </div>


    <main>
        <div class="top-row px-4">
            <a href="https://docs.microsoft.com/aspnet/"
target="_ blank">About</a>
        </div>

        <article class="content px-4"> @Body
        </article>
    </main>
</div>
```

To wrap contents in the layout, one needs to declare where they want to place their components by using the `@layout` directive.

Layouts can be nested just like normal components have child components. To render a layout inside another layout, users must refer to the parent layout in their child layout and render their content inside the child layout.

Here is how to create a layout. Under the `Shared` folder, create a new file named `EShopLayout.razor`:

```
@inherits LayoutComponentBase


<div>

    <p>EShop Blazor Application</p>


    <div>

        @Body

    </div>

</div>
```

First, create a new parent `EShop` layout, and in the second line of `./Shared/ MainLayout.razor`, refer to the `EShop` layout by adding `@layout EShopLayout`. To verify that there are not two layouts together, update `./App.razor` and change the layout for `NotFound` from `@typeof(MainLayout)` to `@typeof(EShoplayout)`.

Run the application and observe the extra label element `EShop Blazor Application` on the top of the Web pages. Browse to an undeclared route, for example, `/eshop`, and the navigation menu will disappear with only the `EShop Blazor Application` label remaining, which means "not found" route will be rendered directly inside the new `EShopLayout`, while the Cart page is rendered in the nested `MainLayout`.

LIBRARIES

In the open-source communities, there are a number of popular Blazor components libraries that users can use in their project.

Fast-Blazor

https://github.com/microsoft/fast-blazor

This is a Blazor component library that implements Microsoft FluentUI. It is lightweight and compatible with .NET 6 applications.

MatBlazor

https://github.com/SamProf/MatBlazor

This library implements common components following material design specifications. It has a complementary demo Web sites and documentation.

Ant Design Blazor

https://github.com/ant-design-blazor/ant-design-blazor

Ant Design is an enterprise level design language by Alibaba and has a strong ecosystem. This library contributes a Blazor implementation to the Ant Design Community

BootstrapBlazor

https://github.com/dotnetcore/BootstrapBlazor

This is also an enterprise-class library. It is implemented based on the popular Bootstrap styles.

CONCLUSION

This chapter covered the basic concepts of components and built an interactive shopping cart page with nested components and databinding between components and models. Readers learned how to pass data down through multiple levels of hierarchies and handle the events emitted by the component. We also introduced the lifecycle of a component and used a special component, layout, to reuse existing components. Finally, readers quickly went through some popular Blazor components in the open-source community.

The next chapter discusses more about the mechanism behind the components and layout and takes some source code as examples to learn the techniques to improve applications' performance.

4

ADVANCED TECHNIQUES FOR BLAZOR COMPONENT ENHANCEMENT

INTRODUCTION

Chapter 3 introduced the Razor components as core building material for a Blazor application. In this chapter, by digging into the source code, readers will go through some more advanced ways to enhance components' features and performances.

STRUCTURE

This chapter discusses the following topics:

- how to reference other components
- how to preserve elements or components
- how to template components
- CSS isolation

In this chapter, we will be understanding the advanced topics around Blazor components. For example, components reference and preservation. We will understand the components template and css isolation as well to help you better organize your code structure.

COMPONENT REFERENCE

Sometimes, users may want to control other components within their own component. In the world of HTML and JavaScript, users usually add an id attribute to the element that will be manipulated. While in Blazor, there is no easy way to get the element by its id in C# code. One way to solve the problem is to use one of the directive attributes introduced in Chapter 3.

The @ref directive attribute allows developers to reference another component, and, in this way, users can invoke the method just from the referenced component instance. For example, users would like to check out the items added to the shopping cart, and they can reference the CartComponent and call the method Checkout from it, just like one would call a method from any other instance in normal C# code.

```
// some other code
  public void Checkout()
  {
    foreach (var item in Cart.Items)
    {
      Console.WriteLine($"Checkout {item.Count} {item.Item.
Name}, the total is {item.Count * item.Item.Price}");
    }
  }
```

First, add a new Checkout method in the CartComponent source code. This method will iterate through all the items in the cart and print out the log displaying the counts, names, and the total prices.

Next, add a @ref directive attribute to the CartComponent in the CarPage. razor and use this component reference as if it is one of the properties of this page class.

```
@page "/cart"
@using EShop.Components;

<PageTitle>Cart</PageTitle>
```

```
<h1>Cart</h1>


<button class="btn btn-danger" @onclick="Buy">Buy</button>
<CascadingValue Value="@_fontSize" Name = "FontSize">
  <CascadingValue Value="@_fontStyle" Name = "FontStyle">
    <CartComponent @ref="cartComponent" Cart="@_cart"
OnCartItemRemoved="OnCartItemRemoved" />
  </CascadingValue>
</CascadingValue>
<button class="btn btn-warning" @onclick="Checkout">Checkout</button>


@code {
    private Models.Cart _cart = new Models.Cart("Brian");
    private string _fontSize = "font-size: 30px;";
    private string _fontStyle = "font-style: italic;";
    private CartComponent cartComponent;
    private void Buy()
    {
        _cart.Add(new Models.CartItem(new Models.ShopItem
("T-shirt", "One of the tops", 5), 2));
        _cart.Add(new Models.CartItem(new Models.ShopItem
("Jacket", "The most popular", 17), 1));
    }


    private void OnCartItemRemoved(Models.CartItem item)
    {
      _cart.Remove(item);
    }


    private void Checkout()
    {
      cartComponent.Checkout();
    }
}
```

Here, place the business logic, checkout, in the Razor component, but in practice, users may want to add more interaction logic between users and the application instead of business logic. Usually, business logic belongs to the model layer.

In this example, there is a public method in the CartComponent, and it is used in the CartPage to display the cart detail to customers. Before adding the @ref directive attribute to the component, users merely depend on the capabilities of the CartComponent by itself. Since users use the @ref directive attribute to catch the reference of this component in the Razor page, they have more flexibility in controlling the behavior of the component and hence be able to add more functionalities to the cart page. It will be like calling a normal C# instance, and one can call any instance member that is marked publicly accessible.

COMPONENTS PRESERVING

In a Web application, it is very common to show a list of variable kinds of data, or a table. It could be a table of employees' pay slips or last month's sales revenue, or simply a list of forecasted weather for the next week. Sometimes, these lists, or data are static. They remain the same through the users' certain experiences. Sometimes, they are dynamic, and users must keep refreshing the data. As a result, the Web application has to keep rerendering itself, and it could consume a lot of resources if there is a huge amount of data to be refreshed.

An example of this would be when one is developing a new feature of a wish list. A wish list is a placeholder where customers can save an item they like for later and not check out for now. One common scenario in this feature is that customers may frequently move items from the cart to their wish list, back and forth, several times while they are shopping. In such cases, the cart item or wish list in the application will be rerendered entirely in conjunction with the frequency that a customer updates it. In particular, when there are a large number of items in the list, there will be performance downgrade, and this will not be welcomed by customers. It is now the developers' responsibility to bring up a solution to boost performance. Luckily, Blazor provides a directive attribute @key to save the data, and users won't have to manually control the rerender algorithm to boost performance.

Create a new file called `WishListComponent.razor` under the `Components` folder and build a wish list component with the corresponding models.

```
<div class="list-group">

    @foreach (var item in WishList!.Items)

    {

        <li originalValue="@item.Item.Name">

            <div class="list-group-item">

                <div class="d-flex w-100 justify-content-between">

                    <p class="mb-1" style="@FontSize">@item.
                    Item.Name</p>

                    <small>

                        <div>

                            <input readonly @bind="item.
UpdateTime" @ bind:format="HH:mm:ss"></input>

                            <i class="p-2 bi bi-box-arrow-up" @
onclick="()=>MoveToCart(item)"></i>

                        </div>

                    </small>

                </div>

                <p class="mb-1">@item.Item.Description</p>

            </div>

        </li>


    }
</div>
```

The corresponding file `WishListComponent.razor.cs` is created for the code behind the component:

```
using Microsoft.AspNetCore.Components;
using EShop.Models;

namespace EShop.Components
```

```
{

    public partial class WishListComponent
    {
        [Parameter]
        public WishList? WishList { get; set; }


        [CascadingParameter(Name = "FontSize")]
        public string? FontSize { get; set; }


        [CascadingParameter(Name = "FontStyle")]
        public string? FontStyle { get; set; }


        [Parameter]
        public EventCallback<WishListItem> OnMovingToCart { get;
        set; }


        private async void MoveToCart(WishListItem item)
        {
            await OnMovingToCart.InvokeAsync(item);
        }

    }

}
```

This time, separate the component logic into a `.razor.cs` file. It is a common pattern in developing WPF projects where the `.xaml` file will be mapped with a `.xaml. cs` file. Blazor shares the same spirit here. The `WishListComponent` is in fact a partial class inheriting `ComponentBase` while partial of the class is UI, another part is pure `C#` code representing the component logic. The wish list models are very similar to the cart and will not be covered here.

Use the `WishListComponent` in the `CartPage`.

```
@page "/cart"
@using EShop.Components;
```

```
<PageTitle>Shopping here!</PageTitle>


<h2>Shopping here!</h2>


<button class="btn btn-danger" @onclick="AddToCart">Add
something to the cart</button>
<CascadingValue Value="@_fontSize" Name="FontSize">
  <CascadingValue Value="@_fontStyle" Name="FontStyle">

    <div>

      <h2>Cart</h2>

      <CartComponent @ref="cartComponent" Cart="@_ cart"
OnCartItemRemoved="OnCartItemRemoved"
OnMovingToWishList="OnMovingToWishList" />

    </div>


    <div>

      <h2>Wish List</h2>

      <WishListComponent @ref="wishListComponent" WishList="@_
wishList" OnMovingToCart="OnMovingToCart" />

    </div>

  </CascadingValue>
</CascadingValue>
<button class="btn btn-warning" @onclick="Checkout">Check-
out</button>

@* some code *@
```

Add the C# code to implement the item switch logic between cart and wish list:

```
@* some code *@
@code {
  private const string USER = "Brian";
  private Models.Cart _cart = new Models.Cart(USER);


  private Models.WishList _wishList = new Models.WishList(USER);
```

```csharp
    private string _fontSize = "font-size: 30px;";
    private string _fontStyle = "font-style: italic;";
    private CartComponent? cartComponent;
    private WishListComponent? wishListComponent;
    private void AddToCart()
    {
       _cart.Add(new Models.CartItem(new Models.ShopItem("T-shirt",
    "One of the tops", 5), 2));
       _cart.Add(new Models.CartItem(new Models.ShopItem
    ("Jacket", "The most popular", 17), 1));
       _cart.Add(new Models.CartItem(new Models.ShopItem("Sun
    glasses", "On sale", 8), 3));
    }


    private void OnCartItemRemoved(Models.CartItem item)
    {
      _cart.Remove(item);
    }


    private void Checkout()
    {
      cartComponent!.Checkout();
    }


    private void OnMovingToCart(Models.WishListItem item)
    {
      _wishList.Remove(item);

      var cartItem = new Models.CartItem(item.Item, item.Count);
      _cart.Add(cartItem);
    }
```

```
private void OnMovingToWishList(Models.CartItem item)
{

  _cart.Remove(item);


  var wishListItem = new Models.WishListItem(item.Item, item.
  Count);_wishList.Add(wishListItem);

}

}
```

The `CarPage`, where cascaded style and fonts are shared between the `CartComponent` and the `WishListComponent` has been updated. Users can now click on the small moving to wish list on the right top corner for each cart item and move it to the wish list. Or click on the similar button on the right top corner to reverse it back.

No performance improvement has been implemented yet. If a user moves an item back and forth, performance will be hurt. Next, add the `@key` directive attribute to each cart or wish list item `div` element to let Blazor know that these elements should be retained and how the cart items are mapped to them.

```
@* some code *@
@foreach (var item in Cart!.Items)
{
    <div class="list-group-item" @key="item.Item.Name">
@* some code *@
```

Use any object to key the element or component. It could be a string, a number, or an instance. Blazor will retain the relationship between the element and the cart item by its name. The best practice is to use the `@key` directive attribute for which the user is developing a list component and may use the item ID to key the component. To retain a mapping, don't forget that `@key` also marks that the relationship should be disposed when there is an instance replacement, and Blazor will rerender the front-end pages.

TEMPLATE COMPONENTS

As the application grows, there will be many places where repeated front-end code could be eliminated by using components. In some cases, this would be an easy replacement. For example, an easy replacement would be when developing a `CartComponent`, `CartItemCountComponent` is used to save the effort allowing customers to update how many items they would like to buy. Untill now, users were dealing with components that were purely developed by writing the HTML code explicitly. In other scenarios, there might be a chance that the consumer of those components will provide the HTML to be rendered inside the user's component.

For example, in the `CartComponent`, one could wrap the contents inside the for each loop to another component, and this new component must have the capability to render the children html in the list group container.

One straightforward way to implement this is to pass the HTML code as string, and the new component will have a string parameter and render the HTML explicitly as follows:

Create `GroupContainer.razor` under the Shared folder:

```
<div class="list-group-item">
    <div class="d-flex w-100 justify-content-between">
        <p class="mb-1" style="@FontSize">@Name</p>
        <small>
            <div>
                @ChildContent
            </div>
        </small>
    </div>
    <p class="mb-1">@Description</p>
</div>
```

`GroupContainer.razor.cs` are created here as well:

```
using Microsoft.AspNetCore.Components;

namespace EShop.Shared
{
    public partial class GroupContainer
    {
        [Parameter]
        public string? Name { get; set; }

        [Parameter]
        public string? Description { get; set; }

        [Parameter]
        public string? FontSize { get; set; }

        [Parameter]
        public RenderFragment? ChildContent { get; set; }
    }
}
```

Now we explicitly use this `GroupContainer` to make sure that every item is rendered in the exact same container:

```
@using Shared

<div class="list-group">
   @foreach (var item in Cart!.Items)
   {
      <GroupContainer Name=@item.Item.Name Description=@item.Item.
Description>
```

```
        <input readonly @bind="item.UpdateTime" @
bind:format="HH:mm:ss"></input>

        <i class="p-2 bi bi-box-arrow-down" @
onclick="()=>MoveToWishList(item)"></i>

        <i class="p-2 bi bi-x-octagon-fill" @
onclick="()=>Remove(item)"></i>

    </GroupContainer>



    @* <CartItemCountComponent @bind-Count="item.Count" @bind-
Count:event="CountChanged" /> *@

    }
</div>
```

Another way to implement an HTML wrapper would be as shown in the codes. It is a convention that when users define a property of type `RenderFragment` with the name `ChildContent`, everything filled inside the component will be rendered where you place the `@ChildContent` in the Razor component. In our example, `@ChildContent` is placed in a `div` element, and when another team or some other developers utilize your `GroupContainer` component, they add an `input` element and two icons in it. These three added elements will be rendered exactly inside the `div` element.

`RenderFragment` is a delegate that uses a `RenderTreeBuilder` to build the UI content, defined as follows:

```
public delegate void RenderFragment(RenderTreeBuilder builder);
```

The preceding code shows the definition of `RenderFragment`, which represents a method with a `RenderTreeBuilder` instance as parameter to customize the content, and there are a few common methods made public to accomplish this objective.

Now that you know `RenderFragment` is a delegate, try writing some HTML elements in pure C# code.

First, add a `RenderFragment` field in `GroupContainer.razor.cs`:

```
using Microsoft.AspNetCore.Components;


namespace EShop.Shared
```

```
{
    public partial class GroupContainer
    {
        [Parameter]
        public string? Name { get; set; }


        [Parameter]
        public string? Description { get; set; }


        [Parameter]
        public string? FontSize { get; set; }


        [Parameter]
        public RenderFragment? ChildContent { get; set; }


        private RenderFragment _descriptionRF = (b) =>
        {
            b.OpenElement(0, "p");
            b.AddAttribute(1, "class", "mb-1");
            b.AddContent(2, "this is a description.");
            b.CloseElement();
        };
    }
}
```

Then use this `RenderFragment` in `GroupContainer.razor` to determine where it will be rendered:

```
<div class="list-group-item">
    <div class="d-flex w-100 justify-content-between">
        <p class="mb-1" style="@FontSize">@Name</p>
```

```
    <small>

        <div>

            @ChildContent

        </div>

    </small>

</div> @_descriptionRF
</div>
```

In the preceding example, users first rendered @_descriptionRF to replace the original p element showing the item description. It looks just like the @ChildContent. Users created a RenderFragment in the corresponding *.razor.cs file. Next to the ChildContent property, users add a private RenderFragment called _ descriptionRF, the name in the Razor file. Given a lambda expression, b is the RenderTreeBuilder.

In the lambdaexpression, OpenElement comes first, the same as when one is writing the HTML code. The user would then type <p> first. Next, call AddAttribute to give the p element a class attribute, just like when class='mb-1' is typed in HTML. The third line, AddContent, gives the p element a content to display. Finally, end the lambda expression by calling CloseElement(), the same as when typing the closing label </p>.

It is all very straightforward, but there is an important aspect missing here— the integer parameter of these first three methods. The integer here plays an important role in the rendering tree. When renumbering these integers in the lambda expression, it still compiles and runs:

```
// some code

private RenderFragment _descriptionRF = (b) =>

{

    b.OpenElement(-3, "p");

    b.AddAttribute(-2, "class", "mb-1");

    b.AddContent(-1, "this is a descrip-
    tion."); b.CloseElement();

};

// some code
```

```
<!--!-->
▼ <div class="list-group"> flex
    <!--!-->
  ▼ <div class="list-group-item">
    ▶ <div class="d-flex w-100 justify-content-between">…</div> flex
      <!--!-->
      <p class="mb-1">this is a description.</p> == $0
    </div>
    <!--!-->
  ▶ <div class="list-group-item">…</div>
    <!--!-->
  ▶ <div class="list-group-item">…</div>
  </div>
</div>
```

FIGURE 4.1 Description RenderFragment.

The sequence can start from any number, as long as they are incremental. One common mistake that developers may make is they use auto incremented index:

```
int index = 0
b.OpenElement(index++, "p");
b.AddAttribute(index++, "class", "mb-1");
b.AddContent(index++, "this is a description.");
b.CloseElement();
```

It seems more reasonable to use an integer tracking the sequence since we are all developers. The difference between Blazor and other UI frameworks is that it uses this sequence to calculate the tree diff with a linear algorithm, although it may work fine in this trivial example. Once users have a more complicated scenario such as if branch or loops autogenerated sequence numbers, it could hurt performance. The key here is the algorithm Blazor takes and compares the old and new rendering with the same sequence. It means for every same sequence number, if the data comes with that number changes, Blazor is convinced that it will rerender that data. In a loop for a list, it is very common that some items will be removed or added in the middle based on business logic, and there will be rerendering for every data that comes after removing or adding, even though most of them remain the same, because the corresponding sequence is changed if one uses auto increment numbers.

Another tip here is always to remember to call `AddAttribute` right after the call of `OpenElement` or `OpenComponent`, otherwise users will encounter the following runtime exception:

```
❸ ▶ crit:                                                    blazor.webassembly.js:1  ⊙
Microsoft.AspNetCore.Components.WebAssembly.Rendering.WebA
ssemblyRenderer[100]
      Unhandled exception rendering component: Attributes may only be added
immediately after frames of type Element or Component
System.InvalidOperationException: Attributes may only be added immediately after
frames of type Element or Component
   at
Microsoft.AspNetCore.Components.Rendering.RenderTreeBuilder.AssertCanAddAttribute()
   at Microsoft.AspNetCore.Components.Rendering.RenderTreeBuilder.AddAttribute(Int32
sequence, String name, String value)
   at EShop.Shared.GroupContainer.<>c.<.ctor>b__18_0(RenderTreeBuilder b) in
C:\Users\Brian\OneDrive\BPBOnline\Chapter4\EShop\Shared\GroupContainer.razor.cs:line
22
   at Microsoft.AspNetCore.Components.Rendering.RenderTreeBuilder.AddContent(Int32
sequence, RenderFragment fragment)
   at EShop.Shared.GroupContainer.BuildRenderTree(RenderTreeBuilder __builder) in
C:\Users\Brian\OneDrive\BPBOnline\Chapter4\EShop\Shared\GroupContainer.razor:line 10
   at Microsoft.AspNetCore.Components.ComponentBase.<.ctor>b__6_0(RenderTreeBuilder
builder)
   at
Microsoft.AspNetCore.Components.Rendering.ComponentState.RenderIntoBatch(RenderBatchBu
ilder batchBuilder, RenderFragment renderFragment, Exception& renderFragmentException)
```

FIGURE 4.2 AddAttribute exception.

Currently, this `RenderFragment` is static, and always renders the same description, but users are required to display specific descriptions for each item. A generic version of `RenderFragment` can be used here:

```
// some code
private RenderFragment<string> _descriptionRF = (desc)
=> (b) =>
{
    b.OpenElement(-3, "p");
    b.AddAttribute(-2,
    "class", "mb-1");
    b.AddContent(-1, desc);
    b.CloseElement();
};
// some code
```

Pass the `Description` as a parameter to the `RenderFragment`:

```
<div class="list-group-item">
    <div class="d-flex w-100 justify-content-between">
        <p class="mb-1" style="@FontSize">@Name</p>
        <small>
            <div>
                @ChildContent
            </div>
        </small>
    </div>
    @_descriptionRF(Description!)
</div>
```

Generic `RenderFragment` is a delegate as well, and it is defined to return a normal `RenderFragment`. It allows developers to render more dynamic content. This generic argument provides a typed parameter to the `RenderFragment` delegate and can be passed to the `RenderTreeBuilder`. Inside the normal `RenderFragment` lambda expression, developers can customize the output with this parameter.

`RenderFragment` provides a way to manually generate HTML elements, but it must be used with caution, otherwise it will easily overcome the benefits it brings. It is recommended not to use `RenderFragment` unless one has a very strong reason to do so.

CSS ISOLATION

CSS style is widely used throughout Web applications. Despite its popularity, there are some common challenges that developers are currently facing. When an application grows larger and more complex, it will be difficult to maintain the style dependencies. It will be hard to locate the style-related bug on deeply nested elements.

Blazor CSS isolation aims to avoid these problems by defining a style dedicated to only one component. It is simple to implement an isolated CSS style. Users only need to name the `css` file prefixed with the name of corresponding Razor file and put them under the same path.

For example, in `GroupContainer`, there is an `<h2>` element:

```
<div class="list-group-item">
<div class="d-flex w-100 justify-content-between">
        <h2>@Name</h2>
        <small>
            <div>
                @ChildContent
            </div>
        </small>
</div>
</div>
@_descriptionRF(Description!)
</div>
```

Create `GroupContainer.razor.css` under the Shared folder with style for `<h2>` element:

```
h2 {
    color: orange;
}
```

In this way, all of the h2 elements in the `GroupContainer` component will have the same orange color. If one inspects the generated Web page html, they may notice that:

```
<h2 b-xk4f1vd9ci>T-shirt</h2>
```

The h2 element was added as an attribute by the compiler in the format of b-{10 characters}. In this case, it is b-xk4f1vd9ci, and this attribute makes the selector more specific. To prove this, bring up the `DevTools` and find h2[b- xk4f1vd9ci] style in `EShop.style.css`. All the isolated css style will be compiled into this file together:

FIGURE 4.3 Compiled isolated CSS style.

Since the `css` is isolated, it will not be applied to the child elements or components. To allow children to inherit the same `css` style, one can use `::deep` to indicate that this style will apply to its children.

Conduct a small experiment here, adding both a parent header and a child header:

```
@* some code *@

<GroupContainer Name=@item.Item.Name Description=@item.Item.
Description>

    <h2>child header</h2>

    <input readonly @bind="item.UpdateTime" @bind:format=
"HH:mm:ss"></input>

    <i class="p-2 bi bi-box-arrow-down" @
onclick="()=>MoveToWishList(item)"></i>

    <i class="p-2 bi bi-x-octagon-fill" @onclick="()=>
Remove(item)"></i>

</GroupContainer>

@* some code *@
```

In `CartComponent.razor`, add an `h2` element, and since it is wrapped inside the `GroupContainer`, this will be the child header. In `./Shared/GroupContainer.razor`, add the code `<h2>parent header</h2>` to the first line, as a parent header. Finally, update the CSS selector from `h2` to `::deep h2`. Run the application to find that the child header is orange, but the parent header is still black. CSS style does not work!

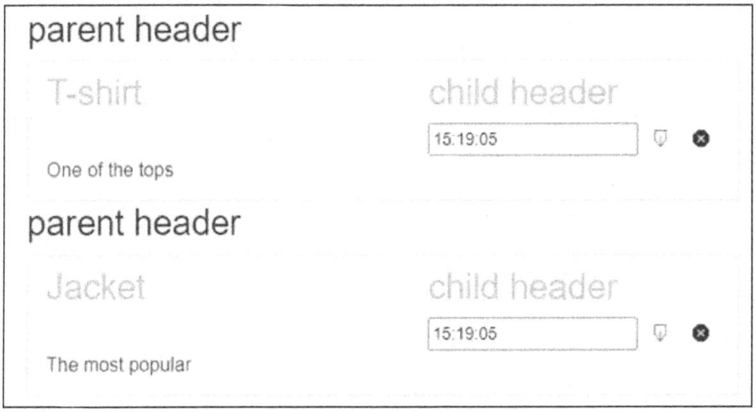

FIGURE 4.4 Inherited css.

That's because the `::deep` selector will not match those elements at the root. Therefore, either wrap the parent header in a `div`, or add another `h2` selector to the `css` file:

```
h2, ::deep h2 { color:
    orange;
}
```

This time, all the headers will be orange.

CONCLUSION

This chapter explored more advanced topics of Blazor components. Starting with components reference, it showed that other components can be referenced just like a variable in plain C# code by adding the @ref directive attribute to the target component. Next, the chapter discussed the technics to preserve the relationship between components with its model. The @key directive attribute helps to retain the mapping and is encouraged to be used inside a list or a loop.

Chapter 4 discussed how to manually generate front-end elements in pure `C#` code. Remember to use `RenderFragment` only when necessary. Finally, the chapter explored `CSS` isolation to avoid dependency chaos and described how this isolation is implemented by the compiler.

Chapter 5 will explore how to build a file uploading components with the knowledge already learned and will discuss how to handle files to or from customers. Some HTTP-related topics will also be covered.

5

FILE UPLOADING IN BLAZOR

INTRODUCTION

Chapter 4 discussed some advanced topics about Blazor components, including components reference, components preserving, and component template. It also introduced the CSS isolation technique to avoid overlap issues. This chapter will demo how users can interact with other users through file uploading and downloading for both Blazor Server and Blazor WebAssembly.

STRUCTURE

This chapter will discuss the following topics:

- file transfer on the internet
- uploading a file
- uploading files to other service providers
- security considerations and best practices

OBJECTIVES

This chapter introduces readers to the protocols that are commonly used to transfer files between clients through the Internet and explores the differences between the protocols HTTP and FTP. Next, the chapter teaches about the `InputFile` component used in the Blazor Framework to allow users to upload their files to the servers. Details will be explained through an EShop feature where customers will upload photos of a purchased item and leave comments for that item.

BUILD COMMENTS FOR ESHOP

File sharing can be a very useful way to communicate between users and the Web application or between users. If it is a social media application, one might want to allow customers to upload their favorite photos, so that other users can leave a comment or share that photo. If it is a business intelligence application, customers may want to download the data as an Excel file or a PDF report. In previous chapters, readers built an EShop application, and it would make their product more competitive if the seller could sign in and post a selected picture for the products on sale or if they could customize a header picture for their home page.

FILE TRANSFER

Two common ways to transfer files on the Internet are HTTP and FTP. HTTP stands for HyperText Transfer Protocol. As the name suggests, HTTP deals with HyperText, which means, the client or Web browser will send a request to retrieve the HyperText from a server. HyperText was introduced by Ted Nelson, an American philosopher and sociologist, in 1956. Hypertext is still text, but a text with more information, linking other HyperTexts by cross- referencing each other. These links between texts are like edges in one huge graph in the world of Internet with texts as the nodes. These nodes are connected to each other, more or less through the links. While at one node, a user can almost travel to any other node directly, or with only a few steps, unlike a bus route, on which the rider must keep traveling to the next stop linearly until their destination, even though the stops in between are not valuable to them at all.

Files are obviously part of the HyperText in our Internet world. HTTP is a one-way communication protocol as discussed in Chapter 2, and a client will initiate a request to get the desired file from the HTTP server. Authentication is not required to get the file, by its nature, through HTTP protocol, although nowadays, developers are adding more and more sophisticated signing-in mechanisms. All of these authentication logics are not required by HTTP. They come from the business.

Alternatively, FTP is born with authentication. FTP stands for File Transfer Protocol. As the name suggests, this protocol is born to share files. Users usually first provide credentials to log in to the server and get permission to upload or download files. Unlike HTTP, FTP is more appropriate for large file transferring, and it is widely used in large enterprises, universities, and institutions.

Nowadays, both HTTP and FTP get their security extensions to HTTPS and FTPS, supporting Transport Layer Security. By enhancing data transfer through encryption algorithms, HTTPS and FTPS have become more and more popular, or even a new must-have requirement in the Internet world. For example, Google Chrome will default to HTTPS starting from version 90. In this chapter, the focus is on file transfer through HTTPS for Web application.

FILE UPLOAD

In both Blazor Server and Blazor WebAssembly, use an `InputFile` component to catch the file from the user's upload. By default, this component will be rendered into an `input` element. In the EShop application, the product owner would like to add a new feature that allows customers to upload their comments with photos for shopping items.

First, build a shop-item page with customized components using the techniques learned in previous chapters.

First, create a new file `Comments.cs` under the `Models` folder:

```
namespace EShop.Models
{
    public class Comment
    {
        public string Content { get; set; }
        public string ImageUrl { get; set; }
        public DateTime CreatedTime { get; set; }
        public Comment(string content, string imageUrl)
        {
            Content = content;
            // ImageUrl = imageUrl;
            ImageUrl = "https://ts1.cn.mm.bing.net/th/id/
```

```
R-C.699defcec-77365c2dcd1bac50a789a46?rik=sk9qvtl%2fpa%2f5eA&
riu=http%3a%2f%2fcdn57. picsart.com%2f179951678001202.jpg&
ehk=SEq86wyqKmauSBKOyess7Qp6gtM56dWG-BQia7SwkJHg%3d&risl=&pid
=ImgRaw&r=0";

            CreatedTime = DateTime.Now;

        }

    }

}
```

Three properties were designed in this Comment model, and for now use a picture from Bing Image to represent the shop item:

```
namespace EShop.Models
{

    public class ShopItem
    {

        public string Name { get; set; }
        public string Description { get; set; }
        public string ImageUrl { get; set; }
        public double Price { get; set; }
        public List<Comment> Comments { get; }
        public ShopItem(string name, string description, double
        price)
        {

            Name = name;
            Description = description;
            Price = price;
            Comments = new List<Comment>();

        }


        public void AddComment(Comment comment)
        {

            Comments.Add(comment);

        }

    }

}
```

A new property of the comments list in the `ShopItem` model and a method to add a comment for this shop item have been added. The comment model has three properties. One is the content of this comment. Another is the image for this shop item that a buyer bought from the `EShop` Web site, and this photo taken from the buyer can be included with this comment. For now, use a random photograph from the Bing Image to display in the application. Later, this default image will be replaced with the one the user uploaded. The last one is an auto-generated time of the comment creation to take note of when the buyer left this comment.

Next, we create a new Blazor component file `Comment.razor` under the `Shared` folder:

```
<div class="Container">

    <p class="Content">@CommentModel.Content</p>
    @if(!string.IsNullOrWhiteSpace(CommentModel.ImageUrl))
    {

        <img class="Image" src="@CommentModel.ImageUrl" />

    }

    <p class="Time">@CommentModel.CreatedTime.ToString("yyyy-mm-dd
HH:MM:ss")</p>

</div>
```

This component will display the content, image, and the date the comment was created.

Next, create the corresponding C# code behind the file `Comment.razor.cs` to hold the model for this component:

```
using Microsoft.AspNetCore.Components;

namespace EShop.Shared
{

    public partial class Comment
    {

        [Parameter]
        public Models.Comment? CommentModel { get; set; }

    }

}
```

Create a corresponding style file `Comment.razor.css` to give the component a nicer look:

```css
.Container {
    border-width: 0 0 1px 0;
    border-style: solid;
    border-color: black;
    margin-bottom: 15px;
}


.Content {
    margin: 1px;
}


.Image {
    width: 300px;
    margin-bottom: 15px;
}


.Time {
    font-size: 12px;
    color: gray;
    margin: 1px;
}
```

Build a shared component for the comment model here. It will display the content of the comment, and the photo user uploaded, together with when the comment was left. Other users who are interested in this shopping item can view the real photo taken by a real buyer, instead of the photo that could be highly augmented by the seller.

Next, construct a new page to display the shop item and the comments about it. Create a new file called `ShopItem.razor` under the `Pages folder.@ page "/shop-item"`:

```
@using EShop.Shared;

<div class="ItemContainer">
    <h1>@Item.Name</h1>
    <h5>$ @Item.Price</h5>
    <p>@Item.Description</p>
</div>

<div class="ItemDisplay">
    <img src="@Item.ImageUrl" />
    <div class="NewComment">
        <input type="text" @bind="Content"/>
        <button class="btn btn-primary NewCommentBtn" @
onclick="AddComment">Leave a comment</button>
    </div>
</div>
<div class="Comments">
    <h4>Comments</h4>
    @foreach(var comment in Item.Comments)
    {
        <Comment CommentModel="@comment" />
    }
</div>
```

Customers will be able to see the name, price, and description of the selected shop item on this new page. Use the newly created Comment component in a foreach loop to list all the comments for this item.

In the corresponding C# code behind the file ShopItem.razor.cs, a model of the ShopItem will be held and a method AddComment will be provided so that customers can click on the button to add their own comments:

```csharp
namespace EShop.Pages
{

    public partial class ShopItem
    {

        public Models.ShopItem Item { get; }
        public string? Content { get; set; }
        public ShopItem()
        {

            Item = new Models.ShopItem("T-shirt", "The best
ever with lower price!", 19.9);

            Item.ImageUrl = "https://ts1.cn.mm.bing.net/
th/id/R-C.614bdee2065be0f1976bdf839c725e26?rik=EJ2vSWnK-
s9a9vQ&riu=http%3a%2f%2fclipart-library.com%2fimg%2f828773.png&eh-
k=avi5QwUJFS0v4Qtu8ggI5Ariopp4uJwf7r5QlOnJQ0o%3d&risl
=&pid=ImgRaw&r=0";


        }


        private void AddComment()
        {

            System.Console.WriteLine("AddComment");

            if (string.IsNullOrWhiteSpace(Content))
            {

                return;

            }


            var comment = new Models.Comment(Content!, "");
            Item.AddComment(comment);


            Console.WriteLine(Content);

        }

    }

}
```

Add a CSS file `ShopItem.razor.css` to make the page look nicer and make the layout more concise:

```css
.ItemContainer {
    display: flex;
    flex-direction: column;
    align-items: center;
}


.ItemDisplay {
    display: flex;
    justify-content: space-around;
}


.NewComment {
    display: flex;
    flex-direction: column;
    width: 300px;
    margin-top: 20px;
    align-items: flex-start;
}


.NewCommentBtn {
    margin-top: 10px;
}


.Comments{
    margin-top: 20px;
}
```

Next, build a new page for displaying shopping items. It shows the shopping item title with its price and description. On the left, there is a graph provided by the seller, and on the right-hand side, customers can leave a comment about the item. For now, do not implement an authentication mechanism, and do not verify the user to be the one that bought this T-shirt before. Basically, anyone can leave that comment. An authentication and authorization system will be built in a later chapter.

Refer to the ShopItem page in Figure 5.1.

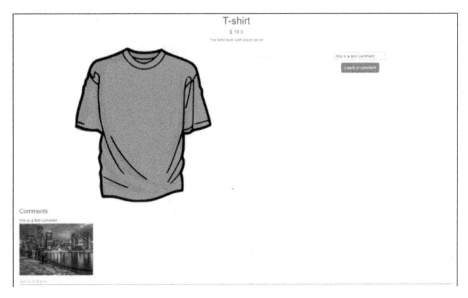

FIGURE 5.1 ShopItem page.

The final thing added is a new page to the navigation menu in `NavMenu.razor` under the `Shared` folder so that users can navigate the showing page with an easy click on the left navigation bar:

```
@* some code *@
        <div class="nav-item px-3">
            <NavLink class="nav-link" href="cart">
                <span class="oi oi-list-rich" aria-hidden=
                "true"></span>
Cart
            </NavLink>
        </div>
        <div class="nav-item px-3">
```

```
            <NavLink class="nav-link" href="shop-item">
                <span class="oi oi-list-rich" aria-hidden=
                "true"></span>
ShopItem
            </NavLink>
        </div>
@* some code *@
```

The skeleton of a shopping item displaying page is almost done, except for the image uploading part. Implement that now and see how the `InputFile` component that comes with Blazor can help achieve that.

Remove the hard coded `ImageUrl` value and use the parameter from the constructor in `Comment.cs`:

```
// some code
        public Comment(string content, string imageUrl)
        {
            Content = content;
            ImageUrl = imageUrl;
            CreatedTime = DateTime.Now;
        }
// some code
```

Add the `InputFile` component in `ShopItem.razor` page and assign the method `UploadImageAsync` to handle the `OnChange` event of the `InputFile` component:

```
        @* some code *@
        <input type="text" @bind="Content"/>
        <InputFile OnChange="@UploadImageAsync" />
        <button class="btn btn-primary NewCommentBtn" @
onclick="AddComment">Leave a comment</button>
        @* some code *@
```

Write the method `UploadImageAsync` in `ShopItem.razor.cs`. Developers can read the file stream through the `InputFileChangeEventArgs` parameter and convert it to a Base64 string:

```csharp
using Microsoft.AspNetCore.Components.Forms;

namespace EShop.Pages
{
    public partial class ShopItem
    {
        public Models.ShopItem Item { get; }
        public string? Content { get; set; }
        private string _base64Image = string.Empty;
        public ShopItem()
        {
            Item = new Models.ShopItem("T-shirt", "The best
ever with lower price!", 19.9);
            Item.ImageUrl = "https://ts1.cn.mm.bing.net/
th/id/R-C.614bdee2065be0f1976bdf839c725e26?rik=EJ2vSWnK-
s9a9vQ&riu=http%3a%2f%2fclipart-library.com%2fimg%2f828773.png&eh-
k=avi5QwUJFS0v4Qtu8ggI5Ariopp4uJwf7r5QlOnJQ0o%3d&risl=&pid=
ImgRaw&r=0";
        }

        private void AddComment()
        {
            System.Console.WriteLine("AddComment");
            if (string.IsNullOrWhiteSpace(Content))
            {
                return;
            }

            var comment = new Models.Comment(Content!,
            _base64Image);
            Item.AddComment(comment);
```

```
        Console.WriteLine(Content);

    }


    private async void UploadImageAsync(InputFileChangeEventArgs
    args)
    {
        using var stream = args.File.OpenReadStream();
        byte[] buffer = new byte[stream.Length];
        await stream.ReadAsync(buffer, 0, buffer.Length);
        _base64Image = $"data:{args.File.ContentType};
        base64,{Convert.ToBase64String(buffer)}";

    }

  }

}
```

Run the application, go to the shop-item page, and open the DevTools. In the Elements tab there is HTML similar to what appears in Figure 5.2.

```
▼ <div class="NewComment" b-ewp9o528pg> flex
  <input type="text" b-ewp9o528pg>
  <!--!-->
  <!--!-->
  <input type="file" _bl_2> == $0
  <!--!-->
  <button class="btn btn-primary NewCommentBtn" b-ewp9o528pg>Leave a comment</button>
  </div>
```

FIGURE 5.2 InputFile render to HTML.

InputFile component will be rendered to an input element with the type attribute of file. To allow users to upload more than one file at once, one may add the attribute multiple to it. OnChange of the InputFile component was assigned a method with the parameter of type InputFileChangeEventArgs to handle the file(s) users uploaded.

First call OpenReadStream to read from the uploaded image stream. By default, an exception will be thrown if the file is larger than 500KB. To override this behavior, users may provide a number to the maxAllowedSize parameter of the OpenReadStream method explicitly. It is not recommended to read the uploaded stream into memory directly, but for demo purposes, that advice is not being followed here, but users should avoid that in their production code. Since saving data through EF core will not be covered in a subsequent chapter, this content will only show the convertion of the uploaded image into a static base64 string to display on the Web page. The `ContentType` used in the example is the standard MIME type that is widely used in the browser. Users rely on this type to convert the stream to a correct bas64 string. When uploading multiple files, users may iterate through the result of the method `GetMultipleFiles` from `InputFileChangeEventArgs`. Each of them can be handled the same as the File property.

TIPS

When one is expecting an image uploaded from users, just like the previous comment example, they may find another method helpful.

Modify the method `UploadImageAsync` in `ShopItem.razor.cs` to use a new method `RequestImageFileAsync` on the `IBrowserFile` type:

```
@* some code *@
private async void UploadImageAsync(InputFileChangeEventArgs args)
{
    var file = await args.File.RequestImageFileAsync(args.File.ContentType, 300, 500);
    using var stream = file.OpenReadStream();
    byte[] buffer = new byte[stream.Length];
    await stream.ReadAsync(buffer, 0, buffer.Length);

    _base64Image = $"data:{file.ContentType};base64,{Convert.ToBase64String(buffer)}";
}
@* some code *@
```

`RequestImageFileAsync` may help the user resize the image from uploading or converting to another format when they provide a specific format. It should be noted that there is no guarantee that the converted `IBrowserFile` will be an image, or even that the conversion can be processed. Since the conversion is running in the JavaScript runtime, the user may find it most suitable to call this method when they are building a Blazor WebAssembly application.

To avoid malicious attacks, the first thing one should do is scan, check, and validate all the files that are provided by outside sources before working on them. In addition, users may also want to upload the customers' files from the client browser directly to a trusted third-party storage service. For example, Azure Storage is most appropriate for these situations, so that the application can safely process the file as a proxy and call the external storage services when one is required to show or use the files. The detail on how to upload to third parties will not be covered in this book, however, since readers are writing C# code, which is the benefit when choosing to build a Web application with Blazor, one can investigate the third-party documents for backend code, and hope they have a C# example.

Finally, it is worth limiting the number of files that a user can upload at once. To achieve that, simply pass an explicit maximum when calling `GetMultipleFiles`. The default number is 10 but remember to change it when there is a less maximum in production.

CONCLUSION

This chapter introduced two popular protocols, HTTP and FTP, that users can leverage to share files between their server and clients. Next the chapter went through a detailed example of how to upload files in Blazor and it discussed a few recommendations and considerations that readers may want to think about when dealing with file uploading.

Chapter 6 discusses how to provide files to customers in Blazor.

6

SERVING AND SECURING FILES IN BLAZOR

INTRODUCTION

The previous chapter introduced how a user can upload files to Blazor by using the `InputFile` Razor component. The chapter also discussed how to protect an application from cybersecurity attacks. Serving files to clients is crucial to the application, especially for those applications that are facing business customers. The requirements often include sales data files generated periodically, statistics downloading to understand more insights, or business intelligence reports. This chapter explores how one can provide users with files, download files from their applications, and the security considerations the same when users upload files.

STRUCTURE

This chapter discusses the following topics:

- middlewares in ASP.NET Core
- serve static files
- serve dynamic files
- security advice

OBJECTIVES

This chapter will describe how requests are handled in ASP.NET Core. The design of is the most important piece to get a whole picture of the ASP.NET Core running mechanism. Next, the chapter introduces how to serve static files or dynamic files in Blazor. Static files are simply static assets saved on the local hard drive while dynamic files require to be generated runtime. The discussion will also touch on some basic security rules to protect servers from attacks when providing files to the clients.

MIDDLEWARE

In Blazor Server, one could choose the static file middleware provided by ASP. NET Core to serve static files to users. Middleware is a new concept that was introduced into ASP.NET Core. It is a pipeline system that is like an assembly line in a manufacturing factory. All the requests from clients will be fed into this pipeline system. Each middleware works as a worker in the assembly line to create, remove, or modify requests and responses. Unlike an assembly line, the middleware pipelines not only pass the requests coming to the next middleware, but they also return the response to the previous one when it reaches the last middleware in the pipeline systems. In addition, each middleware may decide by itself whether or not to pass the requests to the next one. While in a factory, a worker generally cannot control who to work on the products next or where the products go on the assembly line. Figure 6.1 shows the workflow of a request in the middleware system:

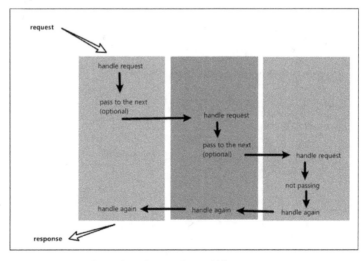

FIGURE 6.1 ASP.NET Core middleware system.

ASP.NET Core comes with a lot of default middlewares, for example, static file middleware. Other common middlewares include Redirection, routing, authentication, authorization, and many more. Even the API controller is implemented by middlewares. All the middlewares follow the very same processing rule illustrated in Figure 6.1. These middlewares together synthesize the robust ASP. NET Core application.

To learn more about the middlewares, the chapter begins by implementing one of them. First, users need to create another EShop project based on Blazor Server and move the EShop with Blazor WebAssembly to a subfolder titled WebAssembly. At the same time, users should create another subfolder, Server, which will contain the code for EShop in Blazor Server mode. To create a Blazor Server EShop, change the directory to the Server folder and run the command `dotnet new blazorserver -n EShop. Server -o`. The code structure will look like the following code:

```
EShop
├──EShop.sln
└──.gitignore
└──.vscode
└──EShop.Server
      ├──Pages
      ├──Shared
      ├──wwwroot
      ├──EShop.Server.csproj
      ├──other folders and files
   └──EShop.WebAssembly
      ├──Pages
      ├──Shared
      ├──wwwroot
      ├──EShop.WebAssembly.csproj
      ├──other folders and files
```

A middleware can be implemented in two ways. The first and simplest way is to code inline middleware. If users want to log every request coming from clients, they can easily use an inline middleware to achieve that. Users can add the inline middleware in `Program.cs` file under the `EShop.Server` project to log every request:

```
using EShop.Server.Data;


var builder = WebApplication.CreateBuilder(args);


// Add services to the container.
builder.Services.AddRazorPages();
builder.Services.AddServerSideBlazor();
builder.Services.AddSingleton<WeatherForecastService>();


var app = builder.Build();


app.Use(async (context, next) =>
{
    string log = $"{context.Request.Scheme}://{context.Request.
Host. Value}{context.Request.Path.Value}";
    Console.WriteLine($"client requests: {log}");


    await next.Invoke();
});


// Configure the HTTP request pipeline.
if (!app.Environment.IsDevelopment())
{
    app.UseExceptionHandler("/Error");
        // The default HSTS value is thirty days. One may want
    to change this for production scenarios. (See https://aka.
    ms/aspnetcore-hsts.)
        app.UseHsts();
}
```

```
app.UseHttpsRedirection();
app.UseStaticFiles();
app.UseRouting();
app.MapBlazorHub();
app.MapFallbackToPage("/_Host");


app.Run();
```

In the preceding code, `Use extension method` is called. This method is used to add an inline middleware delegate to the pipeline system, and users pass a delegate to the method. The delegate has two parameters. The first is the context of the type `HttpContext`, which contains all the information related to the request, and the response as well. Another parameter is called next, which is the next delegate that will be executed in the pipeline system. It in fact points to the next middleware. All the middleware is chained like a linked list, however this list is bidirectional, meaning requests are coming in and going out.

Print out the URLs that clients requested in the debug console. As shown in Figure 6.2, the client first visited the application with the http schema and was directed to port 5001 with a more secure https schema. Thanks to the `UseHttpsRedirection()`, it adds a middleware to redirect http requests to https and forced the clients to use https when they are visiting the EShop application. After that, all the required static files and Blazor components were loaded.

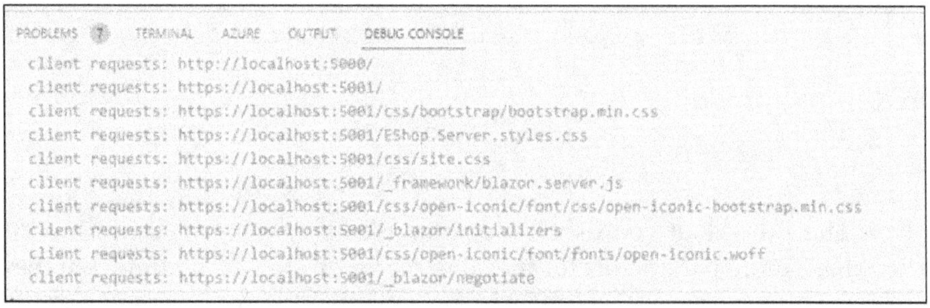

FIGURE 6.2 Inline log middleware.

If users have a more complicated middleware, they might want a dedicated class to act as a middleware in the pipeline system. In fact, there is no such middleware base class provided by the asp.net core framework as long as a class meets two requirements. The first is a public constructor of which the first parameter has the type `RequestDelegate`. The second is a public Invoke or `InvokeAsync` method of which the first parameter has the type `HttpContext`. For example, one can move their logger logic into a class as in the following code:

```
namespace EShop.Server;


public class LoggerMiddleware
{
    private readonly RequestDelegate _next;
    public LoggerMiddleware(RequestDelegate next)
    {
        _next = next;
    }


    public async Task Invoke(HttpContext context)
    {
        string log = $"{context.Request.Scheme}://{context.
Request.Host.Value}{context.Request.Path.Value}";
        Console.WriteLine($"client requests: {log}");


        await context.Response.WriteAsync("hello world!");
    }
}
```

The preceding code shows an example of `LoggerMiddleware`. One may have more parameters for the constructor or Invoke method, but they should make sure that `RequestDelegate` or `HttpContext` comes first. This time in the middleware class, users are not calling `next.Invoke()` to short circuit other middlewares that followed behind. In this way, users revert the request handling direction and start to compose the response returned to the client. The middlewares before `LoggerMiddleware` may choose to alter the response when they see it necessary. Finally, the response will be received by the client from the very first middleware that handles the request.

To add this class of middleware into the pipeline system, users call the `UseMiddleware` extension method in `Program.cs`. It will register middleware to the pipeline. Notice that the order in which a middleware is registered is very important, because if a particular middleware chooses to short-circuit the request, all the middlewares registered after it will be ignored and will not handle the request:

```
using EShop.Server;

usingEShop.Server.Data;


var builder = WebApplication.CreateBuilder(args);


// Add services to the container.
builder.Services.AddRazorPages();
builder.Services.AddServerSideBlazor();
builder.Services.AddSingleton<WeatherForecastService>();


var app = builder.Build();


app.UseMiddleware<LoggerMiddleware>();


// Configure the HTTP request pipeline.
if (!app.Environment.IsDevelopment())
{
    app.UseExceptionHandler("/Error");
        // The default HSTS value is thirty days. Users
    may want to change this for production scenarios, see
    https://aka.ms/aspnetcore-hsts.
    app.UseHsts();
}
```

```
app.UseHttpsRedirection();
app.UseStaticFiles();
app.UseRouting();
app.MapBlazorHub();
app.MapFallbackToPage("/_Host");


app.Run();
```

FIGURE 6.3 Middleware short circuit.

Figure 6.3 is a screenshot of the application when a user browses *http://localhost:5000*. Since the `LoggerMiddleware` short circuits the request pipeline, this time, it will not show the familiar Blazor App home page with menus on the left. Instead, a simple plain text response is returned from the `LoggerMiddleware`.

Move the `LoggerMiddleware` registration after:

```
// some other code
var app = builder.Build();


// Configure the HTTP request pipeline.
If (!app.Environment.IsDevelopment())
{
    app.UseExceptionHandler("/Error");

    // The default HSTS value is thirty days. Users may want
to change this for production scenarios, see https://aka.ms/
aspnetcore-hsts.

    app.UseHsts();
}
```

```
app.UseHttpsRedirection();

app.UseMiddleware<LoggerMiddleware>();

app.UseStaticFiles();
// some other code
```

FIGURE 6.4 Reorder LoggerMiddleware.

Since `LoggerMiddleware` comes after `HttpsRedirection`, when one browses to *http://localhost:5000*, they are redirected to the corresponding https schema endpoint, *https://localhost:5001*.

SERVE STATIC FILES

By default, when one creates a new Blazor Server or Blazor WebAssembly application, serving static files are supported. Since the remainder of middlewares were short-circuited, allow the request to move down through the pipeline system. Update the `LoggerMiddleware.cs` to remove the short circuit:

```
namespace EShop.Server;


public class LoggerMiddleware
{

    private readonly RequestDelegate _next;


    public LoggerMiddleware(RequestDelegate next)
```

```
    {
        _next = next;
    }


    public async Task Invoke(HttpContext context)
    {
        string log = $"{context.Request.Scheme}://{context.Re-
quest.Host.Value}{context.Request.Path.Value}";
        Console.WriteLine($"client requests: {log}");


        // await context.Response.WriteAsync("hello world!");
        await _next.Invoke(context);
    }
}
```

Call the `Invoke` method on the `RequestDelegate` to pass the request to the next middleware:

```
world!
```

```
This is a static file.
```

Add a text file `hello.txt` under the `wwwroot` folder with the preceding content. All the files under `wwwroot` will be served, and you may already find out that all the CSS files are placed under this folder as well:

FIGURE 6.5 Serve static files under wwwroot.

Start the server and browse to *https://localhost:5001/hello.txt*, and the Web browser will display the content from the file `hello.txt`. Similarly, if one navigates to a CSS file, the file will display the style configuration as well.

Sometimes, the files may not be under the default `wwwroot` files. For example, there may be a dedicated assets folder to keep all the graphs or logos together. The browser will indicate that such a file resource cannot be found by posting a 404-error status code.

To support the files under any customized directory, configure the `UseStaticFiles` middleware in `Program.cs`:

```
using EShop.Server;
using EShop.Server.Data;
using Microsoft.Extensions.FileProviders;


var builder = WebApplication.CreateBuilder(args);


// Add services to the container.
builder.Services.AddRazorPages();
builder.Services.AddServerSideBlazor();
builder.Services.AddSingleton<WeatherForecastService>();


var app = builder.Build();


// Configure the HTTP request pipeline.
if (!app.Environment.IsDevelopment())
{
    app.UseExceptionHandler("/Error");
    // The default HSTS value is thirty days. Users may want
to change this for production scenarios, see https://aka.ms/
aspnetcore-hsts.
    app.UseHsts();
}


    app.UseHttpsRedirection();
    app.UseMiddleware<LoggerMiddleware>();
    app.UseStaticFiles(new StaticFileOptions
```

```
{

FileProvider = new PhysicalFileProvider(Path.Combine
        (builder.Environment.ContentRootPath, "Assets")),
RequestPath = "/assets-url"
 });


app.UseRouting();


app.MapBlazorHub(); a
pp.MapFallbackToPage("/_Host");


app.Run();
```

In the preceding code, there appears the static files middleware `StaticFileOptions`. It tells the middleware where the static files were placed and how a client can request them. The first assets string in `PhysicalFileProvider` identifies the physical path of the files folder. The second assets string assigned to `RequestPath` represents the URL path that a user should navigate to get the file. In the example, the user would call *https://localhost:5001/assets-url/Logo_Square.png* to get the logo placed under the `Assets` folder:

FIGURE 6.6 Serve files under another directory.

It works now that users can place files under any folders desired. It's important to note that if they browse the home page, they will find out that it is a plain text page, with no color, no font size, and no style. This is because moving the static files directory from `wwwroot` to `Assets`, means the Web application cannot find those CSS and JavaScript files under the `Assets` folder anymore, however, it can easily be fixed:

FIGURE 6.7 Missing CSS and JavaScript files.

Leave the default `UseStaticFiles` method and call it again in the next line with a customized files directory. In this way, onecan serve any of the many directories as they prefer.

SERVE DYNAMIC FILES

In the previous section, the discussion was how to serve static files to customers. Static files are files that will not change, for example, a Web site logo or a Web site license claim. When a customer requires a statistical report for the past month, it is impossible for developers to prepare such a file in advance and put it under a certain directory. These are dynamic files, and they are generated only when requested or they will change over time. To serve a dynamic file, users need help from JavaScript. Add a new `eshop.js` under the `wwwroot` folder with the following code:

```javascript
function download() {
  const current = new Date();
  const day = current.getDate()
  const month = current.getMonth() + 1
  const year = current.getFullYear()
  const time = year + "/" + month + "/" + day + " " + current.
getHours() + ":" + current.getMinutes() + ":" + current.getSeconds();
  const data = 'hello world!' + "\n" + time;
  const blob = new Blob([data]);
  const url = URL.createObjectURL(blob);
  const anchorElement = document.createElement('a');
  anchorElement.href = url;
  anchorElement.download = 'hello.txt';
  anchorElement.click();
  anchorElement.remove();
  URL.revokeObjectURL(url);
}
```

In the `download` function, users first get the current date and time from the Date object. Then combined with `"hello world!,"` every time a client requests this document, they can generate the content based on the current time. The rest of the function creates an anchor element, which will navigate to the URL and represent the file data through a `Blob` object. Finally, users invoke the click event on the anchor element, remove the element from the DOM, and revoke the URL so that the browser will not keep the reference any longer:

```html
<!DOCTYPE html>
<html lang="en">


<head>

    <meta charset="utf-8" />

    <meta name="viewport" content="width=device-width, initial-scale=1.0, maximum-scale=1.0, user-scalable=no" />

    <title>EShop.WebAssembly</title>

    <base href="/" />

    <link href="css/bootstrap/bootstrap.min.css" rel="stylesheet" />
```

```
    <link href="css/app.css" rel="stylesheet" />
    <link href="EShop.WebAssembly.styles.css" rel="stylesheet" />
</head>

<body>
    <div id="app">Loading...</div>

    <div id="blazor-error-ui">
        An unhandled error has occurred.
        <a href="" class="reload">Reload</a>
        <a class="dismiss">⬚</a>
    </div>
    <script src="_framework/blazor.webassembly.js"></script>
    <script src="eshop.js"></script>
</body>

</html>
```

Next, reference this JavaScript file globally in the index.html so that every page in the EShop application can call this download function just like users would normally do in any JavaScript project:

```
@page "/shop-item"
@using EShop.WebAssembly.Shared;

<div class="ItemContainer">
    <h1>@Item.Name</h1>
    <h5>$ @Item.Price</h5>
    <p>@Item.Description</p>
</div>

<div class="ItemDisplay">
```

```
<img src="@Item.ImageUrl" />
<div class="NewComment">
    <input type="text" @bind="Content"/>
    <InputFile OnChange="@UploadImageAsync" />
    <button class="btn btn-primary NewCommentBtn" @
onclick="AddComment">Leave a comment</button>
</div>
</div>

<button onclick="download()">Download</button>

<div class="Comments">
    <h4>Comments</h4>
    @foreach(var comment in Item.Comments)
    {
        <Comment CommentModel="@comment" />
    }
</div>
```

On the `ShopItem` page, `ShopItem.razor`, add a button to download this "hello world!" file with dynamic date and time. In a production application, JavaScript may depend on the user's input or data from other sources to generate dynamic files. This would require the Blazor application to pass the input or data to JavaScript. It will be accomplished by the interop between Blazor and JavaScript which will be covered in a later chapter.

The previous example represents downloading from a stream that is recommended to serve a file not larger than 250MB. If one is providing a file larger than 250MB to the customers, a better way is to download it from a URL. The steps are basically the same as before, but users will provide the file name and URL directly to JavaScript. The file could in fact be from an external source, or, if a user is implementing a microservice architecture, from another service in your clusters.

SECURITY ADVICE

When users are serving files, it is recommended that downloaded files are located separately from the system files, or code files on the server, as a hacker may acquire the execute permissions on the directory. Placing all the files together prohibits users from applying different security control policies on different types of files.

Users should not forget to revoke the URL; otherwise there may be memory leaks to the clients. They should make sure to perform security checks on the server when they are interacting with customers. Even when they have applied validation or checks on the client side, say, in JavaScript, keep in mind that they need to double-check again as client validations can easily break through.

If they are providing files through any external sources, they should remember to run a security scan before passing them to the customers.

CONCLUSION

This chapter first went through the design of the middlewares pipeline system as a streamline to handle clients' requests. Readers should now understand that `UseStaticFiles` is the default middleware to serve static files to clients, and it can be configured to serve files in different locations. After that, the chapter covered how to serve dynamic files as not all required data can be generated before an application goes online. Last, the chapter covered how to make a server more secure to protect applications.

The next chapter covers some of the most important components or elements that users will regularly interact with and that is customers and forms. The chapter will introduce how to collect data from users with forms, and how to validate the input from users.

CHAPTER

7

Collecting User Input with Forms

INTRODUCTION

This chapter will introduce how a user could provide information to our application and how we will validate the user's input with customized rules. The form has always been a classic element for Web UI, and it is a bridge that connects users and applications with two-direction communications.

STRUCTURE

This chapter will discuss the following topics:

- EditForm
- InputBase
- validation
- custom validation
- form submission
- EditContext
- form state

OBJECTIVES

This chapter will help readers understand how to create forms with Blazor and how to validate users' data with default or customized rules and prompt validation errors if data do not satisfy the rules. Users will also learn the key concepts in Blazor forms, including submission, context, and state.

FORMS

In a Web application, forms are used to collect users' input. A typical example is the register/login page, where a user types their username and password to authenticate; almost all Web applications have this feature. A native HTML `<form>` element works as a container for all kinds of html input elements, including text input, radio buttons, or even files.

In Blazor, users can always use the native `<form>` element to manage users' input data as they did without Blazor. It is recommended to use the `EditForm` that comes with Blazor, and which includes more convenient and advanced data management.

In the EShop application, when there are no clothes of a customer's preferred size, the customer can request their size by filling out a request form, and the EShop staff will then restock the items. The following shows how to implement this feature with native HTML elements.

First, create a new page file called `RequestItem.razor`, under the `Pages` folder of the `EShop.WebAssembly` project. Then add the newly created page to the navigation menu. Find `NavMenu.razor` under the `Shared` folder in the project and update the `<nav>` element:

```
@* some code *@
    <nav class="flex-column">
        <div class="nav-item px-3">
            <NavLink class="nav-link" href="" Match="NavLinkMatch.
            All">
                <span class="oi oi-home" aria-hidden="true">
                </span> Home
            </NavLink>
        </div>
```

```
        <div class="nav-item px-3">
            <NavLink class="nav-link" href="counter">
                <span class="oi oi-plus" aria-hidden="true">
                </span> Counter
            </NavLink>
        </div>
        <div class="nav-item px-3">
            <NavLink class="nav-link" href="fetchdata">
                <span class="oi oi-list-rich" aria-hidden=
"true"></span>
Fetch data
            </NavLink>
        </div>
        <div class="nav-item px-3">
            <NavLink class="nav-link" href="cart">
                <span class="oi oi-list-rich" aria-
                hidden="true"></span> Cart
            </NavLink>
        </div>
        <div class="nav-item px-3">
            <NavLink class="nav-link" href="shop-item">
                <span class="oi oi-list-rich" aria-hidden=
"true"></span>
ShopItem
            </NavLink>
        </div>
        <div class="nav-item px-3">
            <NavLink class="nav-link" href="request-item">
                <span class="oi oi-list-rich" aria-hidden=
"true"></span> RequestItem
            </NavLink>
        </div>
    </nav>
@* some code *@
```

Another `<div>` element navigating to the `request-item` form page has been added. Complete the new page `RequestItem.razor` with the native `<form>` element:

```
@page "/request-item"


<PageTitle>Request Item</PageTitle>


<h2>Please fill in the request form below if you do not find desired item.</h2>


<h3>Native form element</h3>
<form>
    <div>
        <label for="item">Item: </label>
        <input type='text' name='item' id='item' required>
    </div>
    <div>
        <label for="size">Size: </label>
        <select name="size" id='size'>
            <option value="s">Small</option>
            <option value="m">Medium</option>
            <option value="l">Large</option>
        </select>
    </div>

    <div>
        <label for="count">Count: </label>
        <input type='number' name='count' id='count' required
min="1" max="10">
    </div>
```

```
<div>

    <input type='submit' />

</div>

</form>
```

A plain uncustomized form is being used here. It is sufficient to demonstrate the core feature provided by the native `<form>` element. For example, some fields are marked as required, and the form will not be submitted if these fields are empty. Add a `min` and `max` validation to verify that the count value must be between 1 and 10. Refer to Figure 7.1.

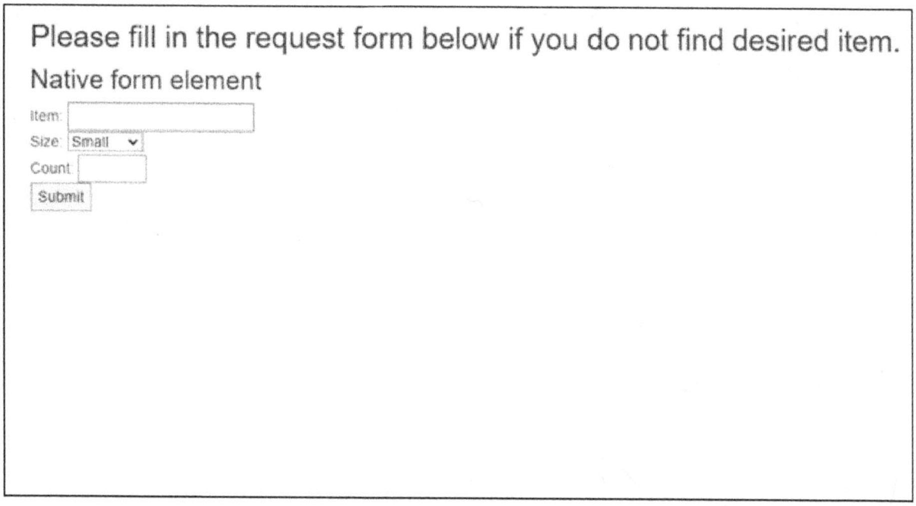

FIGURE 7.1 Native HTML form.

Next, compare the form with a form generated by the `EditForm` component that comes with the Blazor framework.

EditForm

The source code of `EditForm` is located at *https://github.com/dotnet/dotnet/ blob/main/src/aspnetcore/src/Components/Web/src/Forms/EditForm.cs,* and we will show some of the most important sections here:

```csharp
public class EditForm : ComponentBase
{
    private EditContext? _editContext;

    [Parameter]
    public EditContext? EditContext
    {
        get => _editContext;
        set
        {
            _editContext = value;
            _hasSetEditContextExplicitly = value != null;
        }
    }


    [Parameter] public object? Model { get; set; }

    [Parameter] public EventCallback<EditContext> OnSubmit
{ get; set; }

    [Parameter] public EventCallback<EditContext> OnValidSubmit
{ get; set; }

    [Parameter] public EventCallback<EditContext> OnInvalidSubmit {
get; set; }

    protected override void OnParametersSet()
    {
        if (Model != null && Model != _editContext?.Model)
        {
            _editContext = new EditContext(Model!);
        }
    }
```

```csharp
protected override void BuildRenderTree(RenderTreeBuilder
builder)
{
    Debug.Assert(_editContext != null);

    builder.OpenRegion(_editContext.GetHashCode());

    builder.OpenElement(0, "form");
    builder.AddMultipleAttributes(1, AdditionalAttributes);
    builder.AddAttribute(2, "onsubmit", _handleSubmitDelegate);
    builder.OpenComponent<CascadingValue<EditContext>>(3);
    builder.AddAttribute(4, "IsFixed", true);
    builder.AddAttribute(5, "Value", _editContext);
    builder.AddAttribute(6, "ChildContent", ChildContent?.
Invoke(_editContext));
    builder.CloseComponent();
    builder.CloseElement();

    builder.CloseRegion();
}


private async Task HandleSubmitAsync()
{
    Debug.Assert(_editContext != null);

    if (OnSubmit.HasDelegate)
    {
        await OnSubmit.InvokeAsync(_editContext);
    }
    else
    {
        var isValid = _editContext.Validate();


        if (isValid && OnValidSubmit.HasDelegate)
```

```
        {
            await OnValidSubmit.InvokeAsync(_editContext);
        }

        if (!isValid && OnInvalidSubmit.HasDelegate)
        {
            await OnInvalidSubmit.InvokeAsync(_editContext);
        }
    }
}
}
```

The first thing learned is that the EditForm inherits ComponentBase as many other Blazor components do. In the method BuildRenderTree, (introduced in a previous chapter about the advanced Blazor component), EditForm uses the <form> element under the hood as well. It then defined more attributes on the form and cascaded the EditContext to its child components.

The most important parameters of this EditForm component are the Model and the EditContext. The Model could be of any type, while EditContext has a dedicated EditContext type. In general, users will only use one of these two parameters. If a user assigned a model to the Model parameter, a new EditContext will be generated with a simple EditContext constructor that requires one parameter of the model. Otherwise, users are required to assign an EditContext instance directly to the EditContext parameter. In both ways, the EditForm component will have an EditContext parameter that is not null and will cascade it to the children.

The following is information regarding how to replace the native <form> element with the Blazor EditForm component. By default, the namespace Microsoft.AspNetCore.Components.Forms will be imported in the _Imports.razor file, or you could specify this namespace in your razor file with the @using directive.

First, create a new file RequstItem.cs, under the Models folder for the RequestItem model:

```
namespace EShop.WebAssembly.Models;


public enum RequestItemSize
{
    Small,
    Medium,
    Large
}


public class RequestItem
{
    public string EShopItemName { get; set; }
    public RequestItemSize Size { get; set; }
    public int Count { get; set; }
}
```

Use the EditForm component in the RequestItem.razor page, adding the following code to the page:

```
<h3>EditForm component</h3>
<EditForm Model="@_requestItem">
    <p>
        <label>
            Item:
            <InputText id="editform-item" @bind-Value="_requestItem.EShopItemName" />
        </label>
    </p>
    <p>
        <label>
            Size:
            <InputSelect id="editform-size" @bind-Value="_requestItem.Size">
```

```
                <option value=@RequestItemSize.Small>
@RequestItemSize.Small</option>
                <option value=@RequestItemSize.Medium>
@RequestItemSize.Medium</option>
                <option value=@RequestItemSize.Large>
@RequestItemSize.Large</option>
            </InputSelect>
        </label>
    </p>
    <p>
        <label>
            Count:
            <InputNumber id="editform-count" @bind-Value="_
requestItem.Count" />
        </label>
    </p>


    <button type="submit">Submit</button>
</EditForm>
```

Refer to the Figure 7.2.

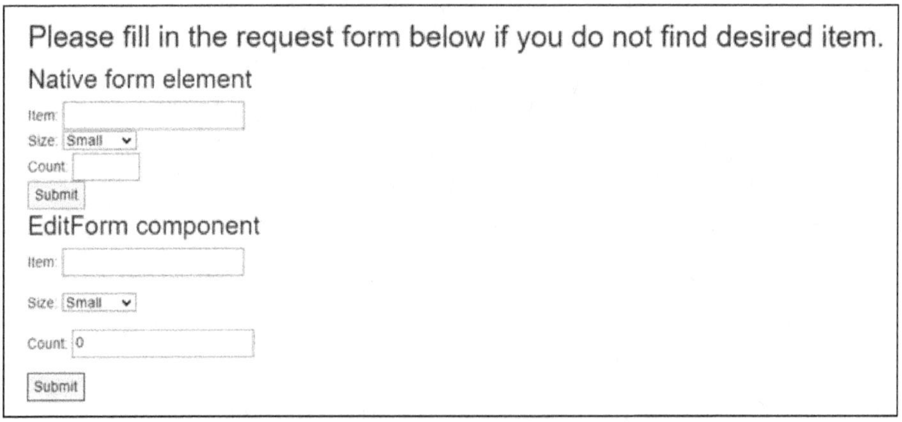

FIGURE 7.2 EditForm.

We are not validating the user's input here, as it will be covered in later sections. In general, it is recommended to use the `EditForm` component because it provides more features than native `<form>` element. These features will be covered in the following sections.

INPUTBASE

In the last simple example, readers may have noticed that Blazor not only provides the `EditForm` component to enhance the development experience, but it also comes with a few `InputXXX` components to replace different types of the native `<intput>` element. For example, `InputText`, `InputSelect` and `InputNumber` were used to replace `<input type='text' />`, `<select></select>` and `<input type='number' />`. These are all components inheriting `InputBase<TValue>`.

`InputBase<TValue>` is an abstract class that sits within the same namespace as `EditForm`. It has a private property of type `EditContext` to receive the cascaded parameter from its parent `EditForm`. Other than that, it has a `Value` parameter of generic type `TValue` to be used as the value of this input, along with a `ValueChanged` callback that will update the bound value. It is intended to use the `Value` parameter with two-way binding, and users may refer to Chapter 6 where this topic was covered.

`InputSelect` component is used to provide a few options for the application users. In the EShop example, people choose their desired clothing size with this component. The code written here does not really follow best practice design principles. Once required to extend the size options, both the code of the enumeration and the form page with the `InputSelect` component must be modified. There is a good chance that one of the modifications might be missed here when users are facing a complex feature. This is when inconsistency comes into play.

To fix that, users can build a customized component inheriting `InputBase<TValue>,` and all it needs is the type of enum used, and then it will automatically show all the available options from that enum type.

Create a new file called `InputEnum.cs` under the `Components` folder:

```
using System.Diagnostics.CodeAnalysis;
using System.Globalization;
using Microsoft.AspNetCore.Components;
using Microsoft.AspNetCore.Components.Forms;
using Microsoft.AspNetCore.Components.Rendering;
```

```
namespace EShop.WebAssembly.Components;


public class InputEnum<Tenum> : InputBase<Tenum>
{
    protected override bool TryParseValueFromString(string?
Value, [MaybeNullWhen(false)] out Tenum result, [NotNullWhen
(false)] out string? validationErrorMessage)
    {
        if (string.IsNullOrWhiteSpace(value))
        {
            result = default;
            validationErrorMessage = $"{nameof(value)} cannot be
            null";

            return false;
        }


        if (Enum.TryParse(typeof(Tenum), value, out object
        convertedEnum))
        {
            result = (Tenum)convertedEnum!;
            validationErrorMessage = null;

            return true;
        }


        result = default;
        validationErrorMessage = $"{nameof(value)} is not valid";


        return false;
    }
```

```csharp
protected override void BuildRenderTree(RenderTreeBuilder
builder)
{
    builder.OpenElement(0, "select");
    builder.AddMultipleAttributes(1, AdditionalAttributes);
    builder.AddAttribute(2, "onchange", EventCallback.Factory.
CreateBinder<string>(this, value => CurrentValueAsString = value,
CurrentValueAsString, null));


    // Add an option element per enum value
    foreach (var value in Enum.GetValues(typeof(Tenum)))
    {
        builder.OpenElement(3, "option");
        builder.AddAttribute(4, "value", value.ToString());
        builder.AddContent(5, value.ToString());
        builder.CloseElement();
    }


    builder.CloseElement(); // close the select element
}
}
```

First, override the abstract method `TryParseValueFromString`, which will parse the input value to an enumeration instance. Next, also override the method `BuildRenderTree` to define how the component is rendered. `InputEnum` wraps the native `<select>` element here. Finally, `InputSelect` is replaced by the `InputEnum`. This time, it only needs to bind with the _ `requestItem.Size`.

VALIDATION

Sometimes, it is necessary to validate user's input before submitting the data to servers, as was done with the native `<form>` element. `EditForm` comes with a simple way for validation, and the following will explore how to validate the same criteria with `EditForm`:

```
<EditForm Model="@_requestItem">

    <DataAnnotationsValidator />


    <p>
        <label>
            Item:
            <InputText id="editform-item" @bind-Value="_requestItem.
EShopItemName" />
        </label>
    </p>
    <p>
        <label>
            Size:
            <InputEnum @bind-Value="_requestItem.Size" />
        </label>
    </p>
    <p>
        <label>
            Count:
            <InputNumber id="editform-count" @bind-Value="_
requestItem.Count" />
        </label>
    </p>


    <button type="submit">Submit</button>
</EditForm>
```

First, add a `DataAnnotationsValidator` in this `EditForm`. This `DataAnnotationsValidator` is a component as well, located under exactly the same namespace, `Microsoft.AspNetCore.Components.Forms`. It has a cascading parameter `EditContext` provided by the parent `EditForm` and it enables the data validation by calling the `EnableDataAnnotationsValidation` method on the `EditContext` with an injected `IServiceProvider` instance.

Here is main part code of the `EditContextDataAnnotationsExtensions`, which builds a few extension methods on `EditContext`:

```
public static class EditContextDataAnnotationsExtensions
{
    public static IDisposable EnableDataAnnotationsValidation(this
EditContext editContext, IServiceProvider serviceProvider)
    {
        return new DataAnnotationsEventSubscriptions(editContext,
serviceProvider);
    }


    // private class DataAnnotationsEventSubscriptions
}
```

This `EnableDataAnnotationsValidation` method will create a private disposable `DataAnnotationsEventSubscriptions` instance. The constructor of this private class `DataAnnotationsEventSubscriptions` is shown as follows:

```
    private sealed class DataAnnotationsEventSubscriptions :
IDisposable
    {
        private static readonly ConcurrentDictionary<(Type
ModelType, string FieldName), PropertyInfo?> _propertyInfoCache
= new();


        private readonly EditContext _editContext;
        private readonly IServiceProvider? _serviceProvider;
        private readonly ValidationMessageStore _messages;


        public DataAnnotationsEventSubscriptions(EditContext
editContext, IServiceProvider serviceProvider)
        {
```

```
        _editContext = editContext ?? throw new
ArgumentNullException(nameof(editContext));

        _serviceProvider = serviceProvider;

        _messages = new ValidationMessageStore(_editContext);


        _editContext.OnFieldChanged += OnFieldChanged;
        _editContext.OnValidationRequested +=
OnValidationRequested;
    }
  }
```

In the constructor, both an `OnFieldChanged` and an `OnValidationRequested` delegate will be attached to the `EditContext` instance by subscribing to the `EditContext`'s event `OnFieldChanged` and `OnValidationRequested` respectively:

```
        private void OnFieldChanged(object? sender,
FieldChangedEventArgs eventArgs)
    {
        var fieldIdentifier = eventArgs.FieldIdentifier;
        if (TryGetValidatableProperty(fieldIdentifier, out var
propertyInfo))
        {


            var propertyValue = propertyInfo.GetValue
(fieldIdentifier.Model);
            var validationContext = new
ValidationContext(fieldIdentifier.Model, _serviceProvider, items: null)
            {
                MemberName = propertyInfo.Name
            };
            var results = new List<ValidationResult>();
```

COLLECTING USER INPUT WITH FORMS • **145**

```
            Validator.TryValidateProperty(propertyValue,
validationContext, results);

            _messages.Clear(fieldIdentifier);

            foreach (var result in CollectionsMarshal.
AsSpan(results))

            {

                _messages.Add(fieldIdentifier, result.
ErrorMessage!);

            }


            _editContext.NotifyValidationStateChanged();

        }

    }
```

In the `OnFieldChanged` method shown previously, the property will be retrieved by its `fieldIdentifier` and the method `TryValidateProperty` of `Validator` is invoked to validate the property. If any violation is detected, the corresponding result will be added to the message list, and the `EditContext` instance will be notified by invoking the method `NotifyValidationStateChanged` on it.

Similarly, when the `OnvalidationRequested` is triggered, the method `TryValidateObject` is called to verify the `Model` of the `EditContext` instance, and an error message will be stored if any are generated, and the `EditContext` instance will receive the notification:

```
        private void OnValidationRequested(object? sender,
ValidationRequestedEventArgs e)
        {
            var validationContext = new ValidationContext(_edit-
            Context.
Model, _serviceProvider, items: null);

            var validationResults = new List<ValidationResult>();

            Validator.TryValidateObject(_editContext.Model,
validationContext, validationResults, true);
```

```
                _messages.Clear();
                foreach (var validationResult in validationResults)
                {
                    if (validationResult == null)
                    {
                        continue;
                    }


                    var hasMemberNames = false;
                    foreach (var memberName in validationResult.
                    MemberNames)
                    {
                        hasMemberNames = true;
                        _messages.Add(_editContext.Field(member-
Name), validationResult.ErrorMessage!);
                    }


                    if (!hasMemberNames)
                    {
                        _messages.Add(new FieldIdentifier(_editCon-
text.Model, fieldName: string.Empty), validationResult.ErrorMes-
sage!);
                    }
                }


    _editContext.NotifyValidationStateChanged();
}
```

Readers should now understand how `EditForm` validates data with `ValidationAttribute`. Next, validate the customers' data with the same rule of native `<form>` element. First, add attributes to the `RequestItem` model class:

```
public class RequestItem
{
    [Required]
    public string EShopItemName { get; set; }
```

```
public RequestItemSize Size { get; set; }

[Required]
[Range(1, 10)]
public int Count { get; set; } = 1;
}
```

Go run the application, fill it in with some invalid data, and click the Submit button, and the input box border will turn red. Refer to Figure 7.3.

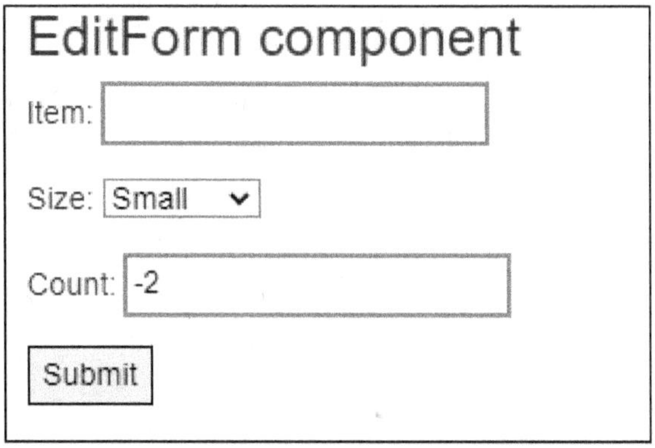

FIGURE 7.3 Validate data with ValidateAttribute.

To help customers understand why the data validation fails, update the EditForm with a ValidationSummary component:

```
<EditForm Model="@_requestItem">

    <DataAnnotationsValidator />

    <ValidationSummary />


    <p>

        <label>

            Item:

            <InputText id="editform-item" @bind-Value="_requestItem.
EShopItemName" />

        </label>
```

```
        </p>
        <p>
            <label>
                Size:
                <InputEnum @bind-Value="_requestItem.Size" />
            </label>
        </p>
        <p>
            <label>
                Count:
                <InputNumber id="editform-count" @bind-Value="_
requestItem.Count" />
            </label>
        </p>


        <button type="submit">Submit</button>
</EditForm>
```

Refer to Figure 7.4.

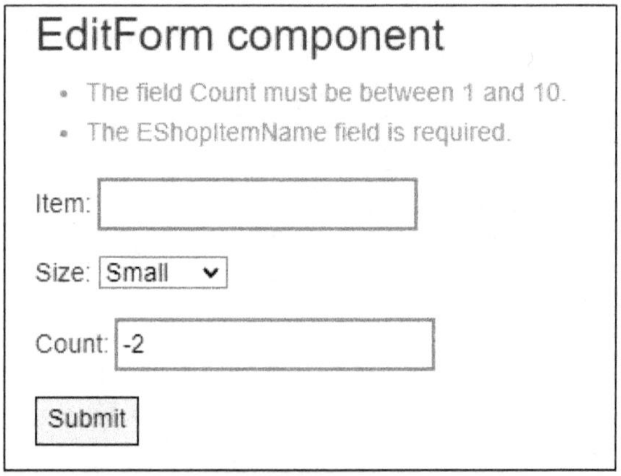

FIGURE 7.4 ValidationSummary.

Both the position of this summary and its content can be easily customized. For example, place the `ValidationSummary` component below the `Submit` button. Build and run again, the summary messages will show below the button as shown in Figure 7.5.

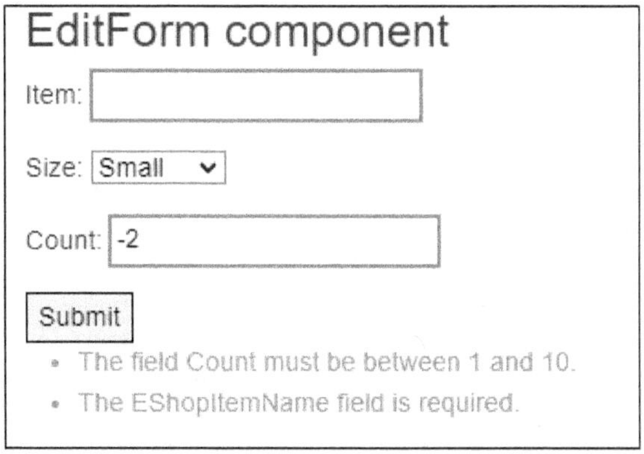

FIGURE 7.5 Move the ValidationSummary below the submit button.

Users can also show the messages under each input field respectively. In this case, use the `ValidationMessage` component. Refer to Figure 7.6.

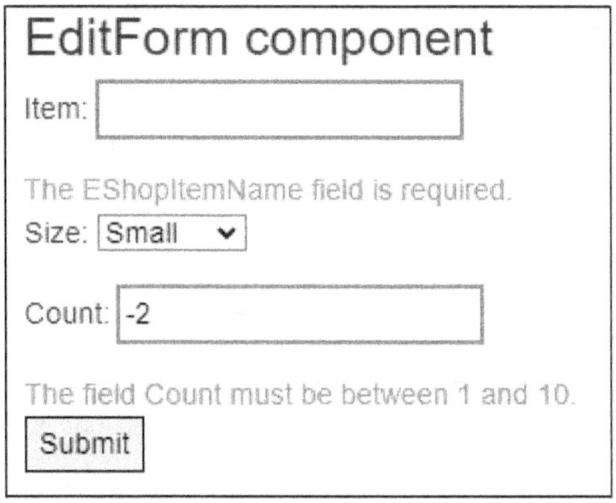

FIGURE 7.6 ValidationMessage for each field.

Customizing validation messages is very straightforward as well. All users have to do is give a string content to the `ErrorMessage` parameter:

```
public class RequestItem
{
    [Required(ErrorMessage = "Please fill in the item name.")]
    public string EShopItemName { get; set; }


    public RequestItemSize Size { get; set; }


    [Required(ErrorMessage = "Please fill in the item count.")]
    [Range(1, 10, ErrorMessage= "You may request no more than 10
    items.")] public int Count { get; set; } = 1;
}
```

Build and run it again, and it will show the new validation message. Refer to Figure 7.7.

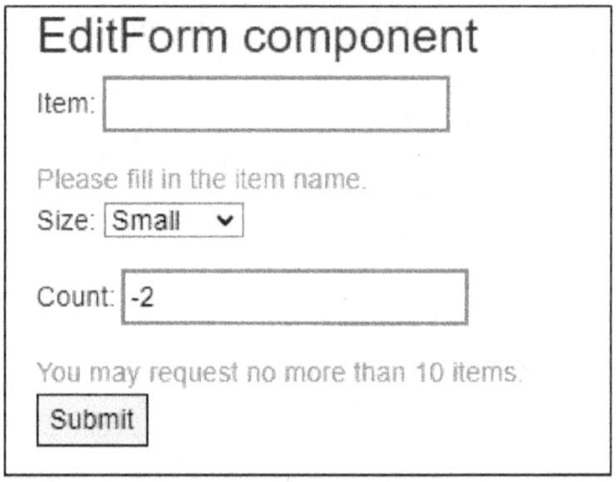

FIGURE 7.7 Customized validation message.

CUSTOM VALIDATION

Data annotations probably meet requirements for the most scenarios, but in some complex cases, developers seek a more customized way to validate users' data both on the client side and from the server side. A custom validation component can help to validate multiple forms in multiple phases.

First, create a customization component, `RequestItemValidator.cs` under the `Components` folder in the `EShop.WebAssembly` project:

```
using Microsoft.AspNetCore.Components;
using Microsoft.AspNetCore.Components.Forms;


namespace EShop.WebAssembly.Components;


public class ValidationMessage
{
    public string Field { get; }
    public string Message { get; }

    public ValidationMessage(string field, string message)
    {
        Field = field;
        Message = message;
    }
}
public class RequestItemValidator : ComponentBase
{
    private ValidationMessageStore _validationMessageStore;

    [CascadingParameter]
    private EditContext EditContext { get; set; }

    protected override void OnInitialized()
    {
        base.OnInitialized();

        _validationMessageStore = new
ValidationMessageStore(EditContext);
```

```
        EditContext.OnValidationRequested += (_, _) => _
validationMessageStore.Clear();

        EditContext.OnFieldChanged += (_, e) => _
validationMessageStore.Clear(e.FieldIdentifier);

    }


    public void Show(IEnumerable<ValidationMessage> validation-
    Messages)

    {

        foreach (var item in validationMessages)

        {

            _validationMessageStore.Add(EditContext.
Field(item.Field), item.Message);

        }


        EditContext.NotifyValidationStateChanged();

    }


    public void Clear()

    {

        _validationMessageStore.Clear();
        EditContext.NotifyValidationStateChanged();

    }

}
```

Create a `ValidationMessage` class here as a container for the validation fields and messages. `RequestItemValidator` is just another component that inherits `ComponentBase`. It must have a cascading parameter of the type `EditContext` so that users can manage the validations. Then users initialize the `ValidationMessageStore` with the cascading `EditContext` and clear messages each time fields change or when validation is requested.

With this validator, add it to our `EditForm` on the `RequestItem` page:

```
<EditForm Model="@_requestItem" OnSubmit="@OnSubmit">
    <RequestItemValidator @ref="_validator" />
```

```
    <p>
        <label>
            Item:
            <InputText id="editform-item" @bind-Value="_
requestItem.EShopItemName" />
        </label>
    </p>
    <p>
        <label>
            Size:
            <InputEnum @bind-Value="_requestItem.Size" />
        </label>
    </p>
    <p>
        <label>
            Count:
            <InputNumber id="editform-count" @bind-Value="_
requestItem.Count" />
        </label>
    </p>


    <button type="submit">Submit</button>


    <ValidationSummary />
</EditForm>
```

Replace the default validator with RequestItemValidator and add a reference to use it in the corresponding C# code.

```
using EShop.WebAssembly.Components;
namespace EShop.WebAssembly.Pages;
public partial class RequestItem
{
```

```csharp
private Models.RequestItem _requestItem = new Models.Re-
questItem(); private RequestItemValidator _validator;

private void OnSubmit()
{
    _validator.Clear();
    var messages = new List<ValidationMessage>();

    // validation logic
    if (_requestItem.Count < 1)
    {
        messages.Add(new ValidationMessage(nameof
(_requestItem.Count), $"{nameof(_requestItem.Count)} must be
positive"));
    }

    if (messages.Count > 0)
    {
        _validator.Show(messages);

        return;
    }

    // submit to the server
    var random = new Random();
    var passServerValidation = random.Next(2) >= 1;
    if (!passServerValidation)
    {
        messages.Add(new ValidationMessage(nameof
(_requestItem.EShopItemName), $"{nameof(_requestItem.
EShopItemName)} does not pass the server validation"));

        _validator.Show(messages);
    }
}
```

During different phases, for example, before or after they are submitted to the server, users can show different validation errors for them. Before a customer clicks on the Submit button, users can validate the input on the client side. Then they can send the data to the server, and the server returns with an expected successful response or the validation messages so that users can show those messages from the server here as well. In the example code, use a Random instance to represent the response from the server, and if the random number is larger than or equal to one, it means that the server accepted the request.

Validation with attributes and a customized validator should be able to cover almost all the scenarios that users will encounter.

FORM SUBMISSION

Since EditForm will be rendered as a native <form> element, users can submit the form to a server with a submit <button> or a submit <input>. There are three event delegates that users can attach to submit a form, and they are OnValidSubmit, OnInvalidSubmit, or OnSubmit.

All of these submitted delegates will be invoked with the instance of EditContext. OnValidSubmit will be triggered when the form is validated successfully without errors, while OnInvalidSubmit will be invoked when the form fails validation. OnSubmit is a more manual and customizable way to submit the form, and developers are responsible for validating the form by calling the Validate method of EditContext or validating in anyway desired on the client side or on the server side.

Please note that in the source code of the EditForm component, it will check if OnValidSubmit or OnInvalidSubmit is assigned while OnSubmit is assigned as well. If that is the case, an exception will be thrown:

```
    if (OnSubmit.HasDelegate && (OnValidSubmit.HasDelegate
|| OnInvalidSubmit.HasDelegate))

    {

        throw new InvalidOperationException($"When supplying
an{nameof(OnSubmit)} parameter to " +

            $"{nameof(EditForm)}, do not also supply
{nameof(OnValidSubmit)} or {nameof(OnInvalidSubmit)}.");

    }
```

EDITCONTEXT AND FORM STATE

`EditContext` is an essential property in `EditForm`. When users assign a model to the `EditForm`, a `RequestItem` instance is in their example. `EditForm` will generate an instance of `EditContext` on this model. Whenever the model is reassigned, the `EditContext` instance will be updated respectively. This `EditContext` is a cascading parameter that will be held by the child components of `EditForm`, as readers have seen in previous examples such as customized input component and validator. It plays the important role of a metadata container for the `EditForm`. `EditContext` holds the information if any fields are modified or if any validation errors occur. It separates the business logic of the model from these metadata.

`FieldIdentifier` is used to identify model properties on the instance level. Unlike reflections in C#, which identify properties on the class level, as long as two instances are of the same type, users will get the same `PropertyInfo` on certain properties, `FieldIdentifier` compares instances reference as well:

```
public override int GetHashCode()
{
    var modelHash = RuntimeHelpers.GetHashCode(Model);

    var fieldHash = StringComparer.Ordinal.GetHashCode(FieldName);

    return (
        modelHash,
        fieldHash
    )
    .GetHashCode();
}


public override bool Equals(object? obj)
    => obj is FieldIdentifier otherIdentifier
    && Equals(otherIdentifier);

public bool Equals(FieldIdentifier otherIdentifier)
{
    return
```

```
            ReferenceEquals(otherIdentifier.Model, Model) &&
            string.Equals(otherIdentifier.FieldName, FieldName,
StringComparison.Ordinal);
    }
```

If the source code of `FieldIdentifier`, implements `IEquatable <FieldIdentifier>` interface and overrides the `GetHashCode` and `Equals` methods, it is always recommended that users override these two methods together. First, the hash code is calculated based on both the model instance and field name. Two `FieldIdentifier` will be tested equally if they are of the same model instance and has the same field name. This is important when users are validating the fields through annotation attributes or customized validators.

While `FieldIdentifier` helps to identify a field, `FieldState` holds information regarding the modified state and validation messages:

```
internal sealed class FieldState
{
    private readonly FieldIdentifier _fieldIdentifier;
    private HashSet<ValidationMessageStore>? _
    validationMessageStores;
    public FieldState(FieldIdentifier fieldIdentifier)
    {
        _fieldIdentifier = fieldIdentifier;
    }


    public bool IsModified { get; set; }


    public IEnumerable<string> GetValidationMessages()
    {
        if (_validationMessageStores != null)
        {
            foreach (var store in _validationMessageStores)
            {
```

```
            foreach (var message in store[_fieldIdentifier])
            {
                yield return message;
            }
        }
    }


    public void
AssociateWithValidationMessageStore(ValidationMessageStore
validationMessageStore)
    {
        if (_validationMessageStores == null)
        {
            _validationMessageStores = new
HashSet<ValidationMessageStore>();
        }


        _validationMessageStores.Add(validationMessageStore);
    }


    public void
DissociateFromValidationMessageStore(ValidationMessageStore
validationMessageStore)
        => _validationMessageStores?.Remove(validationMessage-
        Store);
}
```

The EditContext holds all the FieldIdentifiers and corresponding FieldStates in a dictionary. IsModified property on the FieldState will be set to true when the NotifyFieldChanged method is invoked on the EditContext instance.

Understand that `EditContext` manages the form's state together with `FieldIdentifier` and `FieldState`, and all this management is separated from the model's business logic.

CONCLUSION

This chapter introduced the native `<form>` element in HTML and compared it with the `EditForm` provided by the Blazor framework. We demonstrated the extension capabilities of the `EditForm` by building an `InputEnum` component to easily provide options to customers with enumerations. Readers learned how to validate customers' input with both annotation attributes and customized validators and display error messages as a whole or for each field separately. Finally, the chapter discussed the submission, context, and state management of an `EditForm` instance.

Chapter 8 covers navigation in Blazor and explains how navigation works. Readers will continue to build the EShop project and will also take a look at some Blazor source code to help them understand the mechanism behind it.

NAVIGATING OVER APPLICATION

INTRODUCTION

This chapter will introduce how to navigate between pages. Web applications are created with hyperlinks that enable users to jump through the network. The chapter will explain what a Router class is, and how it equips Blazor with navigation to other Razor components in an application with the help from RouteAttribute class.

STRUCTURE

This chapter will discuss the following topics:

- Router
- RouteAttribute
- NavLink
- route parameters
- navigation events and asynchronous navigation
- ASP.NET core integration

OBJECTIVES

This chapter will help readers understand how to manage navigation in a Blazor application and how a request is mapped to the desired route. Readers will also learn about the components Blazor provides to help navigate to target pages.

ROUTER

There is one file at the project root that has not yet been touched: `App.razor`. This file provides a default backbone component for the WebAssembly application:

```
using Microsoft.AspNetCore.Components.Web;
using Microsoft.AspNetCore.Components.WebAssembly.Hosting;
using EShop.WebAssembly;


var builder = WebAssemblyHostBuilder.CreateDefault(args);
builder.RootComponents.Add<App>("#app"); builder.RootComponents.
Add<HeadOutlet>("head::after");


builder.Services.AddScoped(sp => new HttpClient { BaseAddress =
new Uri(builder.HostEnvironment.BaseAddress) });


await builder.Build().RunAsync();
```

In `Program.cs`, this `App` component is registered into the `RootComponents`, which contains the component mapping for this application. The `Add` method adds the `App` component to this collection.

Look at the `App.razor`:

```
<Router AppAssembly="@typeof(App).Assembly">

    <Found Context="routeData">

        <RouteView RouteData="@routeData" DefaultLayout="@
typeof(MainLayout)" />

        <FocusOnNavigate RouteData="@routeData" Selector="h1" />
```

```
    </Found>

    <NotFound>

        <PageTitle>Not found</PageTitle>

        <LayoutView Layout="@typeof(MainLayout)">

            <p role="alert">Sorry, there's nothing at this
            address.</p>

        </LayoutView>

    </NotFound>

</Router>
```

The `Router` component contains two children, `Found` and `NotFound`, enabling the routing and navigating to all the components placed under the `Pages` folder. It is intuitive that `Found` will be rendered when it is possible to find the matched Router, and `NotFound` will be displayed when no such resource is found. It is a good place to build a uniformed 404 page. For example, one might have seen that github.com has a dedicated page for the 404 result. One can use the `NotFound` section here to implement the same, so there will not be the plain "not found" error from the browser:

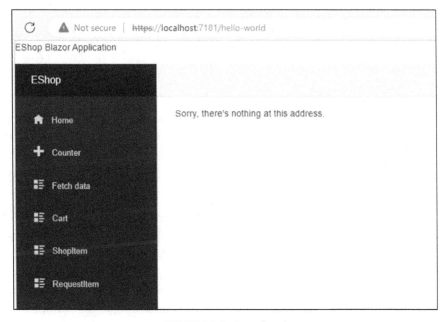

FIGURE 8.1 Page not found.

If users navigate to a "/hello-world" page that does not exist, the page will revert to this NotFound section and display the defined content here.

Other than Found and NotFound, some interesting parameters from the Router component are listed:

```
[Parameter]
[EditorRequired]
public Assembly AppAssembly { get; set; }


[Parameter] public IEnumerable<Assembly> AdditionalAssemblies
{ get; set; }


[Parameter]
[EditorRequired]
public RenderFragment NotFound { get; set; }


[Parameter]
[EditorRequired]
public RenderFragment<RouteData> Found { get; set; }

[Parameter] public RenderFragment? Navigating { get; set; }

[Parameter] public EventCallback<NavigationContext>
OnNavigateAsync { get; set; }
```

The first parameter is AppAssembly. It is assigned by default from the WebAssembly project template. This parameter is used to identify the Assembly that will be scanned, where users add all of the pages, for example, the components under the Pages folder.

The next parameter is AdditionalAssemblies and it is optional if users have more than one assembly holding page component. If one are building an application that goes into the production environment, it will be a good idea to have dedicated assemblies to create pages for different features.

NotFound and Found RenderFragment help render the normal pages and a uniform view for 404 not found. Navigating is also a RenderFragment but not required by the Blazor framework. A developer can use Navigating to render a loading animation when navigating to another page, for example, a progress ring or a progress bar. The last one worth pointing out is OnNavigateAsync, which is an event handler that will be invoked each time before navigating.

ROUTEATTRIBUTE

The last section mentioned that `App.razor` will scan an assembly to determine the routing to each page. The following is a further explanation about how that is achieved with the help of `RouteAttribute`.

`RouteAttribute` for Blazor is located under the namespace `Microsoft.AspNetCore.Components`. Be careful not to mix this up with the `RouteAttribute` from the namespace `Microsoft.AspNetCore.Mvc`. The latter attribute is used to define a route template on ASP.NET Core controllers or actions:

```
namespace Microsoft.AspNetCore.Components;


[AttributeUsage(AttributeTargets.Class, AllowMultiple = true,
Inherited = false)]
public sealed class RouteAttribute : Attribute
{
    public RouteAttribute(string template)
    {
        ArgumentNullException.ThrowIfNull(template);

        Template = template;
    }

    public string Template { get; }
}
```

This `RouteAttribute` has only one parameter, `Template`, and the `Template` is used to define the route `uri` for a component. The Router that was covered in the last section has an internal method called `Refresh`. There are a few occurrences calling this `Refresh` method, in `SetParametersAsync` and `RunOnNavigateAsync`. The `Refresh` method will call its own private method `RefreshRouteTable` which then calls the static `Create` method of `RouteTableFactory` to generate the routing table.

Take a deep look into this `RouteTableFactory.Create()`:

```
public static RouteTable Create(RouteKey routeKey)
{
    if (Cache.TryGetValue(routeKey, out var resolvedComponents))
    {
        return resolvedComponents;
    }

    var componentTypes = GetRouteableComponents(routeKey);
    var routeTable = Create(componentTypes);
    Cache.TryAdd(routeKey, routeTable);
    return routeTable;
}
```

It takes a parameter of type `RouteKey`. The `RouteKey` works as a container to hold the `AppAssembly` and any additional assemblies that need to be scanned:

```
internal readonly struct RouteKey : IEquatable<RouteKey>
{
    public readonly Assembly? AppAssembly;

    public readonly HashSet<Assembly>? AdditionalAssemblies;


    public RouteKey(Assembly appAssembly, IEnumerable<Assembly>
additionalAssemblies)
    {
        AppAssembly = appAssembly;

        AdditionalAssemblies = additionalAssemblies is null ?
null : new HashSet<Assembly>(additionalAssemblies);
    }

    // some code
}
```

As the class name suggests, it works as a key to create a route table. First, RouteTableFactory will check its cache. If components corresponding to the key are found, it will return the components directly. Otherwise, it will generate a new route table and add it to the cache with the key.

To generate the routing table, RouteTableFactory calls the private method GetRouteableComponents. A component is defined as routable only if it implements the IComponent interface while having the RouteAttribute attached. GetRouteableComponents will check not only the AppAssembly but also the AdditionalAssemblies if any:

```
private static List<Type> GetRouteableComponents(RouteKey
routeKey)
{
    var routeableComponents = new List<Type>();
    if (routeKey.AppAssembly is not null)
    {
        GetRouteableComponents(routeableComponents, routeKey.
AppAssembly);
    }


    if (routeKey.AdditionalAssemblies is not null)
    {
        foreach (var assembly in routeKey.AdditionalAssemblies)
        {
            if (assembly != routeKey.AppAssembly)
            {
                GetRouteableComponents(routeableComponents,
                assembly);
            }
        }
    }
```

```
            return routeableComponents;


        static void GetRouteableComponents(List<Type>
    routeableComponents, Assembly assembly)
        {
            foreach (var type in assembly.ExportedTypes)
            {
                if (typeof(IComponent).IsAssignableFrom(type) &&
    type.IsDefined(typeof(RouteAttribute)))
                {
                    routeableComponents.Add(type);
                }
            }
        }
    }
```

Next, `RouteTableFactory` will create the `RouteTable` with the scanned routable components. It iterates through all the components type found in the last step and checks the `RouteAttribute` attached to them. Since each component may have more than one `RouteAttribute` attached, for example, one could define a new page that can be visited by both /route-a and /route-b at the same time, each component type can be mapped to multiple templates:

```
internal static RouteTable Create(List<Type> componentTypes)
{
    var templatesByHandler = new Dictionary<Type, string[]>();
    foreach (var componentType in componentTypes)
    {
        var routeAttributes = componentType.
GetCustomAttributes(typeof(RouteAttribute), inherit: false);
        var templates = new string[routeAttributes.Length];
        for (var i = 0; i < routeAttributes.Length; i++)
        {
```

```
            var attribute = (RouteAttribute)routeAttributes[i];
            templates[i] = attribute.Template;
        }


        templatesByHandler.Add(componentType, templates);
    }

    return Create(templatesByHandler);
}
```

Notice that it retrieves the attribute without inheritance because all the derived child components will share the route template with their parent otherwise.

It will generate the `RouteTable` now. It iterates through the templates dictionary, tries to parse the templates retrieved for each component, and calls the `RouteEntry` constructor to generate new entries to add to the `RouteEntry` list. Last, create the new `RouteTable` with sorted entries:

```
    internal static RouteTable Create(Dictionary<Type, string[]>
templatesByHandler)AU: Define (replace) "it" here.
    {
        var routes = new List<RouteEntry>();
        foreach (var (type, templates) in templatesByHandler)
        {
            var allRouteParameterNames = new
HashSet<string>(StringComparer.OrdinalIgnoreCase);
            var parsedTemplates = new (RouteTemplate,
HashSet<string>) [templates.Length];
            for (var i = 0; i < templates.Length; i++)
            {
                var parsedTemplate = TemplateParser.
ParseTemplate(templates[i]);
                var parameterNames = GetParameterNames
                (parsedTemplate);
```

```
            parsedTemplates[i] = (parsedTemplate,
            parameterNames);


            foreach (var parameterName in parameterNames)
            {
                allRouteParameterNames.Add(parameterName);
            }
        }


        foreach (var (parsedTemplate, routeParameterNames) in
parsedTemplates)
        {
            var unusedRouteParameterNames =
GetUnusedParameterNames(allRouteParameterNames,
routeParameterNames);
            var entry = new RouteEntry(parsedTemplate, type,
unusedRouteParameterNames);
            routes.Add(entry);
        }
    }


    routes.Sort(RoutePrecedence);
    return new RouteTable(routes.ToArray());
}
```

Come back to the Router with a generated RouteTable. It will be called the Route method on the private RouteTable property, Routes. If the client's request path is matched with one of the scanned routes, it will assign the corresponding component type to the Handler property of RouteContext. Finally, users can navigate to the designed component pages. If no match is found, the Handler property will continue to be null and Router will render NotFound as was illustrated before.

A few simplifications have been made to the source code to demonstrate the basic navigation process:

```
var locationPath = NavigationManager.ToBaseRelativePath(_
locationAbsolute);
locationPath = TrimQueryOrHash(locationPath);
var context = new RouteContext(locationPath);
Routes.Route(context);

if (context.Handler != null)
{
    var routeData = new RouteData(
        context.Handler,
        context.Parameters ?? _emptyParametersDictionary);
    _renderHandle.Render(Found(routeData));
}
else
{
    _renderHandle.Render(NotFound);
}
```

NAVLINK

Readers should now understand what is going on beneath when they type a URI in the browser and hit `Enter` to visit a page in Blazor applications. This section examines how to navigate to another page without the customer typing the specific URI.

Users have created a few new pages in the EShop project. Each time a new page is added, users always add a new menu item in the left column. This menu helps customers to wander in the applications.

Under the `Shared folder`, there is a `NavMenu.razor` file, in which were added a few new `NavLink` sections wrapper in a `<div>` element:

```
@* some code *@

<div class="@NavMenuCssClass" @onclick="ToggleNavMenu">

    <nav class="flex-column">

        <div class="nav-item px-3">

            <NavLink class="nav-link" href="" Match="NavLinkMatch.
            All">

                <span class="oi oi-home" aria-hidden="true">
                </span> Home

            </NavLink>

        </div>

        <div class="nav-item px-3">

            <NavLink class="nav-link" href="counter">

                <span class="oi oi-plus" aria-hidden="true">
                </span> Counter

            </NavLink>

        </div>

        <div class="nav-item px-3">

            <NavLink class="nav-link" href="fetchdata">

                <span class="oi oi-list-rich" aria-hidden="true">
                </span>
Fetch data

            </NavLink>

        </div>

        <div class="nav-item px-3">

            <NavLink class="nav-link" href="cart">

                <span class="oi oi-list-rich" aria-hidden="true">
                </span>
Cart

            </NavLink>

        </div>

        <div class="nav-item px-3">

            <NavLink class="nav-link" href="shop-item">

                <span class="oi oi-list-rich" aria-hidden=
"true">
```

```
        </span>
ShopItem

                </NavLink>
            </div>
            <div class="nav-item px-3">
                <NavLink class="nav-link" href="request-item">
                    <span class="oi oi-list-rich" aria-hidden=
"true"></span>
RequestItem
                </NavLink>
            </div>
        </nav>
</div>
@* some code *@
```

In the `<nav>` element, list six `NavLinks`. When customers click on the `NavLink`, they will be taken to the target page defined in the `href` attribute. In an application that will be deployed to the production environment, it is advised to have a string constant holding the page route.

Refer to Figure 8.2.

FIGURE 8.2 Navigation menus.

The best way to understand the NavLink is to read the source code, and readers will soon learn that it is just another component:

```
public class NavLink : ComponentBase, IDisposable
{

}
```

NavLink inherits from ComponentBase and implements an interface IDisposable. First, take a look at the Parameters NavLink exposes:

```
[Parameter]
public string? ActiveClass { get; set; }


[Parameter(CaptureUnmatchedValues = true)]
public IReadOnlyDictionary<string, object>? AdditionalAt-
tributes { get; set; }


[Parameter]
public RenderFragment? ChildContent { get; set; }


[Parameter]
public NavLinkMatch Match { get; set; }
```

Users should be familiar with AdditionalAttributes and ChildContent. One is to capture HTML attributes and later is to render the child element wrapped inside NavLink. ActiveClass is used to render a visual style illustrating customer is visiting the target URI of this NavLink. The last one, Match, is a simple enum that determines if the NavLink is active based on the prefix of the URI or must match the whole URI:

```
public enum NavLinkMatch
{
    Prefix,


    All,
}
```

Another important property in NavLink is the injected NavigationManager, an abstraction for navigation. It exposes an event, LocationChanged and provides a few properties and methods regarding navigation. For example, developers can get BaseUri or an absolute URI from it, or invoke the method NavigateTo on it to visit a specified URI:

```
[Inject] private NavigationManager NavigationManager { get; set; } =
default!;
```

Readers may speculate as to why there is a href attribute assigned to the NavLink, but there are no such parameters. That is because the href attribute is retrieved from the AdditionalAttributes when setting parameters:

```
protected override void OnParametersSet()
    {
        // Update computed state
        var href = (string?)null;
        if (AdditionalAttributes != null && AdditionalAttributes.
TryGetValue("href", out var obj))
        {
            href = Convert.ToString(obj, CultureInfo.
            InvariantCulture);
        }


        _hrefAbsolute = href == null ? null : NavigationManager.
ToAbsoluteUri(href).AbsoluteUri;
        _isActive = ShouldMatch(NavigationManager.Uri);

        _class = (string?)null;
        if (AdditionalAttributes != null && AdditionalAttributes.
TryGetValue("class", out obj))
        {
            _class = Convert.ToString(obj, CultureInfo.
InvariantCulture);
        }


        UpdateCssClass();
    }
```

Here NavLink also checks if current URI matches the target and will assign a Boolean value to the _isActive field. This field is used to determine the visual style when render the NavLink to the customers:

```
private const string DefaultActiveClass = "active";


private void UpdateCssClass()
{
    CssClass = _isActive ? CombineWithSpace(_class,
ActiveClass ?? DefaultActiveClass) : _class;
}


protected override void BuildRenderTree(RenderTreeBuilder
builder)
{
    builder.OpenElement(0, "a");


    builder.AddMultipleAttributes(1, AdditionalAttributes);
    builder.AddAttribute(2, "class", CssClass);
    if (_isActive)
    {
        builder.AddAttribute(3, "aria-current", "page");
    }
    builder.AddContent(4, ChildContent);


    builder.CloseElement();
}
```

In the BuildRenderTree method, it first creates a <a> element, adding html attributes. Notice that ActiveClass, which is active by default, will be added to the class attribute if the current URI matches. Then ChildContent is added as the content of <a> element and finally marks the closed element. Refer to Figure 8.3 in which it shows the rendering results of a NavLink component without matching URL.

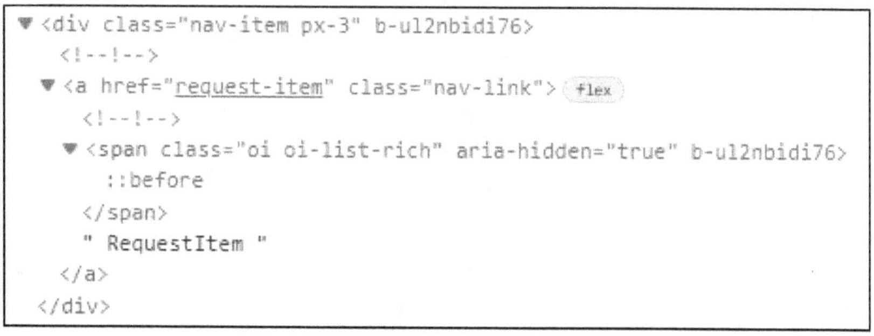

```
▼ <div class="nav-item px-3" b-ul2nbidi76>
    <!--!-->
  ▼ <a href="request-item" class="nav-link"> flex
      <!--!-->
    ▼ <span class="oi oi-list-rich" aria-hidden="true" b-ul2nbidi76>
        ::before
      </span>
      " RequestItem "
    </a>
  </div>
```

FIGURE 8.3 NavLink rendered in html.

Refer to the following Figure 8.4, which shows an active one:

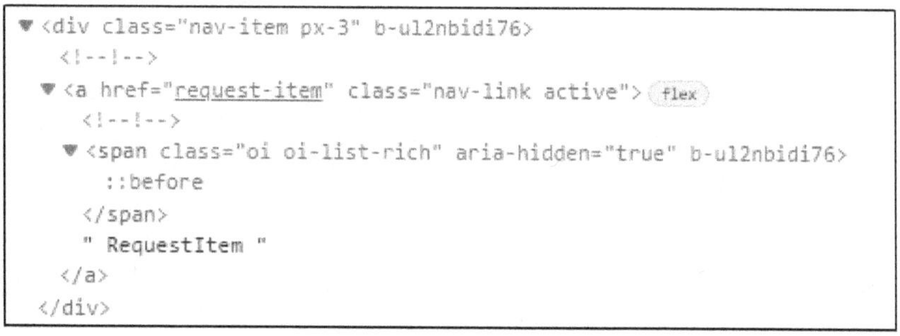

```
▼ <div class="nav-item px-3" b-ul2nbidi76>
    <!--!-->
  ▼ <a href="request-item" class="nav-link active"> flex
      <!--!-->
    ▼ <span class="oi oi-list-rich" aria-hidden="true" b-ul2nbidi76>
        ::before
      </span>
      " RequestItem "
    </a>
  </div>
```

FIGURE 8.4 Active NavLink rendered in html.

NavMenu.`razor.css` defines the visual style for the `NavLink` when it is active, so users will see a semitransparent white background for a matched `NavLink` in Figure 8.2. It is completely up to UI designers or developers to customize the visual effect for the matched `NavLink` by updating the CSS class name or the style:

```
.nav-item ::deep a.active {

    background-color: rgba(255,255,255,0.25);

    color: white;

}
```

The one last thing to do is keep the active status correct. `NavLink` subscribes to the `LocationChanged` event from the injected `NavigationManager` and unsubscribes when disposed in case of memory leakage:

```
protected override void OnInitialized()
{
    NavigationManager.LocationChanged += OnLocationChanged;
}

public void Dispose()
{
    NavigationManager.LocationChanged -= OnLocationChanged;
}

private void OnLocationChanged(object? sender,
LocationChangedEventArgs args)
{
    var shouldBeActiveNow = ShouldMatch(args.Location);
    if (shouldBeActiveNow != _isActive)
    {
        _isActive = shouldBeActiveNow;
        UpdateCssClass();
        StateHasChanged();
    }
}
```

If the application is navigated, `NavLink` will check if it is currently active or not and rerender if necessary.

ROUTE PARAMETERS

Thus far, external and internal navigation has been covered. The next discussion explores the route parameters in detail. Most Web application frameworks will provide at least one way to support route parameters. For example, in NEXT.js, square brackets [] are used to mark the dynamic parameters in a route. In ASP.NET Core, curly braces {} build a route template.

Since Blazor is also a member of the .NET Core family, it uses curly braces {} for the route parameters as well. The route parameter is especially useful when developers are building a page or a template for a mount of similar objects. In EShop, users have built a `ShopItem.razor` with the route `"/shop-item"`, but this page is dedicated to displaying T-Shirts. With help from route parameters, users can reuse this page for other `ShopItem` as well, for example, accessories, shoes, or trousers. To support route parameters, modify the `ShopItem.razor` and `ShopItem.razor.cs`.

First, update the `@page` directive in `ShopItem.razor`. A pair of curly braces with `name` has been added:

```
@page "/shop-item/{name}"
@* some code *@
```

Next, prepare for receiving this parameter in `ShopItem.razor.cs`. Add a `Name` property marked with the `Parameter` attribute and move it to generate an Item model from the constructor to the overridden `OnParametersSet` since the `Name` parameter does not have any value yet in the component constructor. Notice that the route parameter is not case sensitive, so developers can keep their naming conventions:

```
public partial class ShopItem : ComponentBase
{
    [Parameter]
    public string Name { get; set; }


    public Models.ShopItem Item { get; private set; }
    public string? Content { get; set; }
    private string _base64Image = string.Empty;
    protected override void OnParametersSet()
    {
        Item = new Models.ShopItem(Name, "The best ever with lower price!", 19.9);

        Item.ImageUrl = "https://ts1.cn.mm.bing.net/th/id/R-C.614bdee2065be0f1976bdf839c725e26?rik=EJ2vSWnKs9a9vQ&riu=http%3a%2f%2fclipart-library.com%2fimg%2f828773.png&ehk=avi5QwUJFS0v4Qtu8ggI5Ariopp4uJwf7r5QlOnJQ0o%3d&risl=&pid=ImgRaw&r=0";
    }
```

```
    // some code

}
```

Now, customers can not only shop for the T-Shirt that was specified previously, but they can browse any items they like by typing the URI with a desired item name. Refer to Figure 8.5 and Figure 8.6.

FIGURE 8.5 Shop for shoes.

In Figure 8.5, a customer is visiting the page for shoes and in Figure 8.6 the customer is visiting a page displaying accessories information.

FIGURE 8.6 Shop for accessories.

Take note that there is a problem here. If the customer types the URI completely in the browser, the page will show correctly. The issue exists when clicking on the ShopItem nav menu on the left side—it is then it will show a 404 not found message. (See Figure 8.7.)

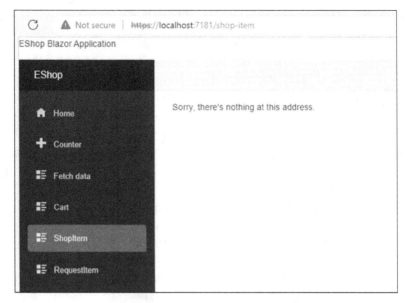

FIGURE 8.7 Shop item page not found.

One simple way to fix this is to add a random name to the end of the `href` attribute for that `NavLink`. Or one could use the optional parameter mechanism to provide a default value for the shop item name. All users need to do here is add a question mark after the name, and check if `Name` property is null before constructing the `Item` model:

```
@page "/shop-item/{name?}"

        protected override void OnParametersSet()
        {
            Name = Name ?? "T-Shirt";
            Item = new Models.ShopItem(Name, "The best ever
with lower price!", 19.9);
            Item.ImageUrl = "https://ts1.cn.mm.bing.net/th/
id/R-C.614bdee2065be0f1976bdf839c725e26?rik=EJ2vSWnK-
s9a9vQ&riu=http%3a%2f%2fclipart-library.com%2fimg%2f828773.png&eh-
k=avi5QwUJFS0v4Qtu8ggI5Ariopp4uJwf7r5QlOnJQ0o%3d&risl=&pid=
ImgRaw&r=0";
        }
```

Customers will view the T-Shirt by default now.

Another tip for route parameters is a pattern to match all the URI until the end of it. It can only be used at the end of a route and must be of type string. The syntax is to add a * before the parameter name, `/shop-item/{*name}`. In this way, the `Name` property will match the following URIs, `"/shop-item/ shoes"` or `"/shop-item/ shoes/size/8"` and its value will be `"shoes"` or `"shoes/size/8"`.

The last tip is route constraint. Just like we have constraints for generic types, we can validate if the route parameter is of the desired type. The syntax is very straightforward, `/{parameter:type}`, parameter represents the parameter name, like the `Name` in the previous example, and the type is the CLR type. With the route constraints, the route parameter must be of the correct CLR type to view the page. Blazor helps developers to easily verify if the route parameter is a valid int before using it as an id to get data from a database. Finally, if one wants to combine the optional parameter with constraints, they should add the question mark after the type, `/{parameter:type?}`.

Other than route, a URI often comes with several query parameters. This feature comes in handy especially when users are displaying an item's gallery. In this case, query parameters can work as a filter. In the EShop example, the shop-item page would be nice to have a size filter so that users can show customers clothes or shoes based on different sizes. To achieve that, they only need to add a parameter to the code behind part, `ShopItem.razor.cs`:

```
[Parameter]
[SupplyParameterFromQuery(Name = "size")]
public int? Size { get; set; }


protected override void OnParametersSet()
{
    Name = Name ?? "T-Shirt";
    Size = Size ?? 5;
    Item = new Models.ShopItem($"{Name} of size {Size}",
"The best ever with lower price!", 19.9);

    Item.ImageUrl = "https://ts1.cn.mm.bing.net/ th/
id/R-C.614bdee2065be0f1976bdf839c725e26?rik=EJ2vSWnK-
s9a9vQ&riu=http%3a%2f%2fclipart-library.com%2fimg%2f828773.
png&eh-k=avi5QwUJFS0v4Qtu8ggI5Ariopp4uJwf7r5QlOnJQ0o%3d&risl=
&pid=ImgRaw&r=0";

}
```

The `Name` field of `SupplyParameterFromQuery` attribute here assigned explicitly is not required if the query name shares the same name with your property, case insensitively. Do not forget to give the query parameter a default value as well.

Refer to Figure 8.8.

FIGURE 8.8 View the shop item with query string.

NAVIGATION EVENTS AND ASYNCHRONOUS NAVIGATION

As introduced in the previous sections, when navigation occurs, `NavigationManager` will emit the event `LocationChanged`. It is a good idea to subscribe to this event if a user is looking for a way to take notes of a customer's footprint.

To subscribe, first create a new file called `App.razor.cs` at the WebAssembly project root and inject the `NavigationManager` instance as a property:

```
using Microsoft.AspNetCore.Components;
using Microsoft.AspNetCore.Components.Routing;


namespace EShop.WebAssembly;


public partial class App : IDisposable
{
    [Inject]
```

```
public NavigationManager NavigationManager { get; set; }

public void Dispose()
{
    NavigationManager.LocationChanged -= OnLocationChanged;
}

protected override void OnInitialized()
{
    NavigationManager.LocationChanged += OnLocationChanged;
}

private void OnLocationChanged(object? sender,
LocationChangedEventArgs e)
{
    Console.WriteLine(e.Location);
    Console.WriteLine(e.IsNavigationIntercepted);
}
}
```

For demonstration purposes, log the event arguments to the console. The Location represents the new URI customers are about to visit. IsNavigationIntercepted indicates whether the Blazor framework intercepts from a browser. For example, if a customer clicks on the Cart in the left menu column, since the Cart is implemented by a NavLink which is in fact <a> element underneath, so it is obviously a navigation behavior from the browser and IsNavigationIntercepted will be true this time. To get a false value, the navigation should be triggered by the NavigateTo method of NavigationManager. To test that, add a button in the ShopItem page and customers will be navigated to the Cart page when clicking it:

```
@* some code *@
<div>
    <button class="btn btn-primary" @onclick="ToCart">To cart</
```

```
    button>
</div>
@* some code *@

        // some code
        [Inject]
        public NavigationManager NavigationManager { get; set; }

        public void ToCart()
        {
            Console.WriteLine("go to cart");

            NavigationManager.NavigateTo("/cart", false);
        }
        // some code
```

NavigationManager is injected in ShopItem.razor.cs and it is a button click event handler invoking the NavigateTo method. Click on the button and check the console log again to see that this time, IsNavigationIntercepted is false because the navigation is not triggered by the browser.

OnNavigateAsync is another event developers can subscribe to on the Router component. This event is invoked before navigating. It can be triggered by the browser or the NavigateTo method of NavigationManager. The argument of this OnNavigateAsync handler is of type NavigationContext, which contains two properties:

```
namespace Microsoft.AspNetCore.Components.Routing;

public sealed class NavigationContext
{
    internal NavigationContext(string path, CancellationToken
cancellationToken)
    {
        Path = path;
```

```
        CancellationToken = cancellationToken;
    }


    public string Path { get; }


    public CancellationToken CancellationToken { get; }
}
```

Path tells a developer what the target URI is and `CancellationToken` is of helpful importance here. With this `CancellationToken` instance, it can be passed to a following async operation, for example, an HTTP request or by saving data to a database in order to cancel them along with a canceled navigation.

ASP.NET CORE INTEGRATION

All the topics that have been discussed so far apply to both Blazor Server and Blazor WebAssembly. When it comes to the route, Blazor Server becomes complex since Blazor Server is essentially a normal ASP.NET Core project. If one creates a sample ASP.NET Core API project and opens the `*.csproj` file from both projects, they will notice that both apps share the same project SDK `Microsoft.NET.Sdk.Web` while Blazor WebAssembly is of SDK `Microsoft.NET.Sdk.BlazorWebAssembly`. That means a developer can add controllers to a Blazor Server project just like any other ASP.NET Core API project:

```
using EShop.Server.Data;


// some code
builder.Services.AddSingleton<WeatherForecastService>();
builder.Services.AddControllers();


// some code
app.MapBlazorHub();
app.MapControllers();
app.MapFallbackToPage("/_Host");


app.Run();
```

Here, modify the `Program.cs` file of the `EShop.Server` project to add the functionality of controllers. Create a `Controllers` folder at the project root with a `HelloController.cs` file in it:

```
using Microsoft.AspNetCore.Mvc;

namespace EShop.Server.Controllers;

[Route("hello")]
public class HelloControler : ControllerBase
{
    [HttpGet]
    public IActionResult SayHi()
    {
        return Content("Hello, world! From Controller.");
    }
}
```

This controller has only one action: saying hello to the world. Now, run the project and go to *https://localhost:7181/hello* in any browser (the port number may be different here), and there will appear plain greetings from the controller. Go to *https://localhost:7181/hello/world*, which does not map to any controllers, and NotFound is rendered in the browser.

Refer to Figure 8.9.

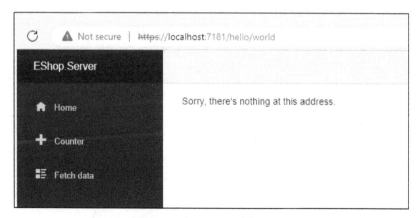

FIGURE 8.9 No controller mapped.

It does not show the default plain HTTP ERROR 404 page from a browser. That is because a fallback to a **/_Host** page is mapped. This fallback is configured with lower priority so the application will try to map a controller endpoint or a Blazor page and if that fails, customers will be routed to this **/_Host** page. In this way, developers can implement both controllers and Blazor pages without interfering with each other in the Blazor Server.

CONCLUSION

This chapter illustrated that the `Router` component works as a backbone for a Blazor application and allows customers to navigate through the application and show a dedicated error page when the URI is not matched. Next, the chapter went into how the `Router` component is implemented to enable the routing with the help from the `RouteAttribute`. The chapter also introduced a `NavLink` component that is a replacement for the <a> element for the native HTML development with a built-in active check. The chapter also discussed more dynamic ways to route through the application and how the pages can handle different types of dynamic routing. Readers also learned the navigation events and asynchronous navigation with cancellation. Finally, the chapter explored how Blazor Server can be developed with traditional API controllers without interfering with each other.

Chapter 9 will discuss .NET and JavaScript interop and how users can call a JavaScript function in .NET code or vice versa. Readers will learn how that is achieved with demonstrations, and that in some scenarios, JavaScript is still a required tool.

9

.NET AND JAVASCRIPT INTEROP

INTRODUCTION

This chapter introduces calling JavaScript functions from Blazor .NET code and .NET methods from JavaScript functions. Blazor helps users code with a minimum of JavaScript. In some scenarios, JavaScript is still necessary to manipulate the document object model (DOM).

STRUCTURE

This chapter discusses the following topics:

- serialization
- loading JavaScript
- initializer
- calling JavaScript from .NET
- JavaScript isolation
- calling .NET from JavaScript
- cache
- element reference
- type safety

OBJECTIVES

The chapter begins by helping readers understand the JSON serialization and deserialization in .NET and holding the techniques to call JavaScript functions from .NET code in Blazor and vice versa. This includes understanding the location to load a JavaScript script, isolating JavaScript, and controlling the cache of static assets, for example, .js files. Finally, readers will understand the reference of elements in JavaScript interop and the type of safety between .NET code and JavaScript functions.

SERIALIZATION

Serialization is a process. This process converts an object instance with its information into a textual or binary format, so that it can be easily stored in a file, a persistent storage database, or be passed to the next service for its handling. The reverse of serialization is called deserialization, which constructs an object instance from the textual or binary data.

Serialization and deserialization are used extensively during JavaScript interop. This section will introduce the built-in library, `System.Text.Json` and how to use it to handle serialization or deserialization. This library comes with the capability to serialize or deserialize from JavaScript Object Notation, also known as JSON. JSON is a textual format target for serialization. It is derived from JavaScript object notation, but it is language independent, which makes it easy to be transferred between computers or services written in different languages. Many products today are adopting the microservices architecture style. JSON is heavily used to exchange information from requests to responses.

JSON is also simple to understand. A typical example illustrates the key value structure of a JSON text:

```
{
  "type": "Blazor",
  "content": "Hello, world!"
}
```

This example uses indents to increase readability. Note that for machines, the JSON content can be more compact to save space and boost the server performance.

To generate the preceding JSON in .NET code, begin by defining a corresponding class and proceed by constructing an instance with the desired property values:

```
public class MyClass
{
    // [System.Text.Json.Serialization.JsonPropertyName("type")]
    public string Type { get; set; }


    // [System.Text.Json.Serialization.JsonPropertyName("content")]
    public string Content { get; set; }
}


var myInstance = new MyClass()
{
    Type = "Blazor",
    Content = "Hello, world!"
};


string jsonString = System.Text.Json.JsonSerializer.
Serialize(myInstance);
```

Even simpler, without defining an explicit class, the exact same JSON string can be converted from an anonymous instance.

```
var myInstance = new
{
    type = "Blazor",
    content = "Hello, world!"
};


string jsonString = System.Text.Json.JsonSerializer.
Serialize(myInstance);
```

By default, the library converts the instance to a compact JSON string. Moreover, there are many configurable behaviors in the process of serialization with `JsonSerializer`. Developers can construct an instance of type `JsonSerializerOptions` and pass it to the `Serialize` method.

LOADING JAVASCRIPT

To call the JavaScript functions or vice versa, users must load the JavaScript code first. There are several ways to complete this task. The first approach is fairly easy and used in the chapter of downloading files. In the `EShop.WebAssembly` project, the file `index.html` was located under the `wwwroot` folder:

```html
<!DOCTYPE html>
<html lang="en">

<head>
    <meta charset="utf-8" />
    <meta name="viewport" content="width=device-width, initial-scale=1.0, maximum-scale=1.0, user-scalable=no" />
    <title>EShop.WebAssembly</title>
    <base href="/" />
    <link href="css/bootstrap/bootstrap.min.css" rel="stylesheet" />
    <link href="css/app.css" rel="stylesheet" />
    <link href="EShop.WebAssembly.styles.css" rel="stylesheet" />
</head>

<body>
    <div id="app">Loading...</div>

    <div id="blazor-error-ui">
        An unhandled error has occurred.
        <a href="" class="reload">Reload</a>
```

```
        <a class="dismiss">▯</a>
    </div>
    <script src="_framework/blazor.webassembly.js"></script>
    <script src="eshop.js"></script>
</body>


</html>
```

In Chapter 8, the external `eshop.js` was loaded in the body section. If one is an experienced front-end developer, they will be able to load an inline script here as well. For the purpose of a demonstration, simply write the JavaScript code in the `<script>` element as done previously:

```
<body>
    <div id="app">Loading...</div>
    <div id="blazor-error-ui">
        An unhandled error has occurred.
        <a href="" class="reload">Reload</a>
        <a class="dismiss">✗</a>
    </div>
    <script src="_framework/blazor.webassembly.js"></script>
<script type="text/javascript">
function download() {
  const current = new Date();
  const day = current.getDate()
  const month = current.getMonth() + 1
  const year = current.getFullYear()
  const time = year + "/" + month + "/" + day + " " + current.
getHours() + ":" + current.getMinutes() + ":" + current.
getSeconds();
  const data = 'hello world!' + "\n" + time;
  const blob = new Blob([data]);
  const url = URL.createObjectURL(blob);
```

```
    const anchorElement = document.createElement('a');
    anchorElement.href = url;
    anchorElement.download = 'hello.txt';
    anchorElement.click();
    anchorElement.remove();
    URL.revokeObjectURL(url);
}
</script>
</body>
```

INITIALIZER

To load the JavaScript code more dynamically, a developer may choose to load them from a JavaScript initializer. This initializer will be executed before or after a Blazor app loads. Developers can use this initializer to control the loading process of a Blazor app, load customized JavaScript code, and configure settings.

The process of building a Blazor application will automatically detect this initializer and import it. The initializer is detected through a naming convention. Name it {NAME}.lib.module.js and place it directly in the wwwroot folder. For example, in the EShop.WebAssembly project, create a new file called EShop.WebAssembly.lib.module.js and put it in the wwwroot folder. In the following code, implement simple HTML indicators to demonstrate that the JavaScript code is loaded successfully:

```
let resources = [];
export async function beforeStart(options) {
    options.loadBootResource = function (_, name, uri) {
        resources.push([name, uri]);
        return uri;
    }
    const before = document.createElement('p');
    before.setAttribute('id', 'beforeStart');
    before.innerText = 'execute beforeStart';
    before.style = 'background-color: red; color: white';
    document.body.appendChild(before);
}
```

```
export async function afterStarted() {
    const after = document.createElement('p');
    after.setAttribute('id', 'afterStarted');
    after.innerText = 'execute afterStarted';
    after.style = 'background-color: green; color: white';
    document.body.appendChild(after);


    if (resources.length > 0) {

        const resourceRow = (row) => `<tr><td>${row[0]}</td>
<td>${row[1]}</td></tr>`;

        const rows = resources.reduce((previewRows, currentRow)
=> previewRows + resourceRow(currentRow), '');


        const resourceTable = document.createElement('table');
        resourceTable.setAttribute('id', 'resources');
        resourceTable.style = 'color: white; width: 100%;
background-color: green; cellpadding: 1;';
        resourceTable.innerHTML = `
<tr>
<th>resource-name</th>
<th>resource-uri</th>
</tr>
${rows}
`;

        document.body.appendChild(resourceTable);
    }

}
```

Both functions, `beforeStart` and `afterStarted` are optional to implement, and a function was assigned to get the requested JavaScript code and the functions were shown in a table at bottom of the page after the Blazor application started. Run the project and navigate to the home page. There is a bar immediately beneath the menu items that reads "execute beforeStart." At the bottom of the page is the appended table s shown in Figure 9.1. In the initializer, a developer may choose to append a `<script>` element to either `beforeStart` function, or `afterStarted` function to load JavaScript code more dynamically:

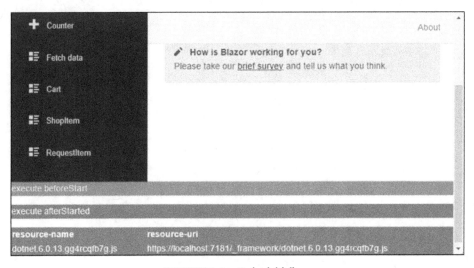

FIGURE 9.1 JavaScript initializer.

CALLING JAVASCRIPT FROM .NET

JSON serialization and deserialization are extensively used in calling JavaScript functions from .NET code. Both are used when passing parameters to a JavaScript function, and when retrieving results, make sure that the object instances bouncing around are serializable.

First let us see how to call a JavaScript function that does not require any parameters and will return void. In *Chapter 6*, we wrote a simple JavaScript function to serve downloadable files to customers with current time in the content. This time, we invoke this function in .NET code:

```
@* some code *@

@* <button onclick="download()">Download</button> *@

<button class="btn btn-primary" @onclick="DownloadAsync">Download
</button>

@* SOME CODE *@
```

In ShopItem.razor, replace the old button directly invoking JavaScript function by a new button called the DownloadAsync method in C# code behind.

In ShopItem.razor.cs, inject a IJSRuntime instance. Call the extension method InvokeVoidAsync to invoke the JavaScript function with the identifier *download*. Note that this identifier is relative to the global variable window:

```
public partial class ShopItem : ComponentBase
{

// some code


    [Inject]
    public IJSRuntime JS { get; set; }

    private async void DownloadAsync()
    {
        await JS.InvokeVoidAsync("download", null);
    }
}
```

To match the global identifier in eshop.js, add the first line as in the following code

example, assigning the download function to window:

```
window.download = download;


function download() {
  // some code

}
```

IJSRuntime is an interface, in which two InvokeAsync methods are defined. The abstract class JSRuntime implements this interface and creates a backbone for invoking JavaScript functions. Refer to the following internal method InvokeAsync as an example:

```
    internal ValueTask<TValue>
InvokeAsync<[DynamicallyAccessedMembers(JsonSerialized)] TValue>(
        long targetInstanceId,
        string identifier,
        CancellationToken cancellationToken,
        object?[]? args)
    {

        var taskId = Interlocked.Increment(ref _nextPendingTaskId);
        var tcs = new TaskCompletionSource<TValue>();
        if (cancellationToken.CanBeCanceled)
        {
            _cancellationRegistrations[taskId] = cancellationToken.
Register(() =>
            {
                tcs.TrySetCanceled(cancellationToken); Clean-
                upTasksAndRegistrations(taskId);
            });
        }
        _pendingTasks[taskId] = tcs;

        try
        {
            if (cancellationToken.IsCancellationRequested)
            {
                tcs.TrySetCanceled(cancellationToken); Clean-
                upTasksAndRegistrations(taskId);

                return new ValueTask<TValue>(tcs.Task);
            }

            var argsJson = args is not null && args.Length != 0 ?
                JsonSerializer.Serialize(args,
                JsonSerializerOptions) :
                null;
```

```
        var resultType = JSCallResultTypeHelper.FromGener-
        ic<TValue>();


        BeginInvokeJS(taskId, identifier, argsJson, resultType,
targetInstanceId);
        return new ValueTask<TValue>(tcs.Task);
    }
    catch
    {
        CleanupTasksAndRegistrations(taskId);
        throw;
    }
}
```

In the given internal method, a `taskId` is obtained at first with the thread-safe `Interlocked.Increment`, and then a new `TaskCompletionSource` instance is created with the return type as the generic argument and the cancellation check is set up. If the invoking function is not cancelled or timed out, `JsonSerializer.Serialize` will be called to serialize the input arguments for the JavaScript functions. Pay attention to the serialization to avoid circular object references in the argument instance as it is not allowed, and serialization will fail. Eventually, the static `InvokeJs` method is called from the static class `InternalCalls`, which is mapped to the functions in the Mono WebAssembly runtime.

Try the dynamic downloading example in *Chapter 6* again with a parameter and a return value. First, modify the JavaScript download function to take a name parameter and return an instance of the invoking status:

```
window.download = download;


function download(name) {
  const current = new Date();
  const day = current.getDate()
  const month = current.getMonth() + 1
  const year = current.getFullYear()
```

```
  const time = year + "/" + month + "/" + day + " " + current.
getHours() + ":" + current.getMinutes() + ":" + current.getSeconds();
  const data = 'hello, ' + name + '!' + '\n' + time;
  const blob = new Blob([data]);
  const url = URL.createObjectURL(blob);
  const anchorElement = document.createElement('a');
  anchorElement.href = url;
  anchorElement.download = 'hello.txt';
  anchorElement.click();
  anchorElement.remove();
  URL.revokeObjectURL(url);


  var status = {
succeed: true,
name: name,
time: current,
  };


  return status;
}
```

This time, say hello to the user and return the invoking status:

```
public class DownloadStatus
{
        [JsonPropertyName("succeed")]
        public bool Succeed { get; set; }

        [JsonPropertyName("name")]
        public string Name { get; set; }

        [JsonPropertyName("time")]
        public DateTime Time { get; set; }
}
```

```
public partial class ShopItem : ComponentBase
{
    // some code

    private async void DownloadAsync()
    {
        var status = await JS.InvokeAsync<DownloadStatus>
("download", "Brian");
    }
}
```

In the C# code behind the `ShoptItem` component, a corresponding `DownloadStatus` class for deserialization was defined, and the username `Brian` was passed to the JavaScript `download` function. Run the application and click on the `Download` button to see the `hello.txt` downloaded this time and will contain the username `Brian` as shown in Figure 9.2.

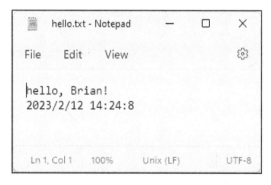

FIGURE 9.2 Invoke JavaScript function with arguments.

JAVASCRIPT ISOLATION

There is another approach to loading JavaScript, used by developers on a daily basis, that has not yet been introduced in the chapter. It is called JavaScript isolation. This technique brings two benefits. The first is that the local JavaScript will not be mixed with global namespace. The second is that if one is a library creator, their consumers will not need to import the corresponding JavaScript code manually. The following is an example that shows moving the loading of eshop.js from index.html to be collocated together with the razor component that calls it. After moving the JavaScript file, rename it ShopItem. razor.js to match the component's name. The global identifier relative to the window is not required in this approach. Users must not forget to export the function this time, otherwise, when it is run, an exception will be thrown: Microsoft.JSInterop.JSException: Could not find 'download' ('download' was undefined):

```
Export function download() {
  // some code
}
```

Next, import this JavaScript code in the C# code behind:

```
Public partial class ShopItem : ComponentBase
{
        // some code


        [Inject]
        public IJSRuntime JS { get; set; }
        private IJSObjectReference? _module;
        // some code


        protected override async Task OnAfterRenderAsync(bool
firstRender)
          {
            if (firstRender)
            {
                _module = await
JS.InvokeAsync<IJSObjectReference>("import", "./Pages/ShopItem.
razor.js");
              }
```

```
        await base.OnAfterRenderAsync(firstRender);

    }


    private async void DownloadAsync()
    {
        if (_module is not null)
        {
            await _module.InvokeVoidAsync("download", null);
        }

    }

}
```

Overriding the `OnAfterRenderAsync` method, imports the JavaScript code if it is the first-time rendering. Provide a `Download` method when the `_module` is not null to invoke the exported `download` function from JavaScript code:

```
@page "/shop-item/{name?}"

@using Eshop.WebAssembly.Shared;


@* some code *@


@* <button onclick="download()">Download</button> *@
<button class="btn btn-primary" @onclick="DownloadAsync">
Download</button>


@* some code *@
```

Finally, in the component, replace the old download button with a new one to call the Download method in C# code behind, to provide the same downloaded file. One must remember to implement the disposal pattern for disposing of any type of JavaScript reference to avoid JavaScript memory leakage.

CALLING .NET FROM JAVASCRIPT

This chapter has introduced how to invoke JavaScript functions from .NET code. Now, it will take a look at the other way around. From JavaScript functions, one may call a static .NET method, an instance .NET method, or methods from a generic class. This section will go through examples of calling these three types of target .NET methods following.

The simplest one is calling a static .NET method from JavaScript code. In .NET code, define a static method to provide a short description for this project. Create a new file called `ProjectUtility.cs`, under a new folder called `Utils` at the project root:

```
using Microsoft.JSInterop;


namespace EShop.WebAssembly.Utils;


public static class ProjectUtility
{
    [JSInvokable("getProj")]
    public static string GetProject(string key)
    {
        if (key == "Description")
        {
            return "This is an EShop project powered by Blazor
            WebAssembly.";
        }


        return "key not found.";
    }}
```

The static `GetProjectDescription` method is marked by a `JSInvokable` attribute with an optional named identifier. If no identifier is specified, the method name will be used as a default identifier. Modify `ShopItem.razor.js` to call this static method once the page is loaded:

```
export function download(name) {

  // some code

}

function getProject(key) {

  DotNet.invokeMethodAsync('EShop.WebAssembly', 'getProj', key)
    .then(data => {

      console.log(data);

    });

}


getProject('Description');
```

In this JavaScript file, add a new function called `getProjectDesc`, in which the `DotNet.invokeMethodAsync` function will be called to invoke the .NET method. `DotNet.invokeMethodAsync` will return a promise and users print out the data returned from the .NET method to the `Console` tab of DevTools in the browser. The first parameter of this method is the assembly's name of the application and the second is the identifier of the .NET method, either a specified name in the `JSInvokable` attribute or the method name itself. There is an optional third parameter which will pass the arguments to the .NET method if necessary. Users may use `DotNet.createJSObjectReference` method to create a data reference passed to the .NET, and the .NET method will receive this parameter as an `IJSObjectReference` instance. Users should dispose of the reference with the `DotNet.disposeJSObjectReference` method before any memory leakage occurs. It is time to run the application and navigate to the shop item page where one will see the short description in the console.

Calling an instance method of .NET requires more work to be done. First, JavaScript has to hold the reference to the instance to call the method on it. Therefore, users should pass the class instance as a `DotNetObjectReference` instance to JavaScript.

The product owner (PO) is usually accountable for user stories (requirements). The PO is going to provide a new page for customers to draw lotteries and the biggest winner will get one thing for free. Assume that there is already a JavaScript function that implements the lottery algorithm, which will help in building the business logic.

First, create a new page called `Lottery.razor` with the corresponding style file. `Lottery.razor.css` under the `Pages` folder:

```
@page "/lottery"


<PageTitle>Lottery</PageTitle>


<h1>Lottery</h1>


<h4>🎊🎊🎊 Welcome to the lottery park. Wish you the best luck!</h4>
<div id="lotteryNo">
    <input id="lotteryTxt" placeholder="please enter the lottery
number you get from the seller."
        @bind="_lotteryNo"></input>
</div>


<div id="drawBtn">
    <button class="btn btn-danger" @onclick="DrawAsync">Draw</button>
</div>


<p id="lotteryResult" class="@_resultClasses">Result: @_
lotteryResult</p>
```

This is a simple page where a customer will enter the lottery number they get from the seller while checking out. Then the customer will click on the Draw button to see if they will get something for free. Give the page a few customized styles in the `Lottery.razor.css`:

```
#lotteryNo {
    margin: 10px;
}
```

```
#lotteryTxt {
    width: 100%;
}


#drawBtn {
    margin: 10px;
}


#lotteryResult{
    color: red;
    font-size: larger;
    font-weight: bold;
}


.hide{
    visibility: hidden;
}
```

Before coding the C# behind in `Lottery.razor.cs`, complete the JavaScript functions first:

```
var reference = {};

function internalDraw(number) {
    var result = 'Thank you for your purchasing!';
    if (number === 'winner') {
        result = 'Congratulations! You win a FREE item!'
    }

    return result;
}
```

```
export function getRef(ref) {

    reference = ref;

}



export function draw(number) {

    var result = internalDraw(number);
    reference.invokeMethodAsync('display', result);

}
```

As has been designed, `internalDraw` will be the function implemented in the JavaScript library and only someone who owns the lottery with the exact content of `winner` will win the prize. The first exported function `getRef` is used to save the instance reference passed from the .NET code. The function `draw` will invoke the method on the .NET instance to display the lottery result to the customer. Turn to `Lottery.razor.cs`, and write the C# code behind, and be ready to pass the instance reference once the page is rendered for the first time:

```csharp
using Microsoft.AspNetCore.Components;
using Microsoft.JSInterop;


namespace EShop.WebAssembly.Pages;


public partial class Lottery : ComponentBase
{
    private string _lotteryNo;
    private string _resultClasses = "hide";
    private string _lotteryResult = string.Empty;
    private DotNetObjectReference<Lottery>? _instanceRef;
    private IJSObjectReference? _module;

    [Inject]
    private IJSRuntime JS { get; set; }
```

```csharp
    protected override async Task OnAfterRenderAsync(bool fir-
    stRender)
    {
        if (firstRender)
        {
            _instanceRef = DotNetObjectReference.Create(this);
            _module = await JS.InvokeAsync<IJSObjectReference>
("import", "./Pages/Lottery.razor.js");
            await _module.InvokeVoidAsync("getRef", _instanceRef);
        }

        await base.OnAfterRenderAsync(firstRender);
    }

    private async void DrawAsync()
    {
        // business logic for lottery drawing
        await _module.InvokeVoidAsync("draw", _lotteryNo);
    }

    [JSInvokable("display")]
    public void DisplayResult(string result)
    {
        _resultClasses = string.Empty;
        _lotteryResult = result;

        StateHasChanged();
    }
}
```

When the page is rendered for the first time, import the corresponding JavaScript file and invoke the `getRef` JavaScript function as was done in the last section. The JavaScript side should hold the reference to the .NET class instance in the variable `reference`. Next, when a customer clicks on the `Draw` button, it will invoke the C# `DrawAsync` method in the code, behind which will then call the JavaScript `draw` function. In the `draw` function, a `third-party` algorithm is used to determine if the customer is a winner. It will display the result by calling the exposed .NET instance method `DisplayResult` with the nickname `display`. Finally, the `hide` style is removed, and the result is shown on the Web page. Invoking a generic method works the same as a normal instance except that the `DotNetObjectReference.Create` is called with a parameter of a generic class instance.

Some advice or rules for JavaScript interop is to use `invokeMethodAsync` instead of `invokeMethod` if one is developing a Blazor Server application. Always make sure that the .NET method exposed to the JavaScript function is public and all the data models transferred between these two worlds can be serialized to a JSON string. There is one way to distinguish whether the code is running in Blazor Assembly or Blazor Server. The static method `RuntimeInformation.IsOSPlatform` can be used to test if users pass a `OSPlatform` struct created from `OSPlatform.Create("BROWSER")` to it. It will return a `Boolean` value that one may pass to a JavaScript function, so that the JavaScript code knows when to call `invokeMethodAsync` or `invokeMethod`.

CACHE

Remember that even with the Blazor framework, JavaScript scripts loaded in any approach are still treated as static assets, which means that they will be cached in client browsers. One common trick is to add a version number parameter to the end of the JavaScript URL and update the version number every time a new version is deployed in the production environment:

```
public partial class Lottery : ComponentBase
{
    // some code


    protected override async Task OnAfterRenderAsync(bool
firstRender)
```

```
    {

        if (firstRender)

        {

            _instanceRef = DotNetObjectReference.Create(this);

            _module = await JS.InvokeAsync<IJSObjectReference>
("import", "./Pages/Lottery.razor.js?v=1");

            await _module.InvokeVoidAsync("getRef", _instanceRef);

        }


        await base.OnAfterRenderAsync(firstRender);

    }


    // some code

}
```

For example, `?v=1` was added while invoking the import. The next time the JavaScript code is modified, users will increase the version number from "v1" to "v2" and as the whole URL becomes different because of this version number, the client browser will treat them as different assets and the cache won't be loaded. Otherwise, even when users update the JavaScript script file, the browser might load the old version it cached on the client side. Keep in mind that if one is developing with Blazor Server, JavaScript scripts are loaded through a normal HTTP request. These HTTP requests will go through all the available .NET Core middleware pipelines, and the developer gets the chance to control the client cache with the cache-control HTTP header in one of these pipelines.

ELEMENT REFERENCE

Sometimes, it is necessary to manipulate HTML elements from a JavaScript function, especially when third-party JavaScript libraries are used. An HTML element is often required to call a function. A new feature comes from the PO and says that when the lottery result shows that the customer wins a free item, play music to celebrate. First, add the audio element to the page, thanks to the music provided by Joystock— *https://www.joystock.org:*

```
@page "/lottery"

<PageTitle>Lottery</PageTitle>

@* some code *@

<p id="lotteryResult" class="@_resultClasses">Result:
@_lotteryResult</

p>


<audio @ref="_audio" src="https://s3.us-east-2.amazonaws.com/
joystock- assets/music/epic.mp3"></audio>
```

The @ref directive attribute in *Chapter 4* can be used to reference a Razor component instance. For a native HTML element, this @ref can be used to capture its reference as well. Unlike a Razor component, an element reference is saved to the ElementReference instance, and no HTML method can be called directly, which means no play() method can be applied on this ElementReference. To resolve this, pass this ElementReference instance to the JavaScript function. Other than the lottery number, when users are invoking the JavaScript draw function, they pass another parameter, an <audio> element:

```
    private async void DrawAsync()
    {
        // business logic for lottery drawing
        await _module.InvokeVoidAsync("draw", _lotteryNo, _audio);
    }
```

The corresponding JavaScript function is then modified to take the <audio> element and play music when there is a winner:

```
function internalDraw(number, audio) {
    var result = 'Thank you for your purchasing!';
    if (number === 'winner') {
```

```
        result = 'Congratulations! You win a FREE item!'
        audio.play();
    }


    return result;
}


export function draw(number, audio) {
    var result = internalDraw(number, audio);
    reference.invokeMethodAsync('display', result);
}
```

Run the application, type the winner on the lottery page, and click on the Draw button to hear the celebration music play.

Be careful when handling element references in the JavaScript functions. Do not manipulate the content of the DOM, which interacts with the Blazor framework. Blazor will lose track of these DOM objects if they are modified by JavaScript function unexpectedly, and it may cause runtime exceptions.

TYPE SAFETY

In JavaScript functions, object types can be interchanged with each other. Contrastingly, in .NET the opposite is observed. Few interchanges are allowed, and developers must be careful while passing the data around. For example, a Boolean in JavaScript must be mapped to the Boolean in .NET and a number in JavaScript must be mapped to Int, Float or Decimal in .NET.

The JsonConverter attribute can be of great help in data type mapping between .NET and JavaScript if used wisely. If the value of enum in .NET is passed to or received from JavaScript functions, a JsonConverter attribute on the enum type can help to break out the limit that enum values can only be passed as integers.

CONCLUSION

This chapter began with the JSON serialization and deserialization that is extensively used in JavaScript interop. The chapter then introduced different approaches to load a JavaScript script, including a more dynamic and customizable way with JavaScript initializer. Next, the chapter invoked JavaScript functions in .NET code, and the JavaScript isolation technique to help maintain a robust application was explained. Calling exposed .NET method and passing the .NET class instance to the JavaScript was also discussed. Finally, readers learned about the cache in client browsers, further detailing how to use element reference to manipulate native HTML elements through JavaScript interop and the type of safety worth attention between JavaScript and .NET.

In Chapter 10, HTTP protocol and communication with other services in both Blazor WebAssembly and Blazor Server will be introduced.

CHAPTER 10

CONNECTING TO THE WORLD WITH HTTP

INTRODUCTION

This chapter introduces the most commonly used HTTP protocol. HTTP protocol is not initially proposed for microservices that are extensively used nowadays, but they soon become a hot spot on the Internet. In the Blazor framework, HTTP is one of the core functionalities that make it possible for customers to use applications. Modern applications do not stand alone anymore, and they must connect to the world to be built upon. For Blazor, users utilize the http client to talk with the world through HTTP protocol. In this framework, there is a predefined service to call other APIs, hence, users can create customized http client services by a factory class instance as well.

STRUCTURE

This chapter discusses the following topics:

- front-end and back-end separation
- HTTP protocol
- CORS
- HttpClient
- HttpClientFactory
- gRPC

OBJECTIVES

This chapter introduces the separation of front-end and back- end code and project, and then aims to help readers understand the most used communication protocol between front-end and back-end called HTTP protocol. Next, readers will understand the limits and risks that come with CORS, when the applications are connecting to the world with HTTP protocol. `HttpClient` and `HttpClientFactory` are two essential types that will be used when the application is communicating with the outside world, and readers will be introduced with the analysis of their source code. Finally, readers will learn about one of the most popular remote procedure protocol (RPC) used and the .proto file that defines the data transferring format and message types.

FRONT-END AND BACK-END SEPARATION

Front-end is a collection of user interfaces that the customers will interact with. Back-end usually provides services or exposes APIs to support customer interactions. There has been a long debate on the separation of front-end and back-end. Users tend to build a Blazor WebAssembly project as a dedicated front-end application and build a Blazor server project as a front-end–back-end coupling application.

A front-end–backend coupling project has brought a few potential benefits. Since both front-end and back-end are in the same project, multiple resources could be shared between the two parts and can protect the back-end APIs from various attacks since they are not exposed. A coupling project also improves the loading speed as there are fewer communication gaps between the front-end and back-end. In general, a front-end–back-end coupling project is recommended when one is building a small project. Alternatively, separated front-end and back-end projects bring more modularity and development layers. Each module can be developed, tested, and deployed independently. As a project grows, it becomes more and more difficult to maintain one single monolithic application. Separated projects allow multiple different tech stacks to be applied in different modules. When the front-end and back-end are deployed separately, communications between them are necessary to support customer interactions. HTTP protocol is the most popular way to communicate in today's applications.

HTTP PROTOCOL

Run the EShop.Assembly application and bring up a preferred browser with its DevTools open. Visit the home page *http://localhost:5117* in the browser, and the `Network` tab in DevTools will show all the http requests sent to the server (see Figure 10.1), which is the EShop application:

FIGURE 10.1 http requests to the server.

HTTP requests are sent based on the HTTP protocol. The protocol is designed for the conversations between the client and server and is used to retrieve static resources initially. The HTTP requests are initiated, each with only one message, by the client which is the browser in our example and the server will respond to that request.

A HTTP request is sent with a dedicated HTTP method. HTTP method defines the operation that the client would like the server to perform. Common HTTP methods are GET, POST, PATCH, PUT, and DELETE. A GET method is usually for retrieving resources from the server. In Figure 10.1, the request with the name `app.css` is a GET request and the server will respond with the CSS content. The POST method is used when a client wants to create a resource on the server. For example, when a new customer is registered, users will send a POST request. PATCH is used less frequently to modify a resource, while a `PUT` method is to replace the target resource with a new one. A `DELETE` request is, by the nature of its name, to remove a target resource.

In addition to the HTTP method, an HTTP request must define the path of the target resource. When the browser sends a request to retrieve app.css, its corresponding target path is `/css/app.css`. If one is requesting a resource at the root, the path is then just a slash (/).

After the HTTP method, the request specifies the protocol version it used to communicate with the server. The most used version is `HTTP/1.1`, while `HTTP/2` is designed for better performance, and `HTTP/3` will use QUIC instead of TCP, under the hood.

Following the introduction to the HTTP method, path, and protocol version, the chapter continues to the introduction of the HTTP header. Headers are essentially key value pairs and allow additional information exchange between the server and client, making the HTTP protocol quite extensible. A new subprotocol can be aligned between certain servers and clients to extend the functionality. There are headers reserved for RFC standards and customized headers agreed between the server and client. Header names are case-insensitive and will be followed with a `colon` (`:`) and the corresponding value. For example, a `host` header indicates the server that the request is sent to.

For a request with POST or PUT method, there is usually a body in the request. In a POST request, the client would like to create a new resource on the server, and the body is the new resource specified in the request.

With all that in mind, send raw HTTP requests to a server with `telnet` and use `JSONPlaceholder` as the fake HTTP API provider.

In the terminal, enter the command `telnet jsonplaceholder.typicode.com 80`. Now the telnet client will be connected to the target server as seen in Figure 10.2.

```
> telnet jsonplaceholder.typicode.com 80
Trying 172.67.149.50 ...
Connected to jsonplaceholder.typicode.com.
Escape character is '^]'.
|
```

FIGURE 10.2 Connect with telnet.

Next, enter a raw HTTP post request and send it. Hit `Enter` twice, before the request is sent as seen in Figure 10.3.

```
> telnet jsonplaceholder.typicode.com 80
Trying 104.21.55.162...
Connected to jsonplaceholder.typicode.com.
Escape character is '^]'.
POST /posts HTTP/1.1
Host: jsonplaceholder.typicode.com
Content-Type: application/json
{"title":"foo", "body":"bar","userId":1}
```

FIGURE 10.3 Send a post request.

Figure 10.3 shows a post request to the server with the target path `/posts`, two headers, and a JSON string as the body. (Tip: If the remote server closes the connection before the request is sent, type the raw HTTP request in a notepad ahead of time and paste it here.)

Almost immediately, a response from the server is received as seen in Figure 10.4.

```
HTTP/1.1 201 Created
Date: Sat, 25 Feb 2023 07:07:32 GMT
Content-Type: application/json; charset=utf-8
Content-Length: 15
Connection: keep-alive
X-Powered-By: Express
X-Ratelimit-Limit: 1000
X-Ratelimit-Remaining: 999
X-Ratelimit-Reset: 1677308878
Vary: Origin, X-HTTP-Method-Override, Accept-Encoding
Access-Control-Allow-Credentials: true
Cache-Control: no-cache
Pragma: no-cache
Expires: -1
Access-Control-Expose-Headers: Location
Location: http:// jsonplaceholder.typicode.com/posts/101
X-Content-Type-Options: nosniff
Etag: W/"f-4jjw4Y8q22Yv1PV9m28FczJgjzk"
Via: 1.1 vegur
CF-Cache-Status: DYNAMIC
Server-Timing: cf-q-config;dur=5.0000016926788e-06
Report-To: {"endpoints":[{"url":"https:\/\/a.nel.cloudflare.com\/report\/v3?s=VTIh
LjhjNIMmAZPiMPPCT8TTRTLftIVU8%2B%2BblmeLglQ2z7kUgW%2FbqudVB5%2BB9yzigE8pfOGzEdfMIU
cXE3VkVH%2Fq%2FXRzJnsasETohD7vXeOT5YWia0uDTsuQkejjgSME4nFoQRyIgkWmxzknJBQL"}],"gro
up":"cf-nel","max_age":604800}
NEL: {"success_fraction":0,"report_to":"cf-nel","max_age":604800}
Server: cloudflare
CF-RAY: 79ee9abe2d53dbe1-LAX
alt-svc: h3=":443"; ma=86400, h3-29=":443"; ma=86400

{
  "id": 101
}
```

FIGURE 10.4 Receive a post response.

An HTTP response is composed in a similar way to an HTTP request. It first indicates the protocol version, with a status code. A status message comes after that. There are some predefined standard RFC status codes and status messages. For example, a code 200 indicates a successful request, and in Figure 10.4, 201 indicates that the desired resource is successfully created.

Starting from the second line in Figure 10.4, it is the identical format with the request. Moreover, the server adds more headers than requests sent, with a JSON body, so that the client knows more details about the new resource created.

HTTP protocol is stateless, and a server will not keep any data between two requests, even when they are requests from the exact same client being received one after the other. With the help of its extensibility, users can build up connections between requests. One common issue that comes with the stateless HTTP protocol is that Web applications are often developed with user identity, and this identity must be retained before those users log out. Headers are a great place for such connections. One way to solve this is to use cookies. The server will return the response with the header set-cookie, the value of cookie-name and cookie-value, along with other rules, like expirations. AU: Edits correct? Please ensure edits have not changed meaning being conveyed here.

CROSS-ORIGIN RESOURCE SHARING

Cross-origin resource sharing (CORS) is a mechanism that determines whether browsers will allow the JavaScript code to access response from a cross-origin server. By default, all the responses for cross-origin requests are blocked.

For example, in Figure 10.1, it records all the requests sent by the browser when visiting the home page of the `EShop.WebAssembly` application. First, a "main" request is sent to get the document on *http://localhost:5117/* and this "main" request defines the origin to be `localhost`. All the requests sent later to a different domain will be blocked by default. Two requests for CSS files, bootstrap.min.css and `app.css` were sent to the local host domain as well, so they are considered secure, and the resources can be loaded successfully. If users try to call an API from another domain, `Microsoft.com`, maybe, the browser will respone with an error message and will block access. This can be easily verified by switching to the console tab in DevTools and typing `fetch` (*'https://www.microsoft.com'*) as shown in Figure 10.5.

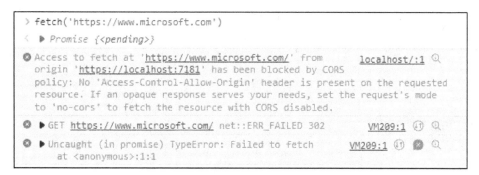

FIGURE 10.5 Same origin security policy.

The resource from cross-domain will be permitted if a valid HTTP header is presented in the response. As it is clearly stated in the error message, Access-Control-Allow-Origin is the required header. When the server sends the response back to the browser, it could add an Access-Control-Allow-Origin header with the value * or a specific URL. When a wildcard is used, it means that any origin can access the resource unless it is used with credentials, which will result in errors.

HTTPCLIENT

With a basic understanding of HTTP protocol, it's time to discuss how to make an HTTP request in a Blazor project. In Blazor applications, there is a pre-defined HttpClient service. The default HttpClient service helps make HTTP to the origin server for the clients. Requests sent to other Web APIs can be implemented by extending the HttpClient service with additional configurations.

By default, when one creates a new Blazor WebAssembly application with the command dotnnet new, program.cs should appear with the HttpClient service registration:

```
using Microsoft.AspNetCore.Components.Web;
using Microsoft.AspNetCore.Components.WebAssembly.Hosting;
using EShop.WebAssembly;
using System.Text.Json;
```

```
var myInstance = new MyClass()
{
    Type = "Blazor",
    Content = "Hello, world!"
};


string jsonString = JsonSerializer.Serialize(my-
Instance); Console.WriteLine(jsonString);


var builder = WebAssemblyHostBuilder.CreateDefault(args);
builder.RootComponents.Add<App>("#app");
builder.RootComponents.Add<HeadOutlet>("head::after");


builder.Services.AddScoped(sp => new HttpClient { BaseAddress =
new Uri(builder.HostEnvironment.BaseAddress) });


await builder.Build().RunAsync();
```

`builder.Services.AddScoped` was called to register the scoped `HttpClient` instance. In the shop item page, use the `HttpClient` instance to get the content of `app.css`. To make the request, modify the `ShopItem.razor.cs` under the pages folder:

```
public partial class ShopItem : ComponentBase
{
    // some code

    [Inject]
    public HttpClient HttpClient { get; set; }

    // some code

    private async void DownloadAsync()
```

```
        {
            if (_module is not null)
            {
                var status = await _module.
InvokeAsync<DownloadStatus>("download", "Brian");
            }

            var json = await HttpClient.GetStringAsync
            ("/foo.json"); var statusAgain = await HttpClient.
GetFromJsonAsync<DownloadStatus>("foo.json");
            Console.WriteLine(statusAgain.Time);
        }
    }
```

First, inject the `HttpClient` instance registered in the `program.cs`. Then in the `DownloadAsync` method, send a **GET** request to get the content of the resource `foo.json`. This JSON file is placed under the `wwwroot` folder with the following content:

```
{
    "succeed": true,
    "name":"foo",
    "time":"2023-02-25"
}
```

The generic extension method `GetFromJsonAsync` helps to send an HTTP GET request and deserialize the response stream to the desired generic type under the hood with a few validations, for example, content length check, or an optional time out check.

HTTPCLIENTFACTORY

When an application connects to multiple backend services, more `HttpClient` instances with different `BaseAddress` are required. One simple way to get these `HttpClient` instances is to register with different names.

In `Program.cs`:

```
builder.Services.AddHttpClient("foo", client =>
    client.BaseAddress = new Uri("https://www.foo.com"));
builder.Services.AddHttpClient("bar", client =>
    client.BaseAddress = new Uri("https://www.bar.com"));
```

Users can register two `HttpClient`, named `foo` and `bar`. To use them in the application, first inject an `IHttpClientFactory` instance. If users are injecting in a `*.razor` page, they should use the following pattern at the start:

```
@inject IHttpClientFactory ClientFactory
```

If you are injecting in `*.razor.cs` C# code behind, use the following code.

```
[Inject]
public IHttpClientFactory ClientFactory { get; set; }
```

Use this `IHttpClientFactory` instance to get the correct `HttpClient` when required, as follows:

```
var client = ClientFactory.CreateClient("foo");
```

One benefit of using a factory pattern is that the factory will cache the corresponding `HttpClientHanlder` instance for each client name while the new `HttpClient` instance is created every time `CreateClient` is called. In most cases, `HttpClientHandler` instances manage the underlying HTTP connection pool by itself, so it saves socket exhaustion and connection delays by reusing them when possible. The `HttpClientHandler`, by default, is cached for two minutes, and to extend the lifetime, developers can call the method `SetHandlerLifetime` when registering the `HttpClient`. Keep in mind that a long-lived `HttpClientHandler` instance might not respond to a DNS change in a timely manner. `HttpClient` instances, however, are meant to be short-lived, as disposing an `HttpClient` instance will not trigger the disposal of `HttpClientHandler` under the hood. Note that `IHttpClientFactory` is not a recommended solution when an application is required to deal with cookies. `IHttpClientFactory` pools `HttpMessageHandler` instances, and there is quite a chance that the `HttpMessageHandler` instance will be reused when creating a new `HttpClient` instance, leading to a shared `CookieContainer` instance. If this is not the behavior desired, avoid using `IHttpClientFactory`.

HTTPCLIENT AGAIN

Another approach to call a Web API is to use a typed `HttpClient`. A typed `HttpClient` is a class wrapped one or more of the registered `HttpClient` instances. Update the example from the previous `HttpClient` section with the typed `HttpClient`.

First, run the following command at the project directory to add a Nuget package:

```
dotnet add package Microsoft.Extensions.Http—version 7.0.0
```

Next, create a new `EShopHttpClient` class in the file `EShopHttpClient.cs` under the `Utils` folder:

```
using System.Net.Http.Json;
using EShop.WebAssembly.Pages;


namespace EShop.WebAssembly.Utils;


public class EShopHttpClient
{
    private readonly HttpClient _httpClient;

    public EShopHttpClient(HttpClient httpClient)
    {
        _httpClient = httpClient;
    }
```

```
public async Task<DownloadStatus> GetDownloadStatusAsync()

{

    var status = await _httpClient.
GetFromJsonAsync<DownloadStatus>("foo.json");


    return status;

}

}
```

In the constructor, inject an `HttpClient` instance, and provide a method to get the `DownloadStatus` asynchronously, and register it in `Program.cs`, replacing the old `HttpClient` registration:

```
builder.Services.AddHttpClient<EShopHttpClient>(sp => new
HttpClient { BaseAddress = new Uri(builder.HostEnvironment.
BaseAddress) });
```

Finally, in `ShopItem.razor.cs`, inject an `EShopHttpClient` instance instead of an `HttpClient` instance, and use it in the `DownloadAsync` method to get the status:

```
public partial class ShopItem : ComponentBase

{

    // some code


    [Inject]
    public EShopHttpClient HttpClient { get; set; }


    // some code


    private async void DownloadAsync()

    {

        if (_module is not null)

        {
```

```
        var status = await _module.
InvokeAsync<DownloadStatus>("download", "Brian");
        }


        var statusAgain = await HttpClient.
GetDownloadStatusAsync();
        Console.WriteLine(statusAgain.Time);
      }

  }
```

gRPC

Remote procedure call (RPC), and the very RPC proposed by Google called gRPC is becoming popular. gRPC provides another option to communicate with other services or clients.

In general, users can invoke a Foo method in a Bar method because these two methods stay in the memory of the same process. Note that with gRPC, an application can call a method in another application as if they are in the same process, even when they are on different machines. We call the application that sends the requests a gRPC client, and the application that reacts to the request is called a gRPC server. Frequently, applications switch their roles from gRPC clients to gRPC servers. Just like many other RPC implementations, developers first define a gRPC service with the parameters and returned types of methods. This interface definition also works in a message format. Thus, in the server application, it will implement the interface and handle client requests.

Readers should now know how to invoke JavaScript functions from .NET code, so it's time to look at another approach. From JavaScript functions, users may call a static .NET method, an instance .NET method, or methods from a generic class. This section will go through each of the examples. Just like HTTP protocol, gRPC works in many different types of machines or servers, and it could be implemented in various languages as well, for example, C#, Go, or Python.

gRPC is better than HTTP API in many ways. First, it has better performance because gRPC uses binary Protobuf which can be quickly serialized or deserialized, unlike JSON serialization in a HTTP request-response pair. gRPC is designed for HTTP/2 and it is born with a better performance compared to HTTP 1.x. Moreover, HTTP/2, gRPC makes it possible to stream with long-lived, real-time communication, be it monodirectional or bidirectional. With a defined `.proto` file, client code can be generated automatically, while HTTP API client requires third-party tools to generate code. Therefore, gRPC is recommended when one is building a microservices cluster, or else network constrain is a common issue in customer use cases. It's important to note that gRPC has limited browser support since it is heavily dependent on HTTP/2 and since HTTP APIs are readable for humans. There are still many convenient HTTP API tools out there to help developers with their daily work. Nevertheless, humans cannot read Protobuf encoding directly, and there are not many gRPC tools that can provide quite those features.

CONCLUSION

This chapter discussed front-end and back-end separation and the requirements for front-end applications to connect with the world. It then introduced the HTTP protocol in detail and explained the format of a raw HTTP request or response. It was noted that CORS as a default security policy is implemented in almost all the modern browsers, and then readers looked at how to get the resources from domains other than the client application itself. Next, the chapter covered how to use predefined `HttpClient`, `IHttpClientFactory` or type `HttpClient` to make a request to the servers. Finally, the chapter explored another option beyond HTTP: gRPC proposed by Google and the advantages and disadvantages when using gRPC as the main communication channel for applications.

Chapter 11 introduces data persistence with EF Core, as data is a vital part of an application. Readers will understand the difference between Blazor WebAssembly and Blazor Server when handling data persistence.

CHAPTER 11

DATA PERSISTENCE WITH EF CORE

INTRODUCTION

This chapter introduces how to persist data in a database with the help of EntityFramework Core. Blazor Server, a stateful Web application, can store customers' data in persistent storage. The chapter will discuss how EntityFramework Core enables applications to perform data access with entities, and readers will learn about model generation from entities, database creation, data querying and saving, and database migration.

STRUCTURE

This chapter discusses the following topics:

- stateless and stateful
- EntityFramework Core
- data entities
- context object
- data update
- data query
- database migration

OBJECTIVES

This chapter aims to help the reader understand one of the most important concepts in back-end development: stateless. Next, readers will be introduced to the nonstateless service, stateful, and an open-source project, EntityFramework Core, that is used popularly in .NET Core projects to persistent data into the selected database. Following will be information that discusses in depth the features that are widely used in EntityFramework Core, such as, entity, context, query, and migration, with detailed examples and source code analysis.

STATELESS AND STATEFUL

The concept of stateless or stateful seems familiar to a senior developer, but they are often confusing for newcomers. A stateless application primarily services clients in isolation. Such an application will not store any relationship between each request or transaction. All the requests are treated as if they all come from completely different clients for the first time. One example is Google Search which will not relate your new search with the last one you searched before. Alternatively, a stateful service will hold a context of the previous requests that future requests or transactions may be affected by. For example, a relational database like Azure SQL database is a typical stateful application that holds all the data that can be modified by a previous request. The next request coming through will usually read the data that has been modified. Often, requests to stateful services will be handled on the same server for the same clients, while a stateless service may handle the requests from the same client on different servers each time. It would be very easy to scale a stateless service horizontally by simply deploying another application instance. For the stateful, as it holds the context, it is not that easy to achieve. Keep in mind, however, that a relational database has always been a key data repository or source for any client facing applications. Later sections will discuss how a Blazor Server application is persisting data in a target relational database.

ENTITYFRAMEWORK CORE

Object-relational mapping (ORM) is a technique that is used to create a bridge, the mapping, between an object-oriented program and a database. In most cases, such a mapping tool is used against a relational database, for example, SQL Server. Typically, one will use SQL to query the relational database:

```
SELECT Id, Name, Latitude, Longitude FROM Cities WHERE Id = 23
```

The previous SQL is an example of retrieving data about a specific city with Id 23 in the table `Cities` from a database. It will return the `Id`, `Name`, `Latitude`, and `Longitude` of the city. A project written by object-oriented programming language would often define a method as follows:

```
var city = cities.GetById(23);
```

An ORM tool can help developers to query the database with a similar method above without particularly paying attention to the SQL running against the database. ORM tools speed up the development for back-end developers and less code is written compared to writing SQL directly in code, while it usually takes more effort to learn an ORM tool in addition to understanding the relational database. For a complex query, ORM tools in general perform worse than using SQL. Many object-oriented languages have ORM tools, and the one that is popularly used with C# is EntityFramework Core, used in most .NET Core projects connecting to a database behind supporting LINQ queries, schema migrations, and change tracking. EntityFramework Core 1.0 was first released back in the summer of 2016. The latest nonpreview version is EF Core 7.0, released at the end of 2022. As a modern object-database mapper, EntityFramework Core works with many different databases, such as SQL Server, Azure SQL Database, or MySQL. There are many databases, and EF Core is quite extensive so one could even write a customized provider.

CONTEXT OBJECT

In EntityFramework Core, a `DbContext` instance represents a connection session with the target database, and developers can use this instance to read from or write to the database. The `DbContext` class is implemented with the repository and unit of work pattern. A repository pattern is by design used to persist data into a database. It dismisses the coupling between the data access layer and the business layer. With that in mind, look at some basic methods implemented in the source code of this `DbContext` class:

```
public class DbContext
{
    public virtual EntityEntry<TEntity> Add<TEntity>(TEntity entity)
        where TEntity : class
    {

        CheckDisposed();
```

```
        return SetEntityState(Check.NotNull(entity, nameof(entity)),
    EntityState.Added);
    }


    public virtual EntityEntry<TEntity> Update<TEntity>(TEntity
    entity)
        where TEntity : class
    {
        CheckDisposed();


            return SetEntityState(Check.NotNull(entity,
    nameof(entity)), EntityState.Modified);
    }


    public virtual EntityEntry<TEntity> Remove<TEntity>(TEntity
    entity) where TEntity : class
    {
        Check.NotNull(entity, nameof(entity));
        CheckDisposed();


        var entry = EntryWithoutDetectChanges(entity);


        var initialState = entry.State;
        if (initialState == EntityState.Detached)
        {
            SetEntityState(entry.GetInfrastructure(), EntityState.
    Unchanged);
        }


        entry.State =
            initialState == EntityState.Added
```

```
                ? EntityState.Detached

                : EntityState.Deleted;


        return entry;

    }



    public virtual TEntity?
Find<[DynamicallyAccessedMembers(IEntityType.
DynamicallyAccessedMemberTypes)] TEntity>(

        params object?[]? keyValues)

        where TEntity : class

    {

        CheckDisposed();


        return Set<TEntity>().Find(keyValues);

    }

}
```

All other implementations in `DbContext` class were removed, and the focus is only on the CRUD methods, namely `Add`, `Remove`, `Update` and `Find`. These methods compose a typical repository class. In such a class, no knowledge is required for the business layer, regarding the persistence technology used in the data access layer. With a `DbContext` instance, developers can manipulate the data in an object-oriented manner as well. In fact, this repository pattern can be used even when the data is coming from a remote API server or a local cache, instead of a direct database. In this case, the repository `DbContext` class works as a mapping layer between the business model and the data layer. In fact, the repository pattern is often implemented as a data access solution in the domain driven design (DDD) pattern. It's important to point out that there is a debate over the necessity of the repository pattern, and the reason is very simple. There are quite a few mature data persistence libraries available, and most of them have already implemented the same capabilities, `DbContext`, for example, so that there is no need for developers to implement just another abstract layer.

Unit of work, however, is another pattern that is implemented in the class. A unit of work represents all of the data operations in a single transaction, and the application sends all of these operations to the database together at once. This is more efficient than if the application sends all the operations one after another. In DbContext class, this pattern is implemented with the method SaveChanges. When users call the Add, Remove or Update methods, no commands are sent to the database. It only saves the cached state of the entity locally, which means that if the application breaks before calling the SaveChanges method, no data modifications will be persisted into the target database:

```
public class DbContext
{

    public virtual int SaveChanges()
        => SaveChanges(acceptAllChangesOnSuccess: true);

}
```

The SaveChanges method with a bool parameter invokes the StateManager to flush all the saved cache into the target database, and this is when the database interaction will be performed. Internally, a StateManager instance will first call the method GetEntriesToSave to get the entries, and then it checks to see if there are any entries to save. If there is no entry, the method can return immediately. Next, the StateManager instance calls another SaveChanges method with a parameter of the entries list. In this SaveChanges method, a last SaveChanges method on the IDatabase interface is invoked. Each database provider will implement the IDatabase with a concrete class. Use InMemoryDatabase and RelationalDatabase as examples:

```
public class InMemoryDatabase : Database, IInMemoryDatabase
{

    private readonly IInMemoryStore _store;


    public override int SaveChanges(IList<IUpdateEntry> entries)
        => _store.ExecuteTransaction(entries, _updateLogger);

}
```

```
public class RelationalDatabase : Database
{

    private IUpdateAdapter? _updateAdapter;


    private IUpdateAdapter UpdateAdapter
        => _updateAdapter ??= Dependencies.UpdateAdapterFactory.
Create();


    protected virtual RelationalDatabaseDependencies
RelationalDependencies { get; }


    public override int SaveChanges(IList<IUpdateEntry> entries)
        => RelationalDependencies.BatchExecutor.Execute(
        RelationalDependencies.BatchPreparer.
BatchCommands(entries, UpdateAdapter),
        RelationalDependencies.Connection);
    }
```

InMemoryDatabase saves updated entries by executing a transaction and RelationalDatabase implements the method by executing batched commands. If developers, for instance, want to call a remote API to get some data, they could even create a concrete class YourRemoteAPI that implements the IDatabase interface and inject it to be used by the DbContext instance by an internal service provider.

Keep in mind that DbContext is not thread safe, which means no sharing of the same instance concurrently. DbContext is designed for a short lifetime, so users should remember to dispose of the instance reasonably to release unmanaged resources.

DATA ENTITIES

Use the Azure SQL Database as the target database for the EShop. Server project. First, create a SQL database resource in Azure Portal. Azure offers a free 12-month trial for those who do not yet have an account. There are plenty of tutorials on how to create a resource in Azure, something that will not be covered in this book. With the Azure SQL Database ready, keep note of the connection string to be used later as shown in Figure 11.1.

FIGURE 11.1 Connection strings of Azure SQL Database.

In Entity Framework Core, there are generally two modes when connecting to a database, `code-first` and `db-first`. Entity Framework Core is capable of creating tables when developers have them designed in C# code. This is called code-first. Entity Framework Core can generate C# code for users if the database already has tables. Start with introducing code-first, then modify the database with new tables and connect to it again with `db-first` mode.

To start with designing database tables, install a NuGet package to the project. Go to the root path of the `EShop.Server` project, and run the following commands:

```
dotnet add package Microsoft.EntityFrameworkCore.
SqlServer—version 7.0.4
```

```
dotnet add package Microsoft.EntityFrameworkCore.
Design—version 7.0.4
```

At the time of the writing of this book, 7.0.4 is the latest stable version. This package depends on `Microsoft.EntityFrameworkCore.Relational` and then on package `Microsoft.EntityFrameworkCore`. As was explained in the previous section, package `Microsoft.EntityFrameworkCore.SqlServer` is responsible for the SQL Server database provider. If one is using a local SQLite database, they may choose to install the package `Microsoft.EntityFrameworkCore.Sqlite`. Azure SQL Database will be used in this chapter.

Next, under the `Data` folder, create a `BaseEntity.cs` file to provide a base class for all of the models:

```
namespace EShop.Server.Data;


public abstract class BaseEntity

{

public int Id { get; set; }

}
```

In this abstract class, define a `TableName` property and an `Id` property, as all the models that represent tables in a database would require them.

Next, create a `ShopItem.cs` file under the `Data` folder with similar properties of the same model in the `EShop.WebAssembly` project, except that the comments list will not be included for now:

```
namespace EShop.Server.Data;


public partial class ShopItem : BaseEntity

{

    public string Name { get; set; }
    public string Description { get; set; }
    public string ImageUrl { get; set; }
    public double Price { get; set; }

}
```

The `ShopItem` entity inherits the abstract `BaseEntity` class and names the mapped table `ShopItem`. There are four properties in the class: `Name`, `Description`, `ImageUrl` and `Price`, representing four columns in the `ShopItem` table.

With the entity defined, it's time to explain how to map the entity model to the table in the target database. One way is using attributes, and the other is fluent API. Some recommend the later method, as it better decouples the business model `ShopItem` class. In this case, with the database mapping, use a class implementing fluent API.

Start mapping by creating a new folder called `EntityTypeConfigurations`, where users place all the mapping configurations and a new base configuration file called:

```
using EShop.Server.Data;

using Microsoft.EntityFrameworkCore;

using Microsoft.EntityFrameworkCore.Metadata.Builders;


namespace EShop.Server.EntityTypeConfigurations;

public abstract class BaseEntityTypeConfiguration<TEntity> :
IEntityTypeConfiguration<TEntity> where TEntity : BaseEntity
{
    protected abstract string TableName { get; }

    protected abstract void ConfigureInternal(EntityTypeBuilder
<TEntity> builder);


    public void Configure(EntityTypeBuilder<TEntity> builder)
    {
        builder.ToTable(TableName); builder.HasKey(e => e.Id);


        ConfigureInternal(builder);
    }
}
```

This abstract base configuration class takes a generic parameter that must be a subclass of `BaseEntity` and defines two abstract members. The first, `TableName`, is used to identify the table in the target database. The second, `ConfigureInternal` method, allows child classes to customize the mapping between entity model and the table.

With the abstract configuration class, create a concrete class to map the `ShopItem` model to the `ShopItem` table:

```
using EShop.Server.Data;

using Microsoft.EntityFrameworkCore;

using Microsoft.EntityFrameworkCore.Metadata.Builders;


namespace EShop.Server.EntityTypeConfigurations;


public class ShopItemEntityTypeConfiguration :
BaseEntityTypeConfiguration<ShopItem>
{
    protected override string TableName => "ShopItem";

    protected override void ConfigureInternal(EntityTypeBuilder
    <ShopItem> builder)
    {
        builder.Property(e => e.Name).IsRequired().
        HasMaxLength(10); builder.Property(e => e.Description);

        builder.Property(e => e.ImageUrl).IsRequired().
HasColumnName("Image");

        builder.Property(e => e.Price).HasDefaultValue(9.9);
    }
}
```

Lambda expressions combined with chaining methods define the bridge between the business model and the target database. For example, use the `Name` property as an example. Lambda expression first identifies the property of a model and then the method `IsRequired` claims that this column cannot be null, and `HasMaxLength` claims that the column will have a length of 10. There are plenty of fluent API available here to customize the constraints on a specific column. Use the method `HasColumnName` to give the column a name other than the name of the property and use `HasDefaultValue` to give the column a default price of 9.9.

DATABASE MIGRATION

The last designing step is to create a concrete `DbContext` class that represents the database and applies all the previous configurations:

```
using EShop.Server.Data;
using EShop.Server.EntityTypeConfigurations;
using Microsoft.EntityFrameworkCore;
namespace EShop.Server;

public partial class EShopContext : DbContext
{
    public EShopContext(DbContextOptions<EShopContext>
options) : base(options) { }

    protected override void OnModelCreating(ModelBuilder model-
    Builder)
    {
        modelBuilder.ApplyConfiguration(new
ShopItemEntityTypeConfiguration());

        base.OnModelCreating(modelBuilder);
    }
}
```

Create a new file called `EShopContext.cs` under the project root path and override the `OnModelCreating` method to apply the customized business model mapping. It is good practice to make the `DbContext` classes and model classes `partial`. In this way, developers can focus only on the necessary part and decouple the properties definition and method implementations.

Next is the final step for creating the `ShopItem` table in the Azure SQL Database. Add the following code to `Program.cs` before calling `builder.Builder()`:

```
builder.Services.AddDbContextFactory<EShopContext>(options
=> options. UseSqlServer(builder.Configuration.
GetConnectionString("Database")));
```

Often, users call the `AddDbContext` extension method, but for Blazor Server applications, it is recommended to call the `AddDbContextFactory` method, otherwise, the developer will have to manage the scope, creation, and lifecycle of a `DbContext` instance.

In `appsettings.json`, add a `ConnectionStrings` section with a key of `Database`, and paste the value of the connection string here:

```
"ConnectionStrings": {
  "Database": "<database connection string>"
}
```

Finally, use a dotnet command line tool to create the corresponding table in Azure SQL Database. Install the tool with the following command:

```
dotnet tool install -global dotnet-ef -version 7.0.4
```

Or update to a specific version if you have it installed:

```
dotnet tool update -global dotnet-ef -version 7.0.4
```

Verify the installation was completed successfully with the following command:

```
dotnet ef
```

It should display results that are similar to those in Figure 11.2.

```
> dotnet ef



        |  _ || _ |
        | _| | _|
        |___||_|

Entity Framework Core .NET Command-line Tools 7.0.4

Usage: dotnet ef [options] [command]

Options:
  --version        Show version information
  -h|--help        Show help information
  -v|--verbose     Show verbose output.
  --no-color       Don't colorize output.
  --prefix-output  Prefix output with level.

Commands:
  database    Commands to manage the database.
  dbcontext   Commands to manage DbContext types.
  migrations  Commands to manage migrations.

Use "dotnet ef [command] --help" for more information about a command.
```

FIGURE 11.2 dotnet ef tool

If anything goes wrong, it's advisable to make sure the dotnet tool path to the PATH environment variable was added:

export PATH="$PATH:/home/brian/.dotnet/tools"

With only lines of commands, a new table will be created in the Azure SQL Database:

```
dotnet ef migrations add create-shopitem-table
```

Refer to Figure 11.3.

```
> dotnet ef migrations add create-shopitem-table
Build started ...
Build succeeded.
Done. To undo this action, use 'ef migrations remove'
```

FIGURE 11.3 Create a migration.

For each migration created, there will be three files. In this case, they are `EShop.Server/Migrations/<datetime>_create-shopitem-table.Designer.cs`, `EShop.Server/Migrations/<datetime>_create-shopitem-table.cs`, and `EShop.Server/Migrations/EShopContextModelSnapshot.cs`. These migration files help to keep track of the current model and generate new migration files when models are modified with evolving features. These migration files can be tracked by a selected source control system. For example, Git:

```
dotnet ef database update
```

Refer to Figure 11.4.

```
> dotnet ef database update
Build started ...
Build succeeded.
info: Microsoft.EntityFrameworkCore.Database.Command[20101]
      Executed DbCommand (114ms) [Parameters=[], CommandType='Text', CommandTimeout='30']
      SELECT 1
info: Microsoft.EntityFrameworkCore.Database.Command[20101]
      Executed DbCommand (108ms) [Parameters=[], CommandType='Text', CommandTimeout='30']
      SELECT OBJECT_ID(N'[__EFMigrationsHistory]');
info: Microsoft.EntityFrameworkCore.Database.Command[20101]
      Executed DbCommand (94ms) [Parameters=[], CommandType='Text', CommandTimeout='30']
      SELECT 1
info: Microsoft.EntityFrameworkCore.Database.Command[20101]
      Executed DbCommand (102ms) [Parameters=[], CommandType='Text', CommandTimeout='30']
      CREATE TABLE [__EFMigrationsHistory] (
          [MigrationId] nvarchar(150) NOT NULL,
          [ProductVersion] nvarchar(32) NOT NULL,
          CONSTRAINT [PK___EFMigrationsHistory] PRIMARY KEY ([MigrationId])
      );
info: Microsoft.EntityFrameworkCore.Database.Command[20101]
      Executed DbCommand (92ms) [Parameters=[], CommandType='Text', CommandTimeout='30']
      SELECT 1
info: Microsoft.EntityFrameworkCore.Database.Command[20101]
      Executed DbCommand (97ms) [Parameters=[], CommandType='Text', CommandTimeout='30']
      SELECT OBJECT_ID(N'[__EFMigrationsHistory]');
info: Microsoft.EntityFrameworkCore.Database.Command[20101]
      Executed DbCommand (97ms) [Parameters=[], CommandType='Text', CommandTimeout='30']
      SELECT [MigrationId], [ProductVersion]
      FROM [__EFMigrationsHistory]
      ORDER BY [MigrationId];
info: Microsoft.EntityFrameworkCore.Migrations[20402]
      Applying migration '20230323131926_create-shopitem-table'.
Applying migration '20230323131926_create-shopitem-table'.
info: Microsoft.EntityFrameworkCore.Database.Command[20101]
      Executed DbCommand (94ms) [Parameters=[], CommandType='Text', CommandTimeout='30']
      CREATE TABLE [ShopItem] (
          [Id] int NOT NULL IDENTITY,
          [Name] nvarchar(10) NOT NULL,
          [Description] nvarchar(max) NOT NULL,
          [Image] nvarchar(max) NOT NULL,
          [Price] float NOT NULL DEFAULT 9.9000000000000004E0,
          CONSTRAINT [PK_ShopItem] PRIMARY KEY ([Id])
      );
info: Microsoft.EntityFrameworkCore.Database.Command[20101]
      Executed DbCommand (93ms) [Parameters=[], CommandType='Text', CommandTimeout='30']
      INSERT INTO [__EFMigrationsHistory] ([MigrationId], [ProductVersion])
      VALUES (N'20230323131926_create-shopitem-table', N'7.0.4');
Done.
```

FIGURE 11.4 Apply migrations to a database.

Once all the migrations are created, this command will execute the SQL commands to the database to reflect the latest model changes. EntityFramework Core will first check if the __EFMigrationsHistory exists and create one if needed. This table keeps track of all the migrations applied to the target database, and only migrations that are not applied yet will be executed. The EntityFramework Core dotnet tool gives users the option to revert back to a specific migration with `dotnet ef database update <migration>`. When that fails, it is still possible to manually revert the migrations by deleting the corresponding records in the __EFMigrationHistory table and running other necessary SQL commands to update the database to a previous state. This is not recommended, and it is best to use the dotnet tool throughout the entire development lifecycle as shown in Figure 11.5.

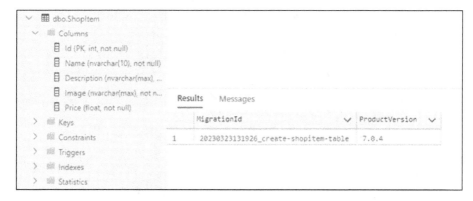

FIGURE 11.5 New tables in Azure SQL Database.

Connect to the Azure SQL Database with your favorite SQL Server client and notice that the ShopItem table has been created as was designed in C# code. There is one record in the __EFMigrationHistory table representing the very first migration.

DATA UPDATE

With a database and a table ready, users can add new available shop items into the table.

First, create a new Blazor page so that EShop employees can add the items. This page should be for authorized employees only. (Authentication and authorization will be discussed in the next chapter.) Currently, this page can be opened by any visitor on the Internet. In the pages folder, create a new AddShopItem.razor file:

```
@page "/add-shop-item"

<div class="ItemContainer">
    <h1>Add Shop Item</h1>
</div>

<div>
    <EditForm Model="@_shopItem" OnValidSubmit="@HandleValidSubmit">
        <div class="container">
            <div class="row">
                <div class="col-1">
                    <label>Name:</label>
                </div>
                <div class="col-4">
                    <InputText @bind-Value="_shopItem.Name" />
                </div>
            </div>

            <div class="row">
                <div class="col-1">
                    <label>Description:</label>
                </div>
                <div class="col-4">
                    <InputText @bind-Value="_shopItem.
                    Description" />
                </div>
            </div>

            <div class="row">
                <div class="col-1">
```

```
                        <label>Price:</label>
                    </div>
                    <div class="col-4">
                        <InputNumber @bind-Value="_shopItem.Price" />
                    </div>
                </div>

                <div class="row">
                    <div class="col-1">
                        <label>Image Url:</label>
                    </div>
                    <div class="col-4">
                        <InputText @bind-Value="_shopItem.ImageUrl" />
                    </div>
                </div>
                <button type="submit" class="btn btn-primary">
                Submit</button>
            </div>
        </EditForm>
</div>
```

This is a simple Blazor form page that was introduced in Chapter 7 with the <EditForm> component. This form is used to collect information on a T-Shirt that is on sale in the EShop application. The corresponding CSS style file AddShopItem.razor.css defines two plain styles:

```
.row {
    margin-top: 20px;
}


.btn-primary{
    margin-top: 20px;
}
```

The C# code "behind" in `AddShopItem.razor.cs` will handle the communication with the target database with the help of the `DbContext` instance:

```
using Microsoft.AspNetCore.Components;
using Microsoft.EntityFrameworkCore;


namespace EShop.Server.Pages;


public partial class AddShopItem : ComponentBase
{
    private EShop.Server.Data.ShopItem _shopItem = new Data.
    ShopItem();


    [Inject]
    public IDbContextFactory<EShopContext> DbFactory { get; set; }


    private void HandleValidSubmit()
    {
        try
        {
            using var context = DbFactory.CreateDbContext();
            context.ShopItems.Add(_shopItem);
            context.SaveChanges();
            _shopItem = new Data.ShopItem();
        }
        catch (Exception ex)
        {
            Console.WriteLine(ex.Message);
        }
    }
}
```

DbFactory instance is injected, and when a user clicks on the Submit button, a new DbContext will be created by the DbFactory. Next, _shopItem is added to the DbSet property of the DbContext instance. The last step is calling the SaveChanges method to persist the new data into the target database. Finally, the context instance is disposed of as the code is running out of the using scope.

Run the application and enter a value for a new T-Shirt that will be on sale, as shown in Figure 11.6.

FIGURE 11.6 Add shop item.

Hit the Submit button, and in the VS Code log window, Entity Framework Core will print out the SQL command to be executed in the database. Note that Entity Framework Core automatically uses parameter variables to prevent SQL injection attacks. Refer to Figure 11.7.

```
info: Microsoft.EntityFrameworkCore.Database.Command[20101]
      Executed DbCommand (166ms) [Parameters=[@p0='?' (Size = 4000), @p1=
'?' (Size = 4000), @p2='?' (Size = 10), @p3='?' (DbType = Double)], Comma
ndType='Text', CommandTimeout='30']
      SET IMPLICIT_TRANSACTIONS OFF;
      SET NOCOUNT ON;
      INSERT INTO [ShopItem] ([Description], [Image], [Name], [Price])
      OUTPUT INSERTED.[Id]
      VALUES (@p0, @p1, @p2, @p3);
```

FIGURE 11.7 Entity Framework Core SQL command.

Connect to the database with the preferred SQL Server client, and run the SQL to list all the data in the ShopItem table. The new T-Shirt is shown in the results as shown in Figure 11.8.

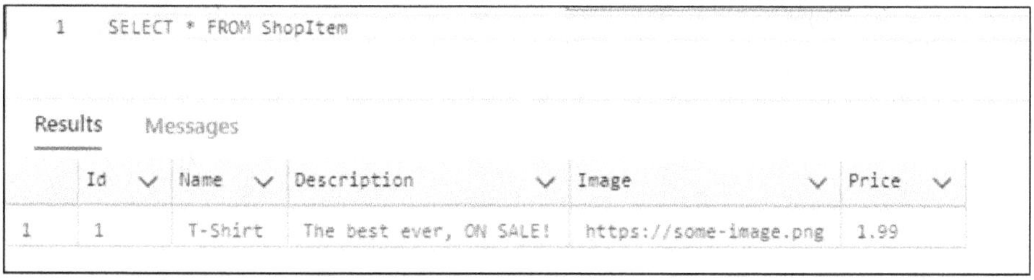

FIGURE 11.8 Check the Azure SQL Database.

In this example, create a `DbContext` instance each time a customer clicks the `Submit` button. Another practice is to create the `DbContext` instance through the `DbFactory` when the component is initialized in the override method `OnInitializedAsync`. Next, manually dispose of the `DbContext` instance in the `Dispose` method of the `IDisposable` interface. In this way, the lifetime of the `DbContext` instance is aligned with the lifetime of the component.

DATA QUERY

Code-first mode was introduced in previous sections. Now, create another table using SQL command first:

```
IF OBJECT_ID('[dbo].[ShopItemComment]', 'U') IS NOT NULL
DROP TABLE [dbo].[ShopItemComment]
GO


CREATE TABLE [dbo].[ShopItemComment]
(
    [Id] INT NOT NULL PRIMARY KEY IDENTITY(1,1),

    [ShopItemId] INT NOT NULL,

    [Content] NVARCHAR(100) NOT NULL


);


ALTER TABLE [dbo].[ShopItemComment] ADD CONSTRAINT
    FK_Comments_ShopItems FOREIGN KEY (ShopItemId)
```

```
REFERENCES dbo.ShopItem (Id)
        ON UPDATE NO ACTION
        ON DELETE CASCADE
GO
```

The SQL command creates a `ShopItemComment` table where the `ShopItemId` column is referring to the record in the table `ShopItem`. Tis will be a one-to-many relationship in which one `ShopItem` record may be related to multiple `ShopItemComment` records. Insert two comments for the T-Shirt `ShopItem` with the following SQL command:

```
INSERT INTO [dbo].[ShopItemComment]
(
  [ShopItemId], [Content]
)
VALUES (
  1, 'I like the T-Shirt!'
),
(
  1, 'It fits me just well.'
)
GO
```

The remote Azure SQL Database has been modified, but local model in C# code has not caught up with the latest changes yet. There are two ways to fix that. One is the `db-first` mode previously introduced. With the following command, Entity Framework Core will regenerate the `EShopContext` and C# model entities for developers.

```
dotnet ef dbcontext scaffold "<Connection String>" Microsoft.
EntityFrameworkCore.SqlServer -t dbo.ShopItemComment -t
dbo.ShopItem -c EShopContext --context-dir . -o ./Data -f
--no-onconfiguring
```

It is the reverse operation of the code-first mode. Users are generating C# code from the remote SQL Server. Unless the database was created before, it is recommended to choose the code-first model, if possible, because all the database updates will be kept track of in the selected code repositories, for example, Git.

Another option is to manually write the code that is generated by the `dotnet ef dbcontext scaffold` command. First, create a `ShopItemComment.cs` file at the same path as `ShopItem.cs`:

```
namespace EShop.Server.Data;


public partial class ShopItemComment : BaseEntity
{

    public int ShopItemId { get; set; }
    public string Content { get; set;
    } public ShopItem ShopItem { get;
    set; }

}
```

To build up the relationship, add a `ShopItem` property that refers to the related `ShopItem` instance which is called the `navigation` property. Add the corresponding navigation property in the `ShopItem` class as well:

```
namespace EShop.Server.Data;


public partial class ShopItem : BaseEntity
{

    public string Name { get; set; }
    public string Description { get; set; }
    public string ImageUrl { get; set; }
    public double Price { get; set; }
    public List<ShopItemComment> ShopItemComments { get; }

}
```

Next, define the `EntityTypeConfiguration` for the `ShopItemComment` model in `ShopItemCommentEntityTypeConfiguration.cs`:

```
using EShop.Server.Data;
using Microsoft.EntityFrameworkCore.Metadata.Builders;

namespace EShop.Server.EntityTypeConfigurations;

public class ShopItemCommentEntityTypeConfiguration :
BaseEntityTypeConfiguration<ShopItemComment>
{
    protected override string TableName => "ShopItemComment";
    protected override void
ConfigureInternal(EntityTypeBuilder<ShopItemComment> builder)
    {
        builder.Property(e => e.Content).IsRequired();
        builder.HasOne(e => e.ShopItem)
            .WithMany(d => d.ShopItemComments)
            .HasForeignKey(e => e.ShopItemId);
    }
}
```

The method `HasOne` was called on the `EntityTypeBuilder` and it claims that each `ShopItemComment` instance is related to one `ShopItem` instance. The next chain methods define the same for `ShopItem` instance in that it has many related `ShopItemComment` instances with a foreign key `ShopItemId` property of the `ShopItemComment` entity. The `EShopContext` is updated to reflect the newly created table as well:

```
public partial class EShopContext : DbContext
{
    public EShopContext(DbContextOptions<EShopContext> options) :
base(options) { }
```

```
    public DbSet<ShopItem> ShopItems { get; set; }
    public DbSet<ShopItemComment> ShopItemComments { get; set; }


    protected override void OnModelCreating(ModelBuilder
    modelBuilder)
    {
        modelBuilder.ApplyConfiguration(new
ShopItemEntityTypeConfiguration());
        modelBuilder.ApplyConfiguration(new
ShopItemCommentEntityTypeConfiguration());


        base.OnModelCreating(modelBuilder);
    }
}
```

Next, build a page to show the `ShopItem` entities saved in the Azure SQL Database. Create a new file called `ShopItem.razor` and acorresponding C# code behind the file `ShopItem.razor.cs` under the `Pages` folder:

```
@page "/shop-item/{id:int}"


<h1>@_model.Name</h1>
<p>@_model.Description</p>


<table class="table">
    <thead>
        <tr>
            <th scope="col">Id</th>
            <th scope="col">Comment</th>
        </tr>
    </thead>
    <tbody>
```

```
        @foreach (var comment in _model.ShopItemComments)
        {
            <tr>
                <th scope="row">@comment.Id</th>
                <td>@comment.Content</td>
            </tr>
        }
    </tbody>
</table>
```

Add a parameter of id with the constraint int as introduced in Chapter 8 and display the Name and Description of the ShopItem. The related ShopItemComment entities are listed in a table container with the Id and Content of each ShopItemComment instance. Query the data in the C# code behind:

```
using Microsoft.AspNetCore.Components;
using Microsoft.EntityFrameworkCore;

namespace EShop.Server.Pages;

public partial class ShopItem : ComponentBase
{
    [Parameter]
    public int Id { get; set; }
    private EShop.Server.Data.ShopItem _model;


    [Inject]
    public IDbContextFactory<EShopContext> DbFactory { get; set; }

    protected override Task OnInitializedAsync()
    {
```

```
        try
        {

            using var context = DbFactory.CreateDbContext();
            _model = context.ShopItems.Where(m => m.Id == Id).
Include(s => s.ShopItemComments).First();
        }
        catch (System.Exception ex)
        {
            Console.WriteLine(ex.Message);
        }

        return base.OnInitializedAsync();
    }
}
```

This time, create the DbContext instance when the component is initialized and dispose it immediately after the data is retrieved. Run the application and go to the URL /shop-item/1, and a Web page similar to Figure 11.9 will be displayed:

FIGURE 11.9 Query related data.

CONCLUSION

This chapter first discussed the difference between a stateless and a stateful service, and readers learned that most relational databases like Azure SQL Database are a type of stateful service. Next, the chapter introduced the EntityFramework Core library that is popularly used as a bridge between the business logic and the data model logic when users are programming an in C#. The chapter then explained in detail how a Context instance works with a repository and unit of work pattern to persist data from the business model. It also demonstrated how to connect to the target database by code-first mode with migrations or db-first mode with manually generated entity model code.

Chapter 12 will enhance the application's security level, protecting data from corruption with authentication and authorization and how it can be combined with Microsoft Account or Azure Active directory to enforce security rules.

12

PROTECTING YOUR APPLICATION WITH IDENTITY

INTRODUCTION

Chapter 11 introduced how to save data persistently in a target database, Azure SQL Database, discussed the design pattern of the DbContext class, and explained the process of handling data with Entity Framework Core in either code-first or db-first mode, leave the EShop item management page open to the public. This chapter introduces how to protect Web content with user authentication and security policy.

STRUCTURE

This chapter discusses the following topics:

- authentication
- AuthenticationStateProvider
- authorization
- role-based authorization
- policy-based authorization
- ASP.NET Core Identity

OBJECTIVES

This chapter will help readers understand how to authenticate customers to present different UI components or enforce rules of accessing components and analyzing the `AuthenticationStateProvider` service with its source code. Next, it will introduce the options to authenticate a customer with a Microsoft account or with the Azure Active Directory. Readers will then understand authorization to control the access granted to a customer, including role-based authorization and policy-based authorization.

AUTHENTICATION

Authentication is about recognizing a user. The user may be a real person, a physical device, or a robot software. Authentication is about the process of verifying identity.

In an application, users are verified by ensuring the credential information and user traits match. Fraud is possible on both sides, either by manipulating the credential stored in the system, or by providing the fake traits during authentication. Authentication usually comes as the first line of defense for an application, although data breaching occurs daily. It makes authentication a must-have defense strategy. There are lots of different approaches to authenticating people, devices, or robots, and they all have their own strengths and weaknesses. The most common way to authenticate is by username and password. This method is adopted by almost every Web application. The idea is to save the username and password, usually encrypted, in a database when a new user signs up. Later, when the user comes back, their username and password will be entered and sent to the server where they are compared with the record in the database. If they match, the service is convinced that they are the one who they claim to be. A good practice is to require customers to update their password regularly, and the more complex the password is, the more secure the account will be. Along with the password authentication method, many Web sites encourage customers to turn on multifactor authentication, which means customers must provide more than one factor to verify themselves.

For example, Microsoft has made an app called Authenticator in which users must either select the correct prompt number in the app or enter the one-time password from the app in the login page every time they sign into their Microsoft account. Other authentication methods include biometric authentication, token authentication, or certificate authentication. Theoretically, there is no authentication approach that can guarantee 100% security, but the more complex the authentication, the more difficult it will be for hackers or malware to break through. Remember that sometimes, a strong authentication is even more important than delivering new features to customers.

AUTHENTICATIONSTATEPROVIDER

This section shows how to build up a password authentication system in `EShop.Server` `AuthenticationStateProvider` can help implement the authentication feature in EShop. `AuthenticationStateProvider` is an abstract class that can provide the authentication information of the current user. Based on that, an `EShopAuthenticationStateProvider` will be built. First, take a look at the source of the class `AuthenticationStateProvider`:

```
public abstract class AuthenticationStateProvider
{
    public abstract Task<AuthenticationState>
GetAuthenticationStateAsync();

    public event AuthenticationStateChangedHandler?
AuthenticationStateChanged;

    protected void
NotifyAuthenticationStateChanged(Task<AuthenticationState> task)
    {
        ArgumentNullException.ThrowIfNull(task);

        AuthenticationStateChanged?.Invoke(task);
    }
}

public delegate void
AuthenticationStateChangedHandler(Task<AuthenticationState> task);
```

Notice that `AuthenticationStateChangedHandler` is a delegate type that takes a Task of `AuthenticationState` as a parameter and returns void. `AuthenticationState` has a read-only User property of the type `ClaimsPrincipal` which will represent the current customer. This delegate type is used to provide an event called `AuthenticationStateChanged` in `AuthenticationStateProvider`. Any client code interested in the authentication event of the current user can subscribe to the event, and they will be able to retrieve the latest user information in the event handler. Another important method in `AuthenticationStateProvider` is `GetAuthenticationStateAsync`. This method must be implemented by the child classes and will provide the latest authentication information as well. `NotifyAuthenticationStateChanged` method, as the name implies, will trigger the `AuthenticationStateChanged` event so that subscribers will know there is a state change of the current user.

Create an `EShopAuthenticationStateProvider`, inheriting the `AuthenticationStateProvider` class in folder Auth for the `EShop.Server` project:

```
using System.Security.Claims;
using Microsoft.AspNetCore.Components.Authorization;

namespace EShop.Server.Auth;

public class EShopAuthenticationStateProvider :
AuthenticationStateProvider
{

    private bool _isSignedIn = false;
    private string _username = string.Empty;


    private string Email { get => $"{_username.Replace(" ", "")}@
eshop.com"; }


    public override Task<AuthenticationState>
GetAuthenticationStateAsync()
    {

        ClaimsIdentity claimsIdentity;
```

```csharp
        if (_isSignedIn)
        {
            var claims = new List<Claim>()
            {
                new Claim(ClaimTypes.Name, _username),
                new Claim(ClaimTypes.Email, Email),
            };

            claimsIdentity = new ClaimsIdentity(claims,
            "EShopAuth");
        }
        else
        {
            claimsIdentity = new ClaimsIdentity();
        }


        var authenticationState = new AuthenticationState(new
ClaimsPrincipal(claimsIdentity));


        return Task.FromResult(authenticationState);
    }


    public void SignIn(string username, string password)
    {
        _username = username;
        _isSignedIn = username == "Brian" && !string.
IsNullOrWhiteSpace(password);


        NotifyAuthenticationStateChanged(GetAuthentication-
        StateAsync());
    }
}
```

In the override method `GetAuthenticationStateAsync`, it first checks if the current user is already signed in. If the result is positive, it will create related Claims for the customer, including username and email information, which is wrapped in the `AuthenticationState` instance and returned as the result of the task. A public `SignIn` method is provided, validating how the user tries to sign in, and will trigger the `AuthenticationStateChanged` event, so that subscribers are aware of the latest `AuthenticationState`. For this example, the name "Brian" is used.

Register the customized `EShopAuthenticationStateProvider` in `Program. cs` with the following code:

```
builder.Services.AddScoped<EShopAuthenticationStateProvider>();
```

Now users have their own `AuthenticationStateProvider`, and can use it in a sign- in page. Before that, first build an `InputPassword` component. Under the `Shared` folder, create a new file called `InputPassword.cs` with the following code:

```
using System.Diagnostics.CodeAnalysis;
using Microsoft.AspNetCore.Components;
using Microsoft.AspNetCore.Components.Forms;
using Microsoft.AspNetCore.Components.Rendering;
namespace EShop.Server.Shared;


public class InputPassword : InputBase<string>
{
    protected override bool TryParseValueFromString(string? value,
[MaybeNullWhen(false)] out string result, [NotNullWhen(false)]
out string? validationErrorMessage)
    {
        result = value;
        validationErrorMessage = null;


        return true;
    }
```

```
protected override void BuildRenderTree(RenderTreeBuilder
builder)

{

    builder.OpenElement(0, "input");
    builder.AddMultipleAttributes(1, AdditionalAttributes);
    builder.AddAttribute(2, "class", CssClass);
    builder.AddAttribute(3, "type", "password");
    builder.AddAttribute(4, "onchange", EventCallback.Factory.
CreateBinder<string>(this, value => CurrentValueAsString = val-
ue, CurrentValueAsString, null));

    builder.CloseElement();

}

}
```

Wrap the native HTML `<input>` element with the customized `InputPassword` component. Add one more model before creating the sign-in page. Create a new file called `SignInFormModel.cs` under the `Data` folder with the following code:

```
namespace EShop.Server.Data;


public class SignInFormModel
{

    public string Name { get; set; }

    public string Password { get; set; }

}
```

The new sign-in page `SignIn.razor` is created under the `Pages` folder.

```
@page "/sign-in"

<PageTitle>Sign In</PageTitle>

@if (_authenticated)

{
```

```
    <h1>Hello, @_model.Name</h1>
}
else
{
    <h1>Sign In</h1>

    <EditForm Model="@_model" OnValidSubmit="@HandleValidSubmit">
        <div class="container">
            <div class="row">
                <div class="col-1">
                    <label>Name:</label>
                </div>
                <div class="col-4">
                    <InputText @bind-Value="_model.Name" />
                </div>
            </div>

            <div class="row">
                <div class="col-1">
                    <label>Password:</label>
                </div>
                <div class="col-4">
                    <InputPassword @bind-Value="_model.Password" />
                </div>
            </div>

            <button type="submit" class="btn btn-primary">
            Submit</button>
        </div>
    </EditForm>
}
```

The preceding code shows if the user has already signed in and will display the welcome prompt when authenticated. If not, the sign-in form appears.

For the C# code behind, write the following code in `SignIn.razor.cs`:

```csharp
using EShop.Server.Auth;
using EShop.Server.Data;
using Microsoft.AspNetCore.Components;
using Microsoft.AspNetCore.Components.Authorization;

namespace EShop.Server.Pages;

public partial class SignIn : ComponentBase
{
    private SignInFormModel _model = new SignInFormModel();
    private bool _authenticated = false;

    [Inject]
    private EShopAuthenticationStateProvider
AuthenticationStateProvider { get; set; }

    private void HandleValidSubmit()
    {
        AuthenticationStateProvider.SignIn(_model.Name, _model.
Password);
    }

    protected override void OnInitialized()
    {
        base.OnInitialized();
        AuthenticationStateProvider.AuthenticationStateChanged +=
OnAuthenticationStateChangedAsync;
    }
```

```
    private async void
OnAuthenticationStateChangedAsync(Task<AuthenticationState>
task)

    {

        var state = await task;

        _authenticated = state.User.Identity.IsAuthenticated;

    }

}
```

In the preceding code, users called the `SignIn` method on the customized `EShopAuthenticationStateProvider` and subscribed to its `AuthenticationStateChanged` event. Users will update the private Boolean field `_authenticated` corresponding to the result we get from the event handler `OnAuthenticationStateChangedAsync`

Run the `EShop.Server` project and navigate to *https://localhost:7181/sign-in* in the browser. Because the user is not authenticated yet, this page will display the sign-in form. Enter the `Name` as `Brian` and any random string in `Password` and hit `Submit`. The page will hide the sign-in form and show the prompt `Hello, Brian` instead. It demonstrated that the user implemented a simple authentication mechanism with the `AuthenticationStateProvider`.

AUTHORIZATION

Authorization means that an authenticated user is given certain permissions to access resources, and in the `EShop` application case, a Web page, maybe. The following sections discuss how to authorize a customer in different ways. First, the `AuthorizeRouteView` component to control the page access is introduced. By default, it considers a user is authorized when they are authenticated, and not authorized when they are not authenticated. Update the `App.razor` at the project root:

```
<CascadingAuthenticationState>

    <Router AppAssembly="@typeof(App).Assembly">

        <Found Context="routeData">

            <AuthorizeRouteView RouteData="@routeData"
```

```
DefaultLayout="@ typeof(MainLayout)">

                <NotAuthorized>

                    <EShop.Server.Pages.SignIn></EShop.Server.
                    Pages.SignIn>

                </NotAuthorized>

            </AuthorizeRouteView>

            <FocusOnNavigate RouteData="@routeData"
            Selector="h1" />

        </Found>

        <NotFound>

            <PageTitle>Not found</PageTitle>

            <LayoutView Layout="@typeof(MainLayout)">

                <p role="alert">Sorry, there's nothing at this
                address.</p>

            </LayoutView>

        </NotFound>

    </Router>

</CascadingAuthenticationState>
```

`App.razor` exposed a `Router` component, the `Router` with a component called `CascadingAuthenticationState` was wrapped. The name of this component is intuitive enough that it will provide a cascading parameter of `AuthenticationState`. That is all the component does. If one reads the source code of the `CascadingAuthenticationState` component, they will notice that there is only one line of code other than C# code behind:

```
@implements IDisposable

@inject AuthenticationStateProvider AuthenticationStateProvider


<CascadingValue TValue="System.Threading.Tasks.
Task<AuthenticationState>" Value="@_currentAuthenticationStateTask"
ChildContent="@ChildContent" />
```

```
@code {

    private Task<AuthenticationState>? _currentAuthentication-
    StateTask;


    [Parameter]
    public RenderFragment? ChildContent { get; set; }


    protected override void OnInitialized()
    {
        AuthenticationStateProvider.AuthenticationStateChanged
+= OnAuthenticationStateChanged;


        _currentAuthenticationStateTask = AuthenticationStateProvider
            .GetAuthenticationStateAsync();
    }


    private void OnAuthenticationStateChanged(Task<Authentica-
tionState> newAuthStateTask)
    {
        _ = InvokeAsync(() =>
        {
            _currentAuthenticationStateTask = newAuthStateTask;
            StateHasChanged();
        });
    }
    void IDisposable.Dispose()
    {
        AuthenticationStateProvider.AuthenticationStateChanged
-= OnAuthenticationStateChanged;
    }
}
```

`CascadingValue` is the only element used here to pass the `Task` of `AuthenticationState` down the components tree to its children. Every time the `AuthenticationStateChanged` is emitted on the injected `AuthenticationStateProvider`, the Task instance will be replaced by the new one from the event argument.

An instance of type `AuthenticationStateProvider` is injected into the `CascadingAuthenticationState` component, but the type `AuthenticationStateProvider` was never registered in `Program. cs`. Only the customized `EShopAuthenticationStateProvider` was registered. It is known that `EShopAuthenticationStateProvider` inherits `AuthenticationStateProvider`, so it is assignable to `AuthenticationStateProvider`. How exactly can that be achieved? Fortunately, when registering a type into the service provider, .NET has an overloaded `AddScoped` method that accepts an instance of `Func` as a factory to create the required instance, and it can be used to register an instance of type `EShopAuthenticationStateProvider` on the type `AuthenticationStateProvider`:

```
builder.Services.AddScoped<AuthenticationStateProvider>(f =>
f.GetRequiredService<EShopAuthenticationStateProvider>());
```

Each time a new instance of type `AuthenticationStateProvider` is required, Lambda expression will be invoked to create one for the application as a factory, and this will provide the value for `CascadingAuthenticationState`.

Next, replace `RouteView` with the new `AuthorizeRouteView` component. `AuthorizeRouteView` inherits `RouteView`, in addition to the Authorization related rendering mechanism. By reading the source code of `AuthorizeRouteView`, users will learn that, by default, it comes with a private `RenderFragment` that will render the plain text `Not authorized` if the user is not authorized and will render the plain text `Authorizing ...` when the user is currently being authorized. Of course, developers may customize the rendering in these two scenarios by providing values to the parameters of `NotAuthorized` and `Authorizing`, respectively:

```
public sealed class AuthorizeRouteView : RouteView
{
    private static readonly RenderFragment<AuthenticationState>
_ defaultNotAuthorizedContent
        = state => builder => builder.AddContent(0, "Not
        authorized");
```

```
    private static readonly RenderFragment _
    defaultAuthorizingContent

        = builder => builder.AddContent(0, "Authorizing...");



    [Parameter]

    public RenderFragment<AuthenticationState>? NotAuthorized
    { get; set; }


    [Parameter]

    public RenderFragment? Authorizing { get; set; }


    [Parameter]

    public object? Resource { get; set; }


    [CascadingParameter]

    private Task<AuthenticationState>?
    ExistingCascadedAuthenticationState { get; set; }


    protected override void Render(RenderTreeBuilder builder)

    {

        if (ExistingCascadedAuthenticationState != null)

        {

            _renderAuthorizeRouteViewCoreDelegate(builder);

        }

        else

        {

            builder.OpenComponent<CascadingAuthenticationState>(0);
            builder.AddAttribute(1,
            nameof(CascadingAuthenticationState.
    ChildContent), _renderAuthorizeRouteViewCoreDelegate);

            builder.CloseComponent();

        }

    }
```

```
    private void RenderAuthorizeRouteViewCore(RenderTreeBuilder
    builder)

    {

        builder.OpenComponent<AuthorizeRouteViewCore>(0);
        builder.AddAttribute(1, nameof(AuthorizeRouteViewCore.
RouteData), RouteData);

        builder.AddAttribute(2, nameof(AuthorizeRouteViewCore.
Authorized), _renderAuthorizedDelegate);

        builder.AddAttribute(3, nameof(AuthorizeRouteViewCore.
Authorizing), _renderAuthorizingDelegate);

        builder.AddAttribute(4, nameof(AuthorizeRouteViewCore.
NotAuthorized), _renderNotAuthorizedDelegate);

        builder.AddAttribute(5, nameof(AuthorizeRouteViewCore.
Resource), Resource);

        builder.CloseComponent();

    }


    private sealed class AuthorizeRouteViewCore : AuthorizeViewCore

    {

        [Parameter]

        public RouteData RouteData { get; set; } = default!;


        protected override IAuthorizeData[]? GetAuthorizeData()

            => AttributeAuthorizeDataCache.
GetAuthorizeDataForType(RouteData.PageType);

}


// some code

}
```

When rendering the `AuthorizeRouteView` component, it will first check if there is an existing cascading Task of `AuthenticationState`. If the result is positive, it will render the `AuthorizeRouteViewCore` directly, otherwise, it will wrap that with a cascading parameter.

The `AuthorizeRouteViewCore` component is the base class to rendering different content based on whether a user is authorized or not. After `AuthorizeRouteViewCore` is initialized in the front-end, it will validate parameters in the override method `OnParametersSetAsync`. First, setting both `ChildContent` and Authorized at the same different is not allowed and an `InvalidOperationException` will be thrown out. Next, it will check if the cascading parameter `AuthenticationState` has been set, and set the field `isAuthorized` to null, in case there is a remaining previous result. It will then retrieve the User property from the `AuthenticationState` and set the field `isAuthorized` again according to whether the user is or is not authorized:

```
public abstract class AuthorizeViewCore : ComponentBase
{

    private AuthenticationState? currentAuthenticationState;

    private bool? isAuthorized;


    [CascadingParameter] private Task<AuthenticationState>?
AuthenticationState { get; set; }



    /// <inheritdoc />

    protected override void BuildRenderTree(RenderTreeBuilder
    builder)

    {

        if (isAuthorized == null)

        {

            builder.AddContent(0, Authorizing);

        }

        else if (isAuthorized == true)

        {

            var authorized = Authorized ?? ChildContent; build-
            er.AddContent(0, authorized?.
Invoke(currentAuthenticationState!));

        }
```

```
        else

        {

            builder.AddContent(0, NotAuthorized?.
Invoke(currentAuthenticationState!));

        }

    }


    protected override async Task OnParametersSetAsync()

    {

        if (ChildContent != null && Authorized != null)

        {

            throw new InvalidOperationException($"Do not specify
both '{nameof(Authorized)}' and '{nameof(ChildContent)}'.");

        }


        if (AuthenticationState == null)

        {

            throw new InvalidOperationException($"Authorization
requires a cascading parameter of type Task<{nameof(Authentica-
tionState)}>.
Consider using {typeof(CascadingAuthenticationState).Name} to
supply
this.");

        }


        isAuthorized = null;


        currentAuthenticationState = await AuthenticationState;

        isAuthorized = await IsAuthorizedAsync(currentAuthenti-
cationState.User);

    }

}
```

The component will render the Authorizing child content when the field `isAuthorized` is null, which means that the application is between the processes of clearing previous result and getting the new authorization result. When `isAuthorized` is true, it will display the content of `Authorized`, or `NotAuthorized`, otherwise. For customers that are not authenticated yet, the sign-in page will be displayed, so the `SignIn` component is assigned to the `NotAuthorized` attribute.

If one builds and runs the application, every page still displays normally, without authentication required, for example, the page to "add shop item" built in the previous chapter. To protect the shop item data from a nonemployee of EShop company, add an Authorize attribute to the component page:

```
@page "/add-shop-item"
@attribute [Authorize]


<div class="ItemContainer">
    <h1>Add Shop Item</h1>
</div>


@* some code *@
```

With this one line of attribute in the page, the page is protected from anyone who is not authorized.

Refer to Figure 12.1.

FIGURE 12.1 Protect page with an Authorize attribute.

Note that the user is visiting `/add-shop-item`, but the browser actually redirects them to the sign-in page. Refer to Figure 12.2.

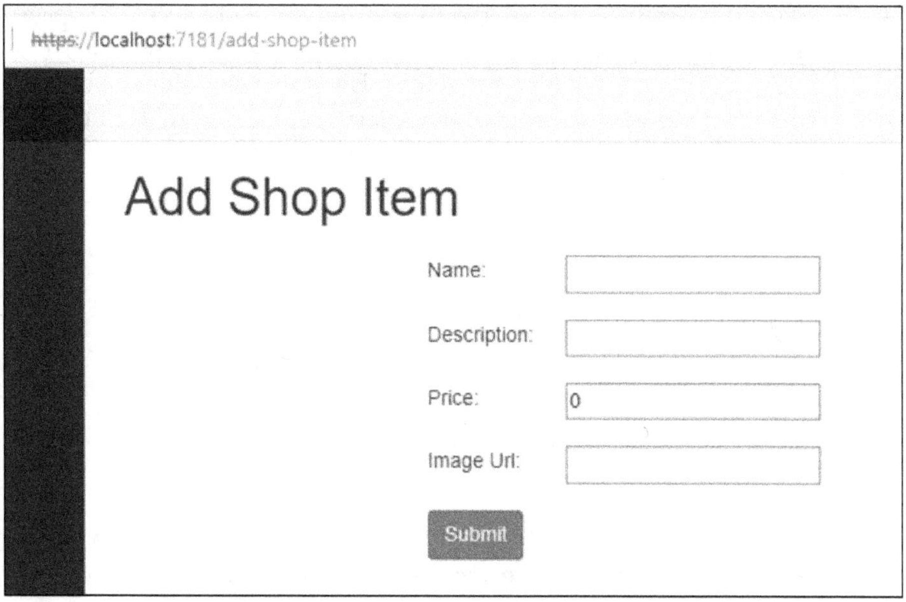

FIGURE 12.2 Visit /add-shop-item when authorized.

When signed in successfully, the browser will redirect back to the "add shop item" page.

Keep in mind that one should only use an Authorize attribute on a page, not on a single child component. If rendering a child component is dependent on the authentication status, use the `AuthorizeView` component to wrap it instead.

ROLE-BASED AUTHORIZATION

In the previous example, all the users who can successfully sign in will be able to add a new shop item in the database, which is obviously not what the PO would desire. A better implementation is allowing only employees of the EShop company to submit the "add shop item" form. Even if a customer is signed in, they should be forbidden from modifying the shop item data.

To put it simply, role-based authorization is assigning an authenticated user a role claim, and later when the user visits a certain page that is protected by specific roles, Blazor will check if the user has one of those specific roles. When the result is positive, the user is authorized to access the page. When the result is negative, `AuthorizeRouteView` will redirect the user to the `NotAuthorized` content rendered. The following shows how to modify `EShopAuthenticationStateProvider` and assign roles to users who are successfully signed in:

```
using System.Security.Claims;
using Microsoft.AspNetCore.Components.Authorization;

namespace EShop.Server.Auth;

public class EShopAuthenticationStateProvider :
AuthenticationStateProvider
{
    private bool _isSignedIn = false;
    private string _username = string.Empty;


    private string Email { get => $"{_username.Replace(" ",
"")}@eshop.com"; }


    public override Task<AuthenticationState>
GetAuthenticationStateAsync()
    {
        ClaimsIdentity claimsIdentity;


        if (_isSignedIn)
        {
            var claims = new List<Claim>()
            {
new Claim(ClaimTypes.Name, _username),
                new Claim(ClaimTypes.Email, Email),
                new Claim(ClaimTypes.Role, _username.
Contains("EShop")?"Employee":"Customer")
            };
```

```
        claimsIdentity = new ClaimsIdentity(claims,
        "EShopAuth");
    }
    else
    {
        claimsIdentity = new ClaimsIdentity();
    }


    var authenticationState = new AuthenticationState(new
ClaimsPrincipal(claimsIdentity));


    return Task.FromResult(authenticationState);
    }


    public void SignIn(string username, string password)
    {
        _username = username;
        _isSignedIn = !string.IsNullOrWhiteSpace(username) &&
        !string.
IsNullOrWhiteSpace(password);


        NotifyAuthenticationStateChanged(GetAuthentication-
        StateAsync());
    }
}
```

In the preceding code example, it's assumed that if the username of the person who is signed in contains EShop, then they are an employee of the EShop company, and an Employee role can be added to them. Otherwise, the user is a potential customer who will buy some clothes in the EShop application at some time, and they are assigned the role of Customer. In AddShopItem. razor, add Roles check to the Authorize attribute.

```
@attribute [Authorize(Roles = "Employee")]
```

Run the application again, and when visiting /add-shop-item, the user will be asked to sign in as before. If the user signs in with the username `Brian`, the page will only display `Hello, Brian`, without redirecting back to the "add shop item" page as shown in Figure 12.3.

FIGURE 12.3 Role-based authorization.

If the user signs in with the username `Brian-EShop` again, the "add shop item" page will be displayed.

POLICY-BASED AUTHORIZATION

Policy-based authorization is more flexible when compared with role-based authorization. In role-based authorization, the application assigns a fixed role to each user and the role is the only rule to check. For policy-based authorization, the rules can go beyond roles. The policy rule could still be a role, but the role could also be a simple email check, a math equation, or a more complex customized handler to determine if the user is authorized.

One scenario could be that the "add shop item" page can only be accessed by users with selected role, and they must be from certain regions for the postal code ends with a particular digit. Apparently, this could not be accomplished by the role-based authorization because the rules mandate more than a simple role check.

To confirm with policy-based authorization, create a new file called `AddShopItem Requirement.cs` under the `Auth` folder with the following code:

```
using Microsoft.AspNetCore.Authorization;

namespace EShop.Server.Auth;

public class AddShopItemRequirement : IAuthorizationRequirement
{
    public char PostalCodeSuffix { get; }
    public string Role { get; }
    public AddShopItemRequirement(char postalCodeSuffix, string role)
    {
        PostalCodeSuffix = postalCodeSuffix;
        Role = role;
    }
}
```

This is a simple data class with two required properties that implements the interface `IAuthorizationRequirement`. This interface does not have any methods defined in it. It works as a generic placeholder for the handler that comes later:

```
public interface IAuthorizationRequirement
{
}
```

Next, create a handler that manages the requirement. Create a new file called `AddShopItemHandler.cs` under the `Auth` folder with the following code:

```
using System.Security.Claims;
using Microsoft.AspNetCore.Authorization;


namespace EShop.Server.Auth;
```

```
public class AddShopItemHandler :
AuthorizationHandler<AddShopItemRequirement>
{
    protected override Task
HandleRequirementAsync(AuthorizationHandlerContext context,
AddShopItemRequirement requirement)
    {
        if (!context.User.HasClaim(c => c.Type == ClaimTypes.Role) &&
!context.User.HasClaim(c => c.Type == ClaimTypes.PostalCode))
        {
            context.Fail();
            return Task.CompletedTask;
        }

        var postalCode = context.User.FindFirstValue(ClaimTypes.
PostalCode);
        var role = context.User.FindFirstValue(ClaimTypes.Role);
        if (postalCode.EndsWith(requirement.PostalCodeSuffix) &&
role == requirement.Role)
        {
            context.Succeed(requirement);
            return Task.CompletedTask;
        }

        context.Fail();
        return Task.CompletedTask;
    }
}
```

In the AddShopItemHandler class, override the HandleRequirementAsync method. If the current matches the customized rule, call the method Succeed on context indicating that this requirement has been successfully evaluated. Otherwise, call method Fail on the context. With the handler, one may even call a remote service API to evaluate the policy, and this is way more powerful than the fixed role-base authorization.

The last step is to modify the Authorize attribute in `AddShopItem.razor` as follows:

```
@attribute [Authorize(Policy = "AddShopItemPolicy")]
```

Register the policy in `Program.cs`:

```
builder.Services.AddAuthorization(config =>
{
    config.AddPolicy("AddShopItemPolicy", p => p.Requirements.
Add(new AddShopItemRequirement('2', "Employee")));
});
```

A more flexible, powerful authorization has been implemented.

ASP.NET CORE IDENTITY

ASP.NET Core Identity is an open-source server library that users may deploy to provide a prebuilt sign-in UI page, and also to manage user data such as passwords, roles, emails, and so on. This saves developers time and effort when they don't have to implement their own authentication and authorization system as was done in previous examples. With the identity library, it is more than easy to integrate with Azure Active Directory or Azure Active Directory B2C. If one is building an application facing business clients who choose to use the Azure Active Directory as their user's system, the ASP.NET Core Identity will be a must-have for developers to build applications with such user authentications.

CONCLUSION

This chapter first went through the concepts of authentication and authorization and then discussed how authentication is implemented with a customized `AuthenticationStateProvider` to sign in a user. Next, the chapter explained how the "add shop item" page demonstrates two different ways to authorize a user, namely, by role-based authorization and policy-based authorization. By comparison, readers were shown that policy-based authorization is more flexible and powerful than role-based authorization.

Chapter 13 will explain how to deploy the EShop application to Kubernetes, running in a cloud environment. Azure Kubernetes Service (AKS) allows users to deploy an application quickly in the Azure Kubernetes cluster while Ops won't have to worry about the maintenance of the infrastructure layer down below.

DEPLOYING WITH DOCKER AND KUBERNETES

INTRODUCTION

Previous chapters implemented a few features for the `EShop` application, including browsing items, adding them to the cart, leaving comments, managing shop items, and authorization. The text discussed many concepts regarding the Blazor Framework.

In this chapter, users will containerize the application and deploy it to the Kubernetes platform on Azure. Modern applications deployed with Docker and K8S enjoy the benefits of standardization, productivity, CI efficiency, and rapid deployment.

STRUCTURE

This chapter discusses the following topics:

- What Is Docker?
- building a Docker image
- image layer
- What Is K8S?
- K8S components
- Deploy to AKS—K8S on Azure

OBJECTIVES

This chapter will help readers understand Docker, one of the most popular container platforms. Docker helps developers to build, share, and run modern cloud native applications in a more efficient and predictable way. Readers will build their own Docker image and understand the layers structure of a Docker image. Next, they will be introduced to Kubernetes and learn about the most important components of Kubernetes. They will then deploy the Docker image manually to the Kubernetes on Azure. Finally, the chapter discusses the GitHub Actions that can be used to automate the AKS deployments.

WHAT IS DOCKER?

Before the era of containers, to deploy an application developers would manually compile the source code and copy and paste the binary files to a server, (e.g., a VM), while maintaining the dependent tools and services. For example, a VM based on Linux and a VM based on Windows require different binary files, therefore users must compile the same source code twice targeting different operating systems. In addition, the application may require a database, for example, an SQL Server to store business data, and developers must manually install it on the target VM. Even more, these apps or services that users depend on may require to have more services or tools installed, and one small change in all of these dependencies might require a huge effort to maintain the entire application family on that VM. Some of these processes can be automated through a CI/CD pipeline, and some of them cannot. Developers, or operators find that the system may be too complex to manage and every time a new version of the application is deployed, unexpected issues will likely occur. It's also important to note that the same application may run well in one environment and crash in another.

Fortunately, Docker provides a uniform platform that allows running Linux- or Windows-based applications in a standardized environment. The idea is that the operating system is like a cargo ship, and every application or service running on the OS is a container. Developers can customize what is inside the container or use a container that is built by other professionals. The running environment of a container is composed so that deploying an application is deploying a series of standard components. Like Lego pieces, developers can choose to build their work (application) upon others' working pieces (database).

A complete Docker is composed of Docker Client, Docker Daemon, Docker Image, and Docker Container. Docker is running under the client-server mode. Docker Daemon is running as a server to take requests from clients, while Docker Client sends requests to Docker Daemon. They can run either on the same machine or on different servers and communicate through sockets or RESTful API. The requests are sent to a Docker Daemon including creating, running, or distributing containers. In this way, the whole process of building, testing, and deploying an application can be fully automated with pipelines.

BUILDING A DOCKER IMAGE

A Docker container is created from a Docker image. Users will build the Docker image out of its definition file called Dockerfile. Before that, users must first install the Docker environment. Instructions for doing so are complex and not covered in this book, but users can follow the instructions from the official Docker Web site based on their operating system. Docker supports Windows, Linux, and MacOS.

Once Docker is installed, run the command `docker--version` in the terminal and they should see a similar output. Refer to Figure 13.1.

```
> docker --version
Docker version 23.0.1, build a5ee5b1
```

FIGURE 13.1 Docker command.

Next, create a new file called `Dockerfile`, under the root folder with the following content:

```
FROM mcr.microsoft.com/dotnet/sdk:6.0

WORKDIR /app

COPY . ./
RUN dotnet restore \
    && dotnet publish ./EShop.Server.csproj -o /publish/
```

```
WORKDIR /publish


ENV ASPNETCORE_URLS="http://0.0.0.0:5000"


ENTRYPOINT ["dotnet", "EShop.Server.dll"]
```

The first line in a Dockerfile must start with a `FROM` command. This command defines the base image that will be used, and it initiates a new build stage. This project is for building a Blazor Server application, so choose the dotnet 6.0 SDK base image from Microsoft. When building applications developed with different languages, users can choose other base images. For example, if one is building a Docker image of a Golang server, they might choose to build their image based on `golang:1.20.4`, or `node:18.16.0` for a `Node.js` application. An image name is separated into two parts by the colon sign. The first part represents the repo of the image. By default, the Docker command will try to pull an image from the Docker Hub. To pull from a customized repo, users need to specify the full repo name. For example, the dotnet SDK image used in the Dockerfile is located under the Microsoft container registry, so the full name is `mcr.microsoft.com/dotnet/sdk:6.0`. Visit the container registry Web page at *https://mcr.microsoft.com/en-us*, and look for necessary images. The second part represents the tag of an image. Under the tags section, the container registry usually lists all the available tags.

Refer to Figure 13.2.

FIGURE 13.2 Docker image tags.

With the repository and tag specified, locate the base Docker image needed. Sometimes, one can even build an image from scratch and Docker provides a special empty image called `scratch`. This is a virtual image that cannot be pulled, run, or tagged. It simply signals an empty image from scratch.

The next line of the Dockerfile uses the `WORKDIR` command. This command specifies the working directory for the image to be /app, and all the following commands will be running under this directory. If the directory does not exist, `WORKDIR` will create that directory.

The third command is `COPY`, which will copy files from the building context to the target image. Here users are copying everything to the working directory, so this line is simply `COPY . .`, and the first dot represents all the files from the building context, and the next dot represents the target path in a relative way. Users are free to use an absolute path as well. Keep in mind that the COPY command will not only copy all the files, but it also keeps the file's meta data, such as file access and modification time.

The next command is `RUN`, followed by shell instructions. The Blazor application will be built and published in this stage.

Then use the `WORKDIR` command again to specify the working directory that contains the published application binary files.

The `ENV` command is used to set up environment variables. All the Dockerfile commands that follow it or the running application can use the environment variables defined here.

The last command is `ENTRYPOINT`. This command defines the running program and the arguments passed to it. This example shows that the running program is `dotnet` and the argument is `EShop.Server.dll`.

Finally, build the image by running the command `docker build ./EShop.Server -t eshopserver:1.0.0` under the root folder, and the terminal should display a similar output as shown in Figure 13.3.

```
> docker build ./EShop.Server -t eshopserver:1.0.0
[+] Building 345.4s (18/18) FINISHED
 => [internal] load build definition from Dockerfile
 => => transferring dockerfile: 204B
 => [internal] load .dockerignore
 => => transferring context: 2B
 => [internal] load metadata for mcr.microsoft.com/dotnet/sdk:6.0
 => [internal] load build context
 => => transferring context: 19.87MB
 => [1/5] FROM mcr.microsoft.com/dotnet/sdk:6.0@sha256:efba5b8cdfdf2b68e8bd6f3fcf58c8670c4fddfdae397a865982ba364582552d
 => => resolve mcr.microsoft.com/dotnet/sdk:6.0@sha256:efba5b8cdfdf2b68e8bd6f3fcf58c8670c4fddfdae397a865982ba364582552d
 => => sha256:efba5b8cdfdf2b68e8bd6f3fcf58c8670c4fddfdae397a865982ba364582552d 1.82kB / 1.82kB
 => => sha256:13cfa02ffefbadbecefbf43ba2514f7ea776d00cd3258414e595d82bef607ff5 2.01kB / 2.01kB
 => => sha256:7543eece699ee04e88f5140f1d1a1c5ff62573f9236de538f8beca6af629489f 7.17kB / 7.17kB
 => => sha256:9e3ea8720c6de96cc9ad544dddc695a3ab73f5581c5d954e0504cc4f80fb5e5c 31.40MB / 31.40MB
 => => sha256:2436f232d04089283ab348e14d6430f339b3b2652272096252202ea0c337aac4 15.17MB / 15.17MB
 => => sha256:c12fd5cada2cee63bdb12538e653c50af66531f211c68af677ed60dbd8eb2b9b 31.63MB / 31.63MB
 => => sha256:a13870fe3303be29f5d281e95c5804efd17582a3082f1128a5f4a2e2215df6ea 156B / 156B
 => => sha256:2c8900f692ad760d73a4d885da5731f2e6bd913b8db4b4075cb859f0000d87c3 9.46MB / 9.46MB
 => => sha256:a1f3127d3b56cf181a8c493aa0d8c668a2f5b5d1204f99ce9fc2a69c18ea6c8f 25.37MB / 25.37MB
 => => sha256:1f82b80d6396caf41ef9d82099ba7e94d36aca74b341ec955d8fc3cc712f3db5 148.55MB / 148.55MB
 => => sha256:8e1ab441189d687a1779f02005936ad3a8c8e3ac540e20ac956425a3c0de5aa6 13.61MB / 13.61MB
 => => extracting sha256:9e3ea8720c6de96cc9ad544dddc695a3ab73f5581c5d954e0504cc4f80fb5e5c
 => => extracting sha256:2436f232d04089283ab348e14d6430f339b3b2652272096252202ea0c337aac4
 => => extracting sha256:c12fd5cada2cee63bdb12538e653c50af66531f211c68af677ed60dbd8eb2b9b
 => => extracting sha256:a13870fe3303be29f5d281e95c5804efd17582a3082f1128a5f4a2e2215df6ea
 => => extracting sha256:2c8900f692ad760d73a4d885da5731f2e6bd913b8db4b4075cb859f0000d87c3
 => => extracting sha256:a1f3127d3b56cf181a8c493aa0d8c668a2f5b5d1204f99ce9fc2a69c18ea6c8f
 => => extracting sha256:1f82b80d6396caf41ef9d82099ba7e94d36aca74b341ec955d8fc3cc712f3db5
 => => extracting sha256:8e1ab441189d687a1779f02005936ad3a8c8e3ac540e20ac956425a3c0de5aa6
 => [2/5] WORKDIR /app
 => [3/5] COPY . ./
 => [4/5] RUN dotnet restore     && dotnet publish ./EShop.Server.csproj -o /publish/
 => [5/5] WORKDIR /publish
 => exporting to image
 => => exporting layers
 => => writing image sha256:4b58c94014818b370509212fd91b47a5b855014462765fe552979ab5554e0207
 => => naming to docker.io/library/eshopserver:1.0.0
```

FIGURE 13.3 Build a Docker image.

Run the command `docker image ls` and see the recently built `eshopserver` image listed. Refer to the Figure 13.4.

```
> docker image ls
REPOSITORY                          TAG        IMAGE ID      CREATED         SIZE
eshopserver                         1.0.0      4b58c9401481  34 minutes ago  986MB
```

FIGURE 13.4 List Docker images.

IMAGE LAYER

An operating system is generally composed of kernel and user spaces. For a Linux system, the root file system can provide the user space support, and Docker images are like a root file system. It contains all the required files, including programs, libraries, configurations or even runtime parameters like the environment variables mentioned in the previous section. Docker images will not contain any dynamic data, and the contents will never change once they are built. As there are too many files to be built into a Docker image, it takes a layer-by-layer approach to build the image. Every layer is built upon the previous layer, which explains why all Dockerfiles must start with the FROM command. After each layer is built, no changes will occur. That means if you remove a file from the previous layer, the file will be marked instead of actually being deleted. When the container of that image finally runs, the file still exists even though one cannot access it anymore. Caution must be used when creating a new image, only adding files that are necessary and cleaning all the cache or extra files before the layer completes its build. One more benefit that comes from the layer structure is that it becomes easy to distribute, share, or reuse layers. All the Dockerfile commands that modify the file systems will normally create a new layer, and the Docker Daemon will determine when it can use a cache if the file system stays the same. For example, if one changes the application published directory to Blazor and build the Docker image again, the Docker Daemon will try to reuse layers any many as it can, and users will see output shows CACHED as in Figure 13.5. Keep in mind that all layers after the modified layer will be rebuilt as well, even when they themselves do not make any files changes, but because the layer they depend on has been updated.

```
) docker build ./EShop.Server -t eshopserver:1.0.0
[+] Building 21.7s (10/10) FINISHED
=> [internal] load build definition from Dockerfile
=> => transferring dockerfile: 282B
=> [internal] load .dockerignore
=> => transferring context: 2B
=> [internal] load metadata for mcr.microsoft.com/dotnet/sdk:6.0
=> [1/5] FROM mcr.microsoft.com/dotnet/sdk:6.0@sha256:efba5b8cdfdf2b68e8bd6f3fcf58c8670c4fddfdae397a065982ba364582552d
=> [internal] load build context
=> => transferring context: 12.69kB
=> CACHED [2/5] WORKDIR /app
=> [3/5] COPY . ./
=> [4/5] RUN dotnet restore     && dotnet publish ./EShop.Server.csproj -o /blazor/
=> [5/5] WORKDIR /blazor
=> exporting to image
=> => exporting layers
=> => writing image sha256:99945f491367aef2673b309f1df4954df25d8f8f54ca6761ac2c1d54dcc8998a
=> => naming to docker.io/library/eshopserver:1.0.0
```

FIGURE 13.5 Docker image layer.

Layers are also valid Docker images, and one can start a container from a layer's image. The layer also comes into play when a new image is pulled. The layers that users already have locally will be skipped, and Docker will only download layers that users don't have.

The following explains how to start a container of the image built with the command,

```
docker run -p 5000:5000 -d eshopserver:1.0.0
```

The argument -p, short for `public`, defines the port that is published for the running container. The first port number represents the port on the host, and the next one represents the port in the container. Usually, users utilize the same port on both sides, but they should decide if they like two different ports. The argument -d, short for `detach`, runs the container in the background, or detached mode. and you will come back to the terminal prompt. The last argument is the image selected to run in the container and the tag defaults to `latest` if omitted.

Now the terminal will display the hash id of the container. Visit *http:// localhost:5000* in the browser to see the exact same page if the application is started with `dotnet run`. Refer to Figure 13.6.

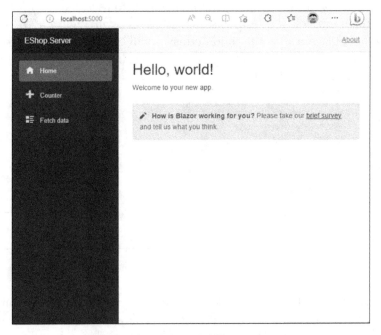

FIGURE 13.6 Start a Docker container.

To stop the container, run the command `docker container stop <hash id>`, and the hash id is from the output of the `docker run` command. Check the container status by using the command `docker container ls -a`, while the `-a` argument is necessary to display stopped containers.

Refer to Figure 13.7.

```
> docker container ls -a
CONTAINER ID   IMAGE            COMMAND                CREATED        STATUS                   PORTS     NAMES
9ea5f7b62096   eshopserver:1.0.0  "dotnet EShop.Server…"  15 seconds ago  Exited (0) 5 seconds ago            elegant_beaver
```

FIGURE 13.7 Container status.

WHAT IS K8S?

Docker containers can help to maintain consistency between different environments as long as users deploy the same image with the same tag in those environments. Another thing to consider is what if one of the containers runs into issues and exits? One simple way to rectify this is to connect to the virtual machine and manually restart the container again. It's important to note that as microservices architecture style is getting more and more popular, one may end up with hundreds or even thousands of containers running in many different virtual machines. It becomes nearly impossible to manually deploy, check, or fix container issues every moment.

Kubernetes, or K8S is an open-source system for automating deployment, scaling, and management of containerized applications. Think of it as a manager that can deploy, check, and restart the container applications and more. Users simply have to define the desired state of their containers to utilize K8S.

K8S COMPONENTS

A Kubernetes system is deployed in a cluster, and there is at least one working machine, called node, in the cluster. To manage the cluster and worker node, Kubernetes provides a group of components named `Control Plane`. `Control Plane` works as the brain of the system, controlling the cluster and responding to the requests and events coming from any clients or nodes. In the `Control Plane` components group, `kube-apiserver` exposes the Kubernetes API to the clients, validates the request data, and works as the front-end. The next component in the group is `etcd`, which is an open source distributed key value database storing all the cluster data, such as Pod status. `kube-scheduler` is the component that is responsible for selecting an appropriate worker node to run the Pod. The `kube-controller-manager` is the component that runs multiple controllers, including Node controller or Job controller. These controllers together control the Node, Job, and communications in a K8S system. The last component in the `Control Plan` group is `cloud-controller-manager`. It allows users to connect the cluster with the cloud provider and will only run the controllers that are specific to the selected cloud provider.

Node components are another group of components that run on every worker node. The first component is an agent called `kubelet`. It takes care of the Pods that run containers and makes sure the Pods are running under the desired state. On every worker node there is a network proxy called `kube-proxy` that maintains the network communications to the Pods. The last component is container runtime and that is responsible for the container runtime. Note that `containerd`, which is used by Docker container as a runtime, is neither the same as Docker container nor the only runtime supported by Kubernetes. The differences between `containerd` and a Docker container are beyond the information contained in this book, so this chapter will only focus on deployment.

DEPLOY TO AKS—K8S ON AZURE

Other than creating and maintaining an on-premises Kubernetes cluster, this section will focus on deploying the EShop.Server application in Azure Kubernetes Services (AKS). AKS is a service offered by Azure. It provides a quick way to deploy cloud-native apps in Azure and automates scaling management. Users will need an Azure account, and a free account with a $200 credit is available from *https://azure.microsoft.com/en-us/free*. To begin, go to *https://portal.azure.com* and click on the `Create a resource` button or search for Kubernetes in the search bar at the top.

Refer to Figure 13.8.

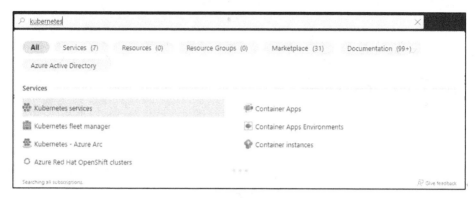

FIGURE 13.8 Search for Kubernetes in the Azure portal.

Click on the first result as in Figure 13.8 to go to the Kubernetes services page. Click the `Create` button and select the first option `Create a Kubernetes cluster` from the drop-down menu as shown in Figure 13.9.

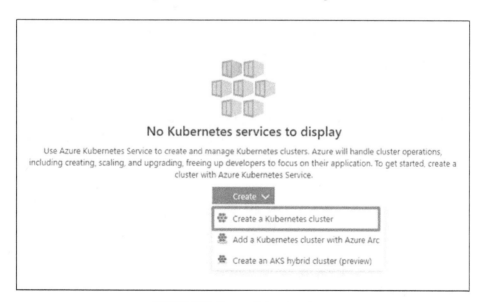

FIGURE 13.9 Create a Kubernetes cluster.

Users will be directed to a new page to submit required information regarding the cluster to be created, as shown in Figure 13.10.

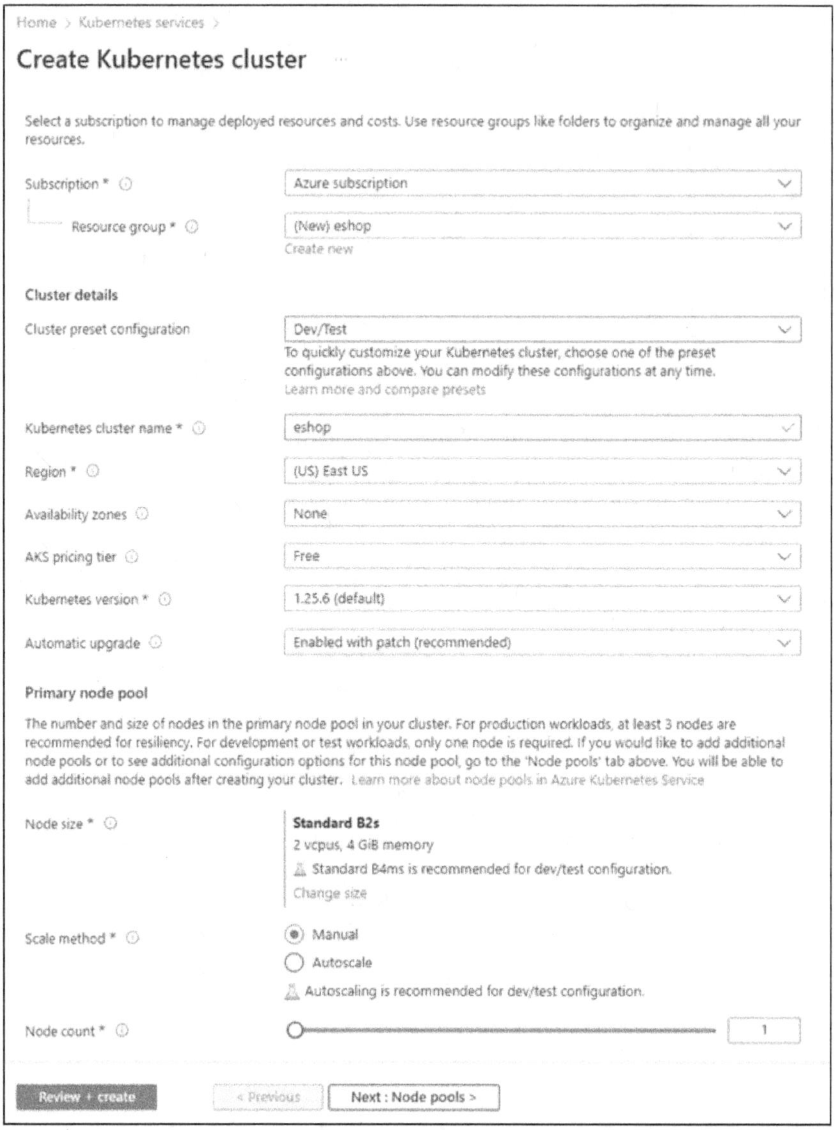

FIGURE 13.10 Required information regarding the new cluster.

First, select an Azure subscription and select a resource group to which the new cluster belongs, or create a new one. It's recommended that users create a dedicated resource group per business line or per feature if their application is large enough. Here, create a new resource group called `eshop`. Next is the `Cluster preset configuration`, and for this, choose Dev/Test since `EShop.Server` is being deployed for the purpose of this demonstartion. Users are free to choose other configurations based on their application loads or performance requirements. Next, give the cluster the name `eshop` as well. Azure provides many available regions around the globe, and it is preferable to choose a region that is closer to potential customers. For this demo, choose the `free tier`, which is more appropriate if one isi still learning or testing with AKS. Choose `Standard B2s` as the `Node size` since there is no strong performance requirement here. Because no scaling is needed, change the `Scale method` from `Autoscale` to `Manual` and assign only `one` node in the cluster. Leave other fields as default and click on the `Review + create` button. Azure will validate the configuration and if it passes, click on the final `Create` button to create the cluster.

Refer to Figures 13.11 and 13.12.

FIGURE 13.11 Creating the cluster.

FIGURE 13.12 Deployment is in progress.

It may take a few minutes to create the cluster, and while Azure is working on that, users will see pages as shown in the preceding screenshots.

When ready, users go to their cluster resource by clicking on the `Go to resource` button on the deployment page. Refer to Figure 13.13.

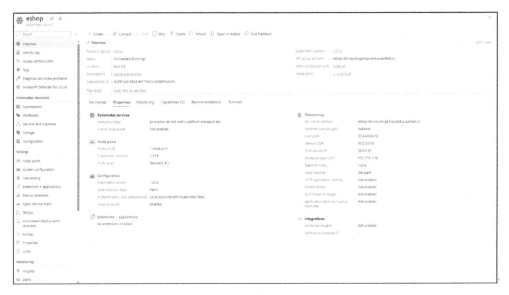

FIGURE 13.13 Cluster resource.

The cluster is ready, however, one more Azure resource is needed, Azure Container Registries (ACR). ACR is a private place to store and manage container images, and it will be used here as the image source for the eshop Kubernetes cluster. Similarly, one can search for container registries in the search bar and create one following the same process. (See Figure 13.14.)

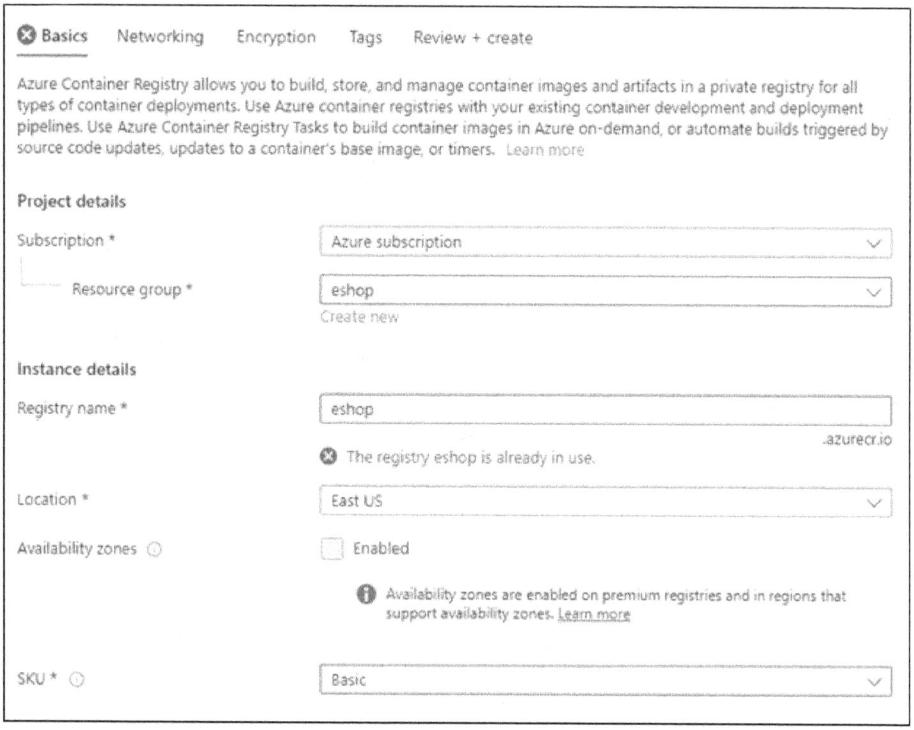

FIGURE 13.14 Create using Azure Container Registries (ACR).

Note that the Registry name must be unique across all Azure Container Registries, so if a name is taken already, one must come up with an alternate. Here, choose the existing eshop Resource group created in the previous step, change the SKU to Basic, and create it.

Once the registry is ready, tag the eshop image and push it up to the Azure Container Registries. By default, a Docker image is tagged for the Docker Hub registry and it should be tagged again, otherwise the Docker image will be pushed to the Docker Hub. To tag the image, run the following command:

```
docker image tag eshopserver:1.0.0 blazoreshop.azurecr.io/
eshopserver:1.0.0
```

Note that the Azure Container Registries server is prepend to the image name. Run `docker image ls` to show all the local images, and to see the newly tagged image.

Refer to Figure 13.15.

```
> docker image ls
REPOSITORY                              TAG     IMAGE ID        CREATED      SIZE
blazoreshop.azurecr.io/eshopserver      1.0.0   99945f491367    6 days ago   986MB
eshopserver                             1.0.0   99945f491367    6 days ago   986MB
```

FIGURE 13.15 Tag the image for Azure Container Registry.

Since the Azure Container Registries is private, users must log in before pushing images. It is recommended to login with an AD service principal in a production environment. For this situation the admin user approach is used for simplicity. Go to the registry resource in Azure portal and turn on Admin user in the Access keys tab. Be sure to save the username and password and keep them in a secure place. Run the following login command:

```
docker login blazoreshop.azurecr.io -u <username> -p
<password>
```

If the terminal displays Login Succeeded then it's okay to push the images. Push the image with the following command:

```
docker push blazoreshop.azurecr.io/eshopserver:1.0.0
```

Refer to the Figure 13.6.

```
> docker push blazoreshop.azurecr.io/eshopserver:1.0.0
The push refers to repository [blazoreshop.azurecr.io/eshopserver]
5f70bf18a086: Pushed
c61432b365d8: Pushed
a2f67bc381a7: Pushed
cea75ca001a6: Pushed
c1564694a634: Pushed
da8534ec9b1e: Pushed
afdc8de34f43: Pushed
8ccc3c25b883: Pushed
a51547ae5e97: Pushed
39a43ba957e5: Pushed
b224b13a335e: Pushed
8553b91047da: Pushed
1.0.0: digest: sha256:5ea1dc03081f76f5f21ef72ced21c88e7b74585ca37a66cab840fefaae1a1566 size: 2844
```

FIGURE 13.16 Push the image to Azure Container Registries.

Double-check the push result in Azure Portal. Go to the registry resource and click on the Repositories menu on the left side to see the new repository just pushed.

Now the image is uploaded, and the Kubernetes cluster is created. The last step before finally deploying the application is to connect the Kubernetes cluster and the registry. Use Azure CLI to accomplish that. Refer to the official Web page `https://learn.microsoft.com/en-us/cli/azure/ install-azure-cli` to install it. Here, the WSL on Windows is being used, so install Azure CLI with the command:

```
curl -sL https://aka.ms/InstallAzureCLIDeb | sudo bash
```

Once Azure CLI is installed, log in with the command:

```
az login --scope https://management.core.windows.net//.
default
```

After a Web page from Azure is prompted, sign in with the Azure Account.

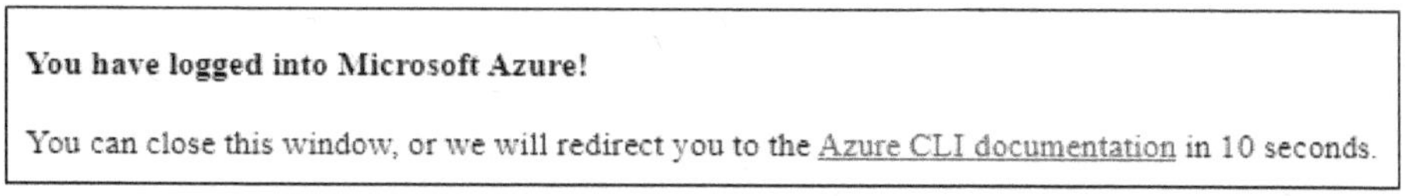

You have logged into Microsoft Azure!

You can close this window, or we will redirect you to the Azure CLI documentation in 10 seconds.

FIGURE 13.17 Azure CLI login.

A successful login will display account information in JSON format in the terminal. Next, run the following command to connect AKS and ACR:

```
az aks update -n <AKS cluster name> -g <resource group>
--attach-acr <ACR id>
```

To find the id of the ACR resource, go to the resource in Azure Portal and click on the `Overview` side menu (which should be the default option), and click on the `JSON View` link in the upper right corner.

In every Kubernetes cluster, pod is the smallest deployable unit. A pod is a running group of one or more containers. These containers share the storage, network, namespace, and running rules. In this case, deploy pods with a single container, `eshopserver`. As mentioned, Kubernetes can take care of the container failure and scaling automatically. In general, users do not create a pod resource directly. They create a Deployments resource instead. The Deployments resource is a declarative way to define the running pods, and the Deployment Controller will make sure that pods are running at the desired state.

In Kubernetes, the clients talk to the Kubernetes API server with a desired final state of the system, instead of commanding the cluster on what operations to take. This desired state is defined in a YAML or JSON format, and YAML will be used here.

Go to the AKS resource in Azure Portal and click on the `Workloads` side menu which directs to the Workloads management page. On this management page, click on the `Deployments` tab, then click on the `Create` button and select "Apply a YAML" in the drop-down menu. In the new page, fill in the following YAML content and click on the `Add` button at the bottom:

```
apiVersion: apps/v1
kind: Deployment
metadata:
  name: eshopserver
  labels:
    app: eshopserver
spec:
  replicas: 2
  selector:
    matchLabels:
      app: eshopserver
  template:
    metadata:
      labels:
        app: eshopserver
    spec:
      containers:
      - name: eshopserver
        image: blazoreshop.azurecr.io/eshopserver:1.0.0
        ports:
        - containerPort: 5000
```

All the Kubernetes YAML follows the same schema, starting with the API version and what kind of workload resources are defined in the YAML. The metadata section defines the name, labels, or namespace. Because a namespace was not specified, it will use the `default` namespace. The spec section defines the configuration of the workload resource, and the detailed configuration differs for different kinds of resources. Here users should first claim that they desire two pods running in the Kubernetes cluster. Then they should define which image should be used for this pod and which port should be exported and listened for the container.

Go back to the Workloads page to see the newly created Deployments resources. It should not take more than a few seconds before the workload is ready. Refer to Figure 13.18.

FIGURE 13.18 Deployed Kubernetes workloads.

Switch to the `Pods` tab, and two new pods should be listed as `Running` as shown in Figure 13.19.

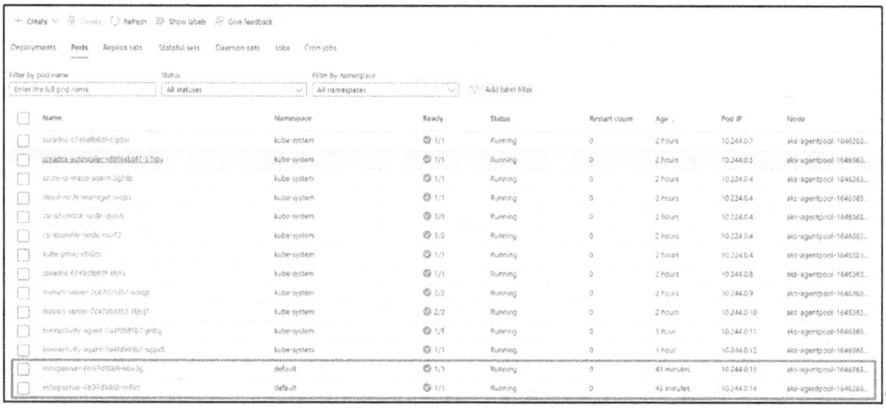

FIGURE 13.19 Running pods in AKS.

The application can only be accessed inside the cluster with the internal Pod IP yet. Expose it to the public Internet by creating a Service in the Kubernetes cluster. Go to the Services and ingresses menu, click on the `Create` button, and select `Apply a YAML` in the drop-down list. Paste the following content into the editor:

```
apiVersion: v1
kind: Service
metadata:
  name: eshopserver-service
spec:
  type: LoadBalancer
ports:
    - port: 80
      targetPort: 5000
      name: http
  selector:
    app: eshopserver
```

It will create a Kubernetes service of type `LoadBalancer`, listening on the container port 5000 and exposing port 80 to the public Internet. In production, users will usually create an ingress controller to expose their application. In Azure, an Application Gateway Ingress Controller, which is a load balancer to manage traffic through applications, can help accomplish that.

Click on the Add button and the Kubernetes service is on the way. An external IP is assigned to the service, and the `EShop` application is exposed to the Internet on *http://<service ip>* .

CONCLUSION

This chapter first introduced Docker, and explored why it is getting popular. Readers then built a Docker image of their own, while the text explained the layer structure of a Docker image and discussed how one can leverage the layers to improve image-building efficiency and device space cost. Next, the chapter introduced the open-source Kubernetes and its components of *Control Plan* and *Work Node*. Together, these components scale, manage containerized applications, and automate deployment. Finally, users explored Azure Container Registries (ACR), used to store Docker images. Users also Azure Kubernetes Service (AKS) used to deploy and run the Docker images.

Throughout the book, readers have learned about WebAssembly, Blazor development, and containerized deployment in Azure, the public cloud. Hopefully, this information will inspire readers to build their own applications!

INDEX